Contemporary Philosophies and Theories in Education

Volume 18

Contemporary Philosophies and Theories in Education signifies new directions and possibilities out of a traditional field of philosophy and education. Around the globe, exciting scholarship that breaks down and reformulates traditions in the humanities and social sciences is being created in the field of education scholarship. This series provides a venue for publication by education scholars whose work reflect the dynamic and experimental qualities that characterize today's academy. The series associates philosophy and theory not exclusively with a cognitive interest (to know, to define, to order) or an evaluative interest (to judge, to impose criteria of validity) but also with an experimental and attentive attitude which is characteristic for exercises in thought that try to find out how to move in the present and how to deal with the actual spaces and times, the different languages and practices of education and its transformations around the globe. It addresses the need to draw on thought across all sorts of borders and counts amongst its elements the following: the valuing of diverse processes of inquiry; an openness to various forms of communication, knowledge, and understanding; a willingness to always continue experimentation that incorporates debate and critique; and an application of this spirit, as implied above, to the institutions and issues of education. Authors for the series come not only from philosophy of education but also from curriculum studies and critical theory, social sciences theory, and humanities theory in education. The series incorporates volumes that are trans- and inner-disciplinary. The audience for the series includes academics, professionals and students in the fields of educational thought and theory, philosophy and social theory, and critical scholarship.

Elias Schwieler

Aporias of Translation

Literature, Philosophy, Education

 Springer

Elias Schwieler
Department of Education
Stockholm University
Stockholm, Sweden

ISSN 2214-9759   ISSN 2214-9767   (electronic)
Contemporary Philosophies and Theories in Education
ISBN 978-3-030-97894-5   ISBN 978-3-030-97895-2   (eBook)
https://doi.org/10.1007/978-3-030-97895-2

This Springer imprint is published by the registered company Springer Nature Switzerland AG
The registered company address is: Gewerbestrasse 11, 6330 Cham, Switzerland

To Ila, Hannah, and Jonah
For your love and support
***
For Olle
Absent but always present
***
In memory of J. Hillis Miller (1928–2021)
For his generosity
A true mentor and a brilliant scholar

Il leur avait seulement donné l'ordre de traverser une forêt dont il ignorait les issues.

(Jacques Rancière, Le maître ignorant – Cinq leçons sur l'émancipation intellectuelle.)

Acknowledgments

Writing this book has been an exciting journey, and there are many people who have been of great help to make it a reality. Early versions of the first two chapters of the book were presented at the annual PESA conference in 2017 and 2018. The opportunity to present my thoughts on the topics of these two chapters was extremely valuable, as was the feedback and comments from those who honored me by attending my presentations. A special thanks goes to PESA's Professor Peter Roberts, who chaired one of my presentations, and who has been very generous with his time and advice ever since we met in Chicago so many years ago now. Special thanks also to Dr. Andrew Gibbons for all the constructive comments during my presentations, and who made me feel welcome and at home at the PESA conferences in both Australia and New Zealand.

I would like to extend my appreciation to the Department of Education at Stockholm University, and especially the higher seminar in philosophy of education, chaired by Professor Klas Roth, who invited me to participate and present at the seminar. Thanks also to Dr. Stefan Ekecrantz for inviting me to participate in a project on critical thinking, funded by the Swedish Research Council. Two of the chapters in the book were written as part of this project, namely "'The Supreme Exertion of Thinking': Censorship, Critique, and Education" and "Toward a Notion of Aporetic Thinking: Translation, Culture, and Critical Thinking."

James M. Magrini has been and continues to be a scholar and friend, whose work and work ethics have influenced me deeply. His encouragement and advice made this book project possible. Thanks, Jim! I am looking forward to our continued collaboration.

Finally, I would like to thank my wife, Ila, for her unwavering support and patience. I love you! And thank you, Hannah and Jonah, my two wonderful kids. You are the light and inspiration that guide me when I most need it.

Contents

Chapter 1
Introduction

My reflections on education in the present study are meant to be seen as an exploration of and confrontation with some aspects of education as they intersect with literature and philosophy. My aim is to pinpoint instances and moments in which education, literature, and philosophy, in a specific context, can be seen to reveal an underlying aporia, which comes to structure the way we read and translate the idea of education, literature, and philosophy, taken separately, as well as in how the three work in a relational interconnectedness.

To be more precise, and provide the reader with an example of the structuring principle of my study, I would like to refer to a monograph by Eli Park Sorensen (2010), titled *Postcolonial Studies and the Literary: Theory, Interpretation and the Novel*. In the introduction to his book, Sorensen describes the development of postcolonial literary studies. He argues that this field of scholarship has turned out both a success and a failure. A success, because "today the field of postcolonial studies occupies an authoritative position of power" (xi) and a failure, "evident in the relation between postcolonial studies and literary texts" (xi). Sorensen suggests that the approach that postcolonial studies takes when it comes to its treatment of literary texts "involves an uncritical 'leap', which translates the literary dimension into a corresponding vocabulary of political concepts and imperatives in a regulative and simplifying way" (x). It is the existence of such a leap that I argue constitutes much of the involvement of literature, as well as philosophy, in education. It is the translation of the literary into examples and illustrations of an educational ideal that leaps across and so, often, neglects the literary, or philosophical, dimension in favor of political, ideological, and activist agendas. My argument is that these agendas are not only political, but epistemological and ontological, and that to leap over the literary and the philosophical, uncritically, does these agendas a disservice, since they undoubtedly have educational good intentions, such as social justice, equity, equality, diversity, etc. The leap that Sorensen identifies in postcolonial studies is in many respects similar to the aporias that I claim are present in the texts I examine in this book. However, an aporia in the sense I use it here is more originary that the leap which Sorensen argues for. Aporia is what makes the leap possible in the first place,

© Springer Nature Switzerland AG 2022
E. Schwieler, *Aporias of Translation*, Contemporary Philosophies and Theories
in Education 18, https://doi.org/10.1007/978-3-030-97895-2_1

it is the *Ur-sprung*, the arche-leap, of any epistemological or ontological conceptualization we make use of to rationalize knowledge. Aporia is the uncertainty, the doubt, that any translation has to take into account.[1] This, then, is the way or path that this book aims to follow, in that it will highlight these aporias in educational, literary, and philosophical texts, in order to take a step back before leaping (in Sorensen's use of the term) and reflect with genuine doubt and concern about the possibilities of education.

I do not presume, in this book, to provide a solution to an educational problem, nor do I treat education from a specific definition. However, my experience and practice as an educationalist stem from higher education, and it is this context that is implied in my readings of the selected texts in the study. Given these preconditions, it is reasonable to introduce the main themes of the study, which will then hopefully serve as guides to the chapters that follow. Hence, I will, in what follows, provide preliminary explications of the guiding themes of the study, namely aporia, translation, and the constellation literature, philosophy, education. I will conclude the introduction with chapter summaries.

Aporia[2]

To begin with the etymology of the word aporia, we find in Liddell and Scott's *Greek-English Lexicon* (1996) (to give a few examples) the following dictionary definitions of ἀπορία and ἄπορος,: difficulty in passing, difficulty, straits, not providing a thing, being at a loss, embarrassment, perplexity, question for discussion, difficulty, puzzle; and for the positive πόρος, for example: means of passing a river, paths, artificial passage over a river, passage through, opening, way or means of achieving, accomplishing, discovering, etc., providing, means of providing, journey, voyage. George Karamanolis and Vasilis Politis (2018) develop some of these dictionary definitions of aporia in the introduction to *The Aporetic Tradition in Ancient Philosophy*, where they provide "the first philosophical image of *aporia*, 'It is like being unable to reach through to a much-desired place'" (p. 1), and they continue to write that "[t]his image goes back to another original everyday use of the term *aporon*, to mean 'un-passable', 'un-traversable'. This image is immortalised by Heraclitus in a very early philosophical statement regarding *aporia*: 'Unless one hopes for that which is not to be hoped for (*anelpiston*), one shall not find it (*ouk*

---

[1] In the book *Heidegger on Literature, Poetry, and Education After the "Turn"* (2018), Magrini and Schwieler touch on doubt and aporia in Heideggerian terms: "To reflect on doubt we must follow the movement of the unknown […], which eludes being represented by metaphysics, science, or hermeneutics but happens as the event of appropriation (*Ereignis*) in the turning and counterturning of the aporia of ontological difference." It is the call for such a reflection that the present study aims to make way for.

[2] I will not italicize the word aporia in this study for two reasons: (1) It is a word that is in common use in the English language; (2) it is one of the main themes of the present study.

exeurēsei). For it is hard to search for (*anexereunēton*) and to reach through to (*aporon*)' (fragment DK18)" (p. 1).[3] As Karamanolis and Politis point out, this aporetic fragment concerns aporia as such, it is a statement about the passage, πόρος, through the impasse, ἀπορία. This, because there is no path out of the ἀπορία, since it is unexplored and undiscovered, which means that we must expect the unexpected, and see the possibilities in the impossible. We must be open to that which is not already given as appearance, knowledge, or understanding.

In the same anthology, John Palmer (2018) gives a clear and concise definition of aporia in his contribution, titled "Contradiction and *Aporia* in Early Greek Philosophy": "An *aporia* is, essentially, a point of impasse where there is puzzlement or perplexity about how to proceed. Aporetic reasoning is reasoning that leads to this sort of impasse, and an *aporia*-based method would be one that centrally employs such reasoning. One might describe *aporia*, more basically, as a point where one does not know how to respond to what is said" (p. 9). Thus, an aporia is both the impasse itself and the state of mind caused by the aporia, it functions as both subject and object of philosophical thinking. However, as Heraclitus's fragment D 18 intimates, the aporia is first and foremost an aporia of aporia, that is, the statement about aporia is aporetic itself, the understanding of aporia goes by way of nonunderstanding, and the knowledge of aporia goes by way of nonknowledge. Thus, we must hope for or expect that which cannot be hoped for or expected, and it cannot be hoped for or expected because there is no passage through to that which can be hoped for or expected. This approach of conceiving of aporia by way of Heraclitus differs from how aporia is employed in Plato and Aristotle. In Plato's early dialogues, often referred to as the aporetic dialogues, Socrates's famous method of reasoning ends in his interlocutors not knowing how to follow through with the argument and they come to an impasse.[4] However, Aristotle was the first

---

[3] This is Karamanolis and Politis's translation of Heraclitus's: "ἐὰν μὴ ἔλπηται ἀνέλπιστον οὐκ ἐξευρήσει, ἀνεξερεύνητον ἐὸν καὶ ἄπορον." The aporia of this fragment is perhaps best expressed in Diels's (1906) translation into German: "*Wenn er's nicht erhofft, wird er das Unverhoffte nicht finden. Denn unerforschlich ist's und unzugänglich*" (p. 65). C.f. Kahn's translation which reads: "He who does not expect will not find out the unexpected, for it is trackless and unexplored" (p. 105). Kahn interprets the fragment as being concerned with "the difficulty of cognition from the side of the object. [...] Even if the *logos* [i.e. reason, knowledge, etc.] is common to all, so that the structure of reality is 'given' in everyday experience, recognition comes hard. It requires the right kind of openness on the part of the percipient – what Heraclitus calls 'hope' or 'expectation'. [...] And it requires inquiry and reflection" (p. 105). The fragment in question, VII (D 18), is grouped together with VIII (D 22), XI (D 35), and X (D 123) by Kahn because, as he states, "of their common imagery of searching, finding, being hard to find" (p. 105).

[4] In Plato, aporia serves as part of the means to acquire knowledge, that is, aporia is a moment of learning, in that Socrates's interlocutors gain insight into their own limitations, but also a deeper knowledge of what virtue is. As James Magrini (2018) states, in his *Plato's Socrates, Philosophy and Education*, about the resolution in *Theaeteus*: "Socrates inspires him [Theaeteus] through exhortation and encouragement, because even though the dialogue ends in *aporia*, a 'constructive' moment of learning has occurred: Socrates has brought the best out of Theaeteus because the value of the philosophical pursuit has been instilled in him. Theaeteus admits that the pursuit of such philosophical questions regarding the nature of knowledge, wisdom, and other virtues has already

philosopher to use aporetic reasoning in a systematic way. As Friedemann Buddensiek states in the chapter "*Aporia* in Aristotle's *Metaphysics Beta*" in the anthology *The Aporetic Tradition in Ancient Philosophy*:

> At the beginning of *Metaphysics Beta* Aristotle presents a list of *aporiai* which he then carefully elaborates in the main part of B. These *aporiai* concern the science of the first principles and the first principles themselves. They consist of pairs of important, though incompatible views concerning that science and the principles – views that others have held as well as other views that might arise. The *aporiai* are raised, as it seems, because the awareness and discussion of them as well as the solution to them is a means to accessing those principles: The *aporiai* are mentioned and presented not only because they concern that science and its principles, but because their discussion (their '*diaporein*') is helpful or necessary for establishing that science and for finding and grasping the principles. (p. 137)

Hence, in Aristotle the aporias are posed in order to set up an argument with the aim of clearing up problems facing our understanding of science and its principles. These aporias are in other words not meant to be unsolvable; on the contrary, they are posed more as a rhetorical strategy to understand the fundamental principles governing science.

My approach in this study takes its cue more form the way I have described aporia in Heraclitus, than how it is used in Plato or Aristotle. I am interested in those moments in which an aporia becomes a performative enactment of itself as aporia, when it translates itself into what it is, namely an aporia of aporia. An aporia of translation, then, is just such an event; that is, when translation and aporia are the mirror image of one another, or each the other's echo. This is, furthermore, an event that deconstructs the origin of aporia, aporia as original, and translation respectively.

---

inspired his sense of *philosophical understanding*. For in the *care* of Socrates' *midwifery*, Theaeteus admits, to his own surprise, that Socrates brought about the best in him by transforming his disposition, opening him to an authentic philosophical attitude that Theaeteus never imagined could be experienced (Tht. 210b)" (p. 82). Another important reading of aporia in Plato is Sean Kirkland's (2012) *The Ontology of Socratic Questioning in Plato's Early Dialogues*, in which he provides an extensive reflection on the etymology of aporia and the word's relation to *poros* (a way through or over an impasse) and *peras* (end, limit, boundary). More importantly, he compares the notion of *meletē* (usually translated as exercise, practice, but which Kirkland translates, in the context of Plato, as concern and being concerned) and aporia, which, as he suggests, are two words for expressing the same condition. Thus, Kirkland notes that "the originally passive suffering that is at the very heart of *meletē* would seem to indicate that, no matter how valid or persuasive, no *logos* can ever *generate* the condition of being concerned in its most fundamental sense. Our concerns can be made more poignant or more pressing or less so through discourse of argumentation, and what concerns us might be clarified and refined through investigation or analysis. However, we cannot properly speaking *create* or *compel meletē*, either in ourselves or in others. It is simply not in our power to do so, for *meletē* in its original sense is not the *act* of a subject at all, but, as its grammar insists, an undergoing, a *pathos* triggered through the affective contact with that which places us in a relation of concern" (p. 103). This condition, then, describes aporia as well. Hence, the notion of being concerned that Krikland puts forth here is of importance to the way I read Derrida's use of the word concerned in Chap. 6. Moreover, *meletē* and aporia as an undergoing and not an act of a subject correlates with my use of aporia in this study.

Translation

Jacques Rancière (1991), in *The Ignorant Schoolmaster: Five Lessons in Intellectual Emancipation* (*Le Maître ignorant: Cinq leçons sur l'émancipation intellectuelle*), tells the story of Joseph Jacotot and how he is delegated to teach Flemish students French without the students knowing a word of French and Jacotot not knowing a word of Flemish. Jacotot assigns them the didactic novel *The Adventures of Telemachus, son of Ulisses* (*Les aventures de Télémaque, fils d'Ulysse*) by François Fénelon, written in 1693–94, to read in French together with the Flemish translation of the book. Fénelon's *Télémaque*, as its title suggests, is the story of Ulysses's son and recounts Telemachus's travels and explorations, and his transformation from being a selfish youth into a mature man ready to rule. The story could, in other words, be said to inscribe itself in the long tradition of didactic literature spanning from Hesiod's *Work and Days* (ca 700 BC) to the German *Bildungsroman*, and on to such modern works as the popular novel *Sofie's World* (*Sofies verden*) written by Jostein Gaarder in 1991. In fact, Rancière's *The Ignorant Schoolmaster* could itself be viewed as part of the didactic tradition in philosophy and literature. Thus Rancière, a philosopher, in *The Ignorant Schoolmaster*, broaches the themes pedagogy, teaching, learning, literature, translation, in relation to the topic that constitutes the main concern in much of his work, namely emancipation. The following is a passage in which Rancière addresses translation as intertwined with these themes:

> Understanding is never more than translating, that is, giving the equivalent of a text, but in no way its reason. There is nothing behind the written page, no false bottom that necessitates the work of an *other* intelligence, that of the explicator; no language of the master, no language of the language whose words and sentences are able to speak the reason of the words and sentences of a text. The Flemish students had furnished the proof: to speak about *Télémaque* they had at their disposition only the words of *Télémaque*. Fénelon's sentences alone are necessary to understand Fénelon's sentences and to express what one has understood about them. Learning and understanding are two ways of expressing the same act of translation. There is nothing beyond texts except the will to express, that is, to translate. If they had understood the language by learning Fénelon, it wasn't simply through the gymnastics of comparing the page on the left with the page on the right. It isn't the aptitude for changing columns that counts, but rather the capacity to say what one thinks in the words of others. If they had learned this from Fénelon, that was because the act of Fénelon the writer was itself one of translation: in order to translate a political lesson into a legendary narrative, Fénelon transformed into the French of his century Homer's Greek, Vergil's Latin, and the language, wise or naïve, of a hundred other texts, from children's stories to erudite history. He had applied to this double translation the same intelligence they employed in their turn to recount with the sentences of his book what they thought about his book. (pp. 9–10)

Jacotot's students are using translation to learn French from a book that translates, as Rancière points out, the narratives and languages of classical literature and poetry. His students not only learn the French language but are also exposed to Fénelon's didactic intent in the *Télémaque*. But translation also teaches the students to express their thoughts about Fénelon's novel; being able to express more than the literal translation of the words in one language into another, they learned how to appropriate the text and what it had to say. They learned how to translate, without the direction of a teacher, both the literal and the figurative dimensions of Fénelon's translation. As Rancière contends: "Learning and understanding are two ways of expressing the same act of translation" (p. 10). In Rancière's narrative, we find how translation is employed in order to develop the students' autonomy and freedom in and of both language and thought. In other words, Rancière is telling the story of emancipation through translation.

It is important to remember, when considering Jacotot's choice of literature, the enormous influence that Fénelon's novel has had, not only on education and politics, but on Enlightenment thought overall. In his study *The Political Philosophy of Fénelon*, Ryan Patrick Hanley (2020) lists among Fénelon's admirers Montesquieu, Rousseau, Hume, Bentham, Godwin, Leibniz, Herder, Goethe, Thomas Jefferson, and Robespierre (p. 1). And among Fénelon's writings the *Télémaque* was the work that had the most profound impact, since it constitutes at once a political tract, his foremost work on political reform, his literary masterpiece, and his major work on education. As Hanley states, Fénelon's "principal work on education is of course *Telemachus*":

> A work distinguished by a highly self-conscious approach to both the theory and practice of education. Not only is it obviously didactic, offering subtle (and sometimes less subtle) lessons for the prince to whom it is addressed, it also famously offers a model of idealized educational practice in its detailed depiction of the teacher-student relationship of Mentor and Telemachus. [...] *Telemachus*, as readers have long appreciated (and sometimes lamented), is fundamentally the work of a moralist, an exercise in what we today might call "character formation." (pp. 25–26).

Thus, in *The Ignorant Schoolmaster*, we encounter not only layer upon layer of translations, but we are also faced with the fact that Rancière's work on education and emancipation tells us about the teacher Jacotot's pedagogical method, which entails using Fénelon's *Télémaque*, a work that, as Hanley points out, and just like Ranciére's, interweaves both politics and education. One could claim, then, that Rancière is doing something similar to Fénelon, when he writes that "the act of Fénelon the writer was itself one of translation: in order to translate a political lesson into a legendary narrative" (p. 10). Ranciére is, in consequence, engaging both Jacoto's and Fénelon's pedagogy, and by this double reading enacts a translation of them into his own pedagogy of emancipation. Although Jacotot's narrative might not be legendary it corresponds to Rancière's project of reading, or rather, translating historical records and stories of emancipation. Translating here implies making these records and stories available and so exposing them to an audience that might not otherwise have access to them. Fénelon's allegorical translation of Homer's *Ulysses*, with its aim of instructing its readers also presupposes the reader's translation of the allegory by coming to an understanding of its relevance outside of the story itself. This is the function of allegory; it is meant to teach us something indirectly, in a way that we are forced to translate, and so learn what the text is not telling us explicitly. However, Fénelon's novel, just as Jacotot's pedagogical method, does not require an instructor or explicator to reveal the other language of the text. As Rancière states: "Understanding is never more than translating, that is, giving the equivalent of a text, but in no way its reason. There is nothing behind the written page, no false bottom that necessitates the work of an *other* intelligence, that of the explicator; no language of the master, no language of the language whose words and sentences are able to speak the reason of the words and sentences of a text" (p. 9). Rancière, in other words, identifies translation as a fundamental feature of learning and understanding, a feature that as such is emancipating in that it does not require someone or something form the outside to explain and correct, or as Rancière maintains, "an *other* intelligence" (p. 9) that would impose an established and determined meaning on the translation.

Translation is in this way the structural possibility of meaning and understanding. It is that arche-writing that precedes reason, method, analysis, and explanation. The act of translation is an act of reading that exposes the aporia of language as such and language as a referential medium. It is that which makes possible Rancière's story of Jacotot's pedagogical method of translation, since Rancière's narrative in itself is a translation of the events that make up the story Jacotot is concerned with, installing a "supplement of fiction"[5] into Rancière's philosophical narrative, which in turn builds on Fénelon's fictional novel that stages the education of his readers to become just rulers. Translation, to put it differently, interrupts the determining division between literal and figural language, or to use a notion borrowed from Rancière, the *partage*, the simultaneous division and partaking of the literal and the figural. Thus, the aporia of translation, as I conceive of it in this study, is precisely the undecidability that irrupts out of the act of translating. The aporia of translation is the unnamable event of difference that makes translation as such possible. This way of conceiving of translation is the reason why I have, in this study, not focused exclusively on texts that thematize, analyze, or make use of translation explicitly. Rather, my aim is to point to aporias of translation in texts where we perhaps do not expect to find them. That being said, many of the texts in the study do concern translation in one or another way.

Literature, Philosophy, Education

Education, just as many other disciplines in higher education, frames its content according to determined rules, regulations, and laws, which must be followed in order to qualify what is taught, studied, and researched within education as being proper to education as a discipline. What is perhaps different when it comes to the discipline of education is that it appropriates and applies concepts, content, and methods from other disciplines, that is, it is fundamentally interdisciplinary: it crosses borders, it traces passages over and across disciplines, it figures itself as being, to use the language adopted in this study, πόρος (*poros*), a passage, a way, an

---

[5] See Jacques Derrida's (2002) "The University Without Condition" for his use of the "supplement of fiction" and its relation to the Kantian "as if."

opening. Education as a discipline is thus a passage through, an opening, a way or means of achieving, accomplishing, discovering, a means of providing for something, a journey or voyage. These figures of education, moreover, describe what is often stated as a general purpose of education, that is, it constitutes a transformation that is enacted by learning, often described by using the metaphor of travelling, as a person undertaking a journey in order to gain insight and knowledge, to open up new worlds, and thus undergo some kind of change. Teaching and learning is, furthermore, often characterized as taking place on a stage, that it constitutes some sort of performance, where we act in order to teach and in order to learn. The simile between education and a stage play also describes the formalized nature of education, in which the students and teachers work through certain acts, with a specific content. Education is in this way similar to the stage play in that it is governed by a determined form with a corresponding content. The teachers translate this content to the students who in turn translate it into something understandable that they can appropriate and learn from. The metaphor of the journey and of the stage play to describe education will be touched on in the chapters that follow, although my main concern will be on the aporia of the πόρος. In other words, my central focus is on the impasse of education, when it does not simply function as a journey or passage across a river of ignorance, misunderstanding, or incomprehension – situations where the staging of an educational content does not deliver straight forward meanings to be appropriated and learned. These situations, or events, which we must suffer and endure, are precisely what I call aporias of translation.

In line with the notion of aporias of translation as something that we *undergo*, and not something which we can *choose* and *act on*, my stance toward education as a project in this study is to problematize instances of education as they figure in specific educational, literary, and philosophical contexts. I will, for example, address aesthetic education, social justice education, the discourse of diversity, formal versus informal education, the problematics of rationality and critical thinking, or critique, as it shapes and governs certain aspects of formalized higher education. By bringing together the three main themes of the study, literature, philosophy, and education, my aim is to explore singular aspects of education which, explicitly and implicitly, highlight their importance in the way they shape, form, and inform our thinking, as well as our opinions about what is considered to be the purpose of education in the world and society we inhabit.

To introduce the three themes, I would like to address them by referring to a critic and teacher who has informed my own thinking and teaching on these themes, namely J. Hillis Miller. In the short essay "The Imperative to Teach," Miller (2005) asks the following questions: "Is teaching a contingent addition to 'literary study', or to 'humanistic study' generally? Or, to put it more simply, does reading, the reading of a poem, a novel, or a philosophical text, for example, require teaching it, or lead inevitably to teaching it?" (p. 326). His response is a reflection on teaching and reading, and the place of the humanities in universities today. Miller points out that teaching in the humanities seems to be viewed differently than teaching in the natural or applied sciences. Since reading literary or philosophical texts does not have any use value for society and is "detached from 'the real world', as opposed to research in science, with its presumed 'applied' usefulness" (p. 327), as Miller suggests here, there is a demand for the teaching of these texts within the humanities. Why? Because, Miller continues, "our society feels reading literature or philosophy can only be justified if it is firmly attached to the social and socializing activity of teaching, the passing on and reinforcing of the values of that society through the canonical teaching of canonical works" (p. 327). This also broaches the issue of applying taken for granted, received, meanings of literary and philosophical texts to exemplify or explain, for example social or cultural, phenomena outside the text. In education, this is a conventional way of using literature and philosophy, which I, in this study, want to highlight and problematize. However, to go outside the text is not in itself the problem; it is what we do all the time when we read; that is, we attempt to relate our reading to our experiences of the world outside the text. And teaching is one of the most important activities that lets us venture outside the text in an attempt to, as Miller writes, "verify its referential and performative validity, that is, to find out whether it tells the truth and whether it can be efficacious in helping us and our students in living our lives, in making judgments and decisions 'in the real world'" (p. 327). The problem, or challenge, is rather the impossibility of verifying a text's referential or performative validity. As Miller points out:

> The impossibility of distinguishing for certain between literal and figurative language in the text, that is to say, the interference of rhetoric in grammar and logic does not mean that no text is truthfully referential but that neither reader, nor teacher, nor student [...] can ever be certain whether or not the text is truthfully referential. [...] There is no way to tell for sure, and the reader-teacher is suspended in the extreme discomfort of responding to an imperative call which at the same time he or she is altogether unable to fulfill. (p. 328)

Thus, as teachers and students, we cannot choose, or act on, a verified, truthful meaning or interpretation of a text, but must instead, through a concerned reading, undergo the ambivalence of not being able to know and so decide on what the text is referring to or what it makes happen, that is, what it performs. We are, in other words, caught in an aporia of translation, since there is an imperative to translate, to teach, and understand the text, but as soon as we do, we are undermined by the inadequacy of our own reading. Hence, Miller argues: "The teaching of literature, in fact, is neither a one-way street, nor a two-way street, but a permanent impasse, or a road impassable for an indefinite time, while it is 'under construction'" (p. 329). Nevertheless, this does not mean that we cannot or should not teach, study, and read literature, philosophy, and other texts in the humanities. "Far from it," Miller assures us: "Teaching happens all the time, I am happy to say. But it happens as the patient, iterated, and reiterated demonstration, out there in the open, whatever the teacher may think he or she is doing, of the impasse I have tried to define" (p. 329). What Miller describes, in his essay, is precisely the predicament that a careful, rhetorical, or deconstructive reading and teaching practice finds itself in. When there is nothing that with absolute certainty can be predicted, calculated, or measured by applying rational logic or a scientific method that would determine and assign an authorized meaning to a text, when there is not even any kind of performative promise of social justice or emancipation, when there is no assurance of any formative or transformative outcome that can be measured, evaluated, and assessed, and so accounted for, the social efficiency and accountability of education is undermined.

Given this predicament, what the present study suggests, and which I hope will be its contribution to teachers and students alike (if I am to envision a desired outcome of the study) is that it will speak to educators and students in new ways that might inspire them to recognize and embrace the unique and developing "life-projects" of education, which constitutes processes of "learning" – *becoming other to oneself* – with the understanding that learning (reading, translating) occurs in its most authentic form as a concerned undergoing, and is not to be found in any "actualized" or "authorized" concrete or objectified results standing outside or beyond either the individual or the educational process itself, in a way that would devalue the process and render it disposable.[6] Moreover, I contend that it is in the moments of aporia, when these educational processes are disrupted or deconstruct, when we have to remain concerned, μελέτη (*meletē*), in the face of an impasse, or other boundaries, limits, and limitations, seemingly impossible to cross over, it is then, in those moments, that we can truly begin to undergo, and eventually translate, the experience of education as an act of *possible* emancipation. And this, I argue, should be a major concern, perhaps most of all, to education as a discipline.

Chapter Summaries

In Chap. 2 of the study, "The Education of Death," I aim to explore how education is depicted in Thomas Bernhard's novel *Gargoyles*. I start out by referring to a passage in Hegel's *Phenomenology of Spirit* where a dialectic is staged in his discussion of culture, wealth, and state power. I am particularly interested in Hegel's use of the word "*Verkherung*" and its translation by A. V. Miller as "perversion" and how it can be used to analyze Bernhard's *Gargoyles*. When it comes to Bernhard's novel I note that both it and Hegel's *Phenomenology of Sprit* can be read as journeys of transformation, and so belonging to the *Bildungsroman* genre. The protagonist in the novel that is of main interest is the deranged Prince Saurau, who utters a sentence which I pay particular attention, namely: "The only attainable goal of study is death" [*Das einzige erreichbare Lernziel ... ist der Tot*]." I then go on to explore irony in relation to education and dialectics, a discussion which continues my reflections on Hegel and Bernhard. This, in turn, leads me to broach the question of translation, and how my notion of it is informed by irony and dialectics. Next, I analyze Jean-Luc Nancy's *Hegel: The Restlessness of the Negative* from the perspective of his translation of Hegel, specifically a sentence from §590 in the Phenomenology of Spirit where Hegel mentions the death of signification. I then relate the question of translation to Nancy's translation of Hegel as exhibiting the death of signification in

---

[6] I would like to thank James Magrini for providing me with the inspiration to rephrase and develop this sentence. Magrini's original sentence will appear in a forthcoming essay that we are co-authoring.

itself, but also how it ties in to my reading of Hegel and Bernhard. From my reading of Nancy I continue by invoking Freud's *Beyond the Pleasure Principle* and how the death drive figures in Prince Saurau's idea of death. My next step is to introduce Kant into my analysis, together with Derrida's reading of Kant, as well as Derrida's own thoughts on aporia in his work *Aporias*. Importantly, Derrida brings up translation in the context of Kant's famous statement that one cannot learn philosophy, but only learn how to philosophize, and also finds an aporia at work in Kant's statement. Moreover, Derrida broaches the etymology of aporia and its relation to passage and crossing the ultimate border, that is, death. Derrida's reading of aporia brings me, finally, to consider aporia and Bernhard's *Gargoyles* in which the aporia of an education of death is staged and enacted, in other words, translated.

Chapter 3 of the study is titled "The Supreme Exertion of Thinking": Censorship, Critique, and Education" and explores the censored chapter "At Tikhon" in Dostoevsky's novel *Demons*. I highlight the pedagogical situation which develops in the encounter between the novel's protagonist Stavrogin and the monk Tikhon, an encounter which raises the question of critique, censorship, and education more generally. This leads me to broach Derrida's reading of how Kant relates to censorship, which makes it possible for me to connect translation with a certain censuring effect that exposes its aporetic character. I then extend my argument by developing a notion of critique in relation to Heidegger's use of the word *Auseinandersetzung* (confrontation) and how Walter Benjamin's thinking on critique and translation ties into my analysis of education, translation, and aporia. I conclude the chapter with some reflections on ethics and confrontation (*Auseinandersetzung*) as critique, or what Heidegger calls "the supreme exertion of thinking."

Chapter 4 continues my reflections on translation, critique, and education, specifically addressing the idea of "critical thinking" as a measurable outcome of higher education. One of the main texts I consider is Sarah Maitland's important book *What is Cultural Translation?* My aim is to confront the notions of culture and translation in Maitland's study in order to probe their limits and aporias. I then continue by considering a specific debate within the critical thinking discourse in higher education, which is played out between proponents of a discipline specific view of critical thinking and an idea of critical thinking as being independent of discipline and so viewed as a generic skill that can be applied in any discipline by using formal logic and rational reasoning. This leads me to consider Jon Elster's critique of Edward Said's reading of Jane Austen's *Mansfield Park*. This critique highlights the epistemological divide between analytic and continental philosophy and theory, which, it could be argued, has extended into what is termed the "culture wars," where proponents of rationalism stand against the perceived relativity of postmodernism and poststructuralism. In the chapter, I argue for a stance that recognizes the aporetic nature of knowledge, culture, history, and education, and against the reductionist tendencies of reasoning that applies strict formal logic and rational thinking in such texts as, for example, Elster's "Hard and Soft Obscuritanism in the Humanities and Social Sciences." My alternative is to see critique as translation, but a notion of translation as the aporetic possibility of literary and philosophical texts as such.

The title of Chap. 5 is "The Nature of Learning and the Aporia of 'Words'" and begins with a reading of figures of learning in Heidegger and Aristotle, and what these two philosophers view as the nature, or essence, of learning. This entails considering Aristotle's principle of non-contradiction, and education related to that which requires no proof. According to Heidegger it is thinking that require no proof and so it is thinking that we still have not learned properly. To search for the matter of thinking, Heidegger says, is the fundamental challenge we are facing, and this means questioning scientism and formal logic, which hinders the way we can prepare for a thinking that ponders the matter for thinking as such. This means that we must disregard Aristotle's principle of non-contradiction and be prepared to think through the aporia that can lead us to learn, in a more fundamental way, what the matter for thinking is. Heidegger turns to poetry in order to reflect on the nature of learning and the matter for thinking, and in the chapter, I consider his reading of Stefan George's poem "Words," in which Heidegger reflects on what learning means and what it entails for thinking. I extend my consideration of Heidegger's view on learning by referring to the way he deals with it in "What is a Thing?" In Heidegger, learning and thinking are strictly related to the thinking of Being as such, which is a thinking that can only happen as something unexpected and unanticipated, as that which is not governed by the principle of non-contradiction, in other words, as an aporia. Hence, I argue that the thinking of Being necessarily involves a translation of a fundamental aporia, and that to prepare for such translations is to engage in another way of learning than the kind of learning that is ruled by scientism and an adherence to formal logic.

Chapter 6, "The Aporias of Translation in Poetry and Aesthetic Education: Reading John Ashbery" develops a reading of John Ashbery's poetry, with a special focus on his poems "One Hundred Multiple-Choice Questions" and the long prose poem *Three Poems*. The emphasis of my reading lies on the nature of poetic meaning and how determined meanings inform education and specifically aesthetic education to develop a sensitivity to art, empathy, and virtue in its students. To problematize the idea of poetic meaning as transferable and transformative I refer to Blanchot's insistence on the difference between poetic meaning and rational discourse. Poetic meaning, Blanchot holds, cannot be paraphrased or translated, but is expressed precisely as that which is lost in translation, analysis, and paraphrase. This brings me to consider the rhetorical figure catachresis in relation to poetry and aesthetic education. I pay special attention to Gayatri Spivak's notion of the "double bind," which I compare to catachresis and aporia. Furthermore, Spivak's double bind is in itself a necessary questioning of aesthetic education in its historical and cultural situatedness, informed by enlightenment thought and positivist rationality. Next, I introduce Stephen Fredman's analysis of *Three Poems* and his suggestion to define Ashberey's poem as translative and reliant on what Fredman calls not-understanding, which relates to the way Ashbery characterizes his poetry in an interview; Ashbery is trying, as he says, to capture the "experience of experience." In Fredman's reading, Ashbery's poem becomes an educational journey, with a clear goal, which is to learn what has been learned. I then consider the Kantian "as if" (*als ob*) and how it figures in Ashbery's poem, which brings me to introduce

Bataille's notions of the counter-project, nonknowledge, and the sovereign moment. These notions bring into relief Ashbery's project in *Three Poems* as a counter-project, which means that it works against itself toward its own disruption. In the poem, the sought after moment, when the word that will explain everything, never comes, since it cannot be anticipated, but only arrives as the unspoken and unfulfilled performative utterance which leaves the audience hanging in suspense, even after the performance is over. In other words, the translation in and of the poem ends in aporia. I conclude the chapter with some reflections on aesthetic education and how Ashbery's poetry breaks up the system of aesthetic education seen as a transformative process with the aim of cultivating character through determined poetic meaning. I contrast Ashbery's poetry with the utilitarianism of J. S. Mill's idea of aesthetic education with its purpose of transferring the effect of, for example, beauty into virtue that can be acquired if one reads or perceives art in a predetermined manner. I end the chapter by speculating if another aesthetic education is possible, one which might consider, for example, the play drive in Schiller's *The Aesthetic Education of Man* as an alternative to the emphasis on work, labor, and meaning, which we still find in aesthetic education today.

In the last chapter of the study, Chap. 7, titled "Translating the Other: Diversity and the (Ir)responsibility of Teaching," I address a concept that is commonly used in the discourses in the humanities and the social sciences, namely the concept of the other. This concept is also an intrinsic part of another concept that has come to play an integral part in the discourse within higher education, namely the concept of diversity. In the chapter, I trace these two concepts, the other and diversity, to some of their philosophical origins and how they have been used in later theory, such as Cultural Studies and critical pedagogy, but I also relate the concept of the other to Sharon Todd's important study *Learning from the Other: Levinas, Psychoanalysis and Ethical Possibilities in Education*, which does not address diversity as such, but rather what Todd calls Social Justice Education. As Todd points out, the concept of the other is both a concept appropriated in education to designate a marginalized subject, and a philosophical concept with different epistemological and ontological implications. These two stances toward the other are often fused, not to say confused, with the consequence that it becomes theoretically vague. Hence, I refer to how the concept of the other is thought in Levinas's and Derrida's thinking, which necessarily brings with it a consideration of ethics and responsibility and how these additional concepts are tied to their thinking of the other. Next, I relate the practice of teaching to Derrida's notion of "irresponisibilization" and how the discourses on ethics are inevitably caught in an aporia, which becomes a challenge for teaching, since teaching must apply or translate what it teaches. Thus, I suggest that teaching must consider its other as what Derrida calls "arche-writing," which constitutes the very possibility of reflecting on and so also the possibility of teaching the other. Remaining concerned in teaching thus means recognizing the aporia of translation, which is also, as J. Hillis Miller suggests, an imperative to teach.

References

Derrida, J. (2002). The university without condition. In P. Kamuf (Trans.), *Without Alibi* (pp. 202–237). Stanford University Press.

Diels, H. (1906). *Die Fragmente der Vorsokratiker (Erster Band)*. WeidmannscheBuchhandlung.

Hanley, R. P. (2020). *The political philosophy of Fénelon*. Oxford University Press.

Karamanolis, G., & Politis, V. (2018). Introduktion. In G. Karamanolis & V. Politis (Eds.), *The Aporetic tradition in ancient philosophy* (pp. 1–8). Cambridge University Press.

Kirkland, S. D. (2012). *The ontology of Socratic questioning in Plato's early dialogues*. State University of New York Press.

Magrini, J. M. (2018). *Plato's Socrates, philosophy and education*. Springer.

Magrini, J. M., & Schwieler, E. (2018). *Heidegger on literature, poetry, and education after the "turn": At the limits of metaphysics*. Routledge.

Miller, J. H. (2005). The imperative to teach. In J. Wolfreys (Ed.), *The J. Hillis Miller reader* (pp. 326–329). Stanford University Press.

Palmer, J. (2018). Contradiction and *Aporia* in early Greek philosophy. In G. Karamanolis & V. Politis (Eds.), *The Aporetic tradition in ancient philosophy* (pp. 9–28). Cambridge University Press.

Rancière, J. (1991). *The ignorant schoolmaster: Five lessons in intellectual emancipation* (K. Ross, Trans.). Stanford University Press.

Sorensen, E. P. (2010). *Postcolonial studies and the literary: Theory, interpretation and the novel*. Palgrave Macmillan.

Chapter 2
The Education of Death

*Ein Mißverständnis setzt uns in die Welt der Mißverständnisse,
die wir als nur aus lauter Mißverständnissen zusammengesetzt
zu ertragen haben und mit einem einzigen großen
Mißverständnis wieder verlassen, denn der Tod ist das größte
Mißverständnis.*

Thomas Bernhard, Der Untergeher

*One misunderstanding casts us into the world of
misunderstanding, which we must put up with as a world
composed solely of misunderstandings and which we depart
from with a single great misunderstanding, for death is the
greatest misunderstanding of all.*

Thomas Bernhard, The Loser

Introduction: *Verkehrung* in Hegel's Dialectics

I will begin this chapter by referring to a passage in Hegel's (1977) *Phenomenology of Spirit*, more precisely §491 in A. V. Miller's translation. The passage will serve as the point of departure for a reading of the text which constitutes my main concern in the chapter, namely Thomas Bernhard's novel *Gargoyles*. The passage in the *Phenomenology* that I want to highlight is the place in Hegel's text where he discusses culture (*Bildung*) in relation to state power and wealth. Hegel does this by, not surprisingly, invoking the movement of dialectics. "Existence" (*das Dasein*), Hegel writes,

> is really the perversion of every determinateness into its opposite, and it is only this alienation that is the essential nature and support of the whole. We have now to consider this process in which the moments are stirred into life and given an existence of their own; the alienation will alienate itself, and the whole will, through this alienation, return into its Notion. (p. 300)

© Springer Nature Switzerland AG 2022
E. Schwieler, *Aporias of Translation*, Contemporary Philosophies and Theories in Education 18, https://doi.org/10.1007/978-3-030-97895-2_2

[das Dasein ist vielmehr die Verkehrung jeder Bestimmtheit in ihre entgegengesetzte, und nur diese Entfremdung ist das Wesen und Erhaltung des Ganzen. Diese verwirklichende Bewegung und Begeistung der Momente ist nun zu betrachten; die Entfremdung wird sich selbst entfremden, und das Ganze durch sie in seinen Begriff sich zurücknehmen.] (p. 662)

Reading the passage, we recognize many of the words that characterize Hegel's vocabulary in the *Phenomenology*, and, as indicated, also the movement of dialectics which is a distinctive mark of what could be called Hegel's style, besides being, needless to say, his method of doing philosophy. The word that stands out in the above-cited passage and that also signals the movement of dialectics is "perversion," and as we can see in the German original of the text the word Hegel uses in German is "*Verkehrung*." Now, *Verkehrung* can in addition to perversion mean reversal, which perhaps more clearly indicates the oscillating movement implied in dialectics. But even though reversal is the obvious and literal translation tied to dialectics, Miller here chooses to use perversion in his translation to add something to the movement that Hegel is trying to describe. Miller's translation thus tells us that the movement of dialectics in Hegel is more than a simple reversal of what is determined; the dialectical movement is reversing and perverting the determinateness into its opposite, which means it is not a simple and straight forward movement of negativity, but a turning out of shape of what is determined into what it is not, although still related to it by being its opposite. Moreover, it is existence (*das Dasein*), Hegel says, that is the perversion of determinateness. Existence alienates what is determined and in so doing supports the whole, that is to say, what is determined and fixed. Thus, *Verkehrung* as reversal, perversion, and alienation is the "essential nature and support of the whole," i.e. every determinateness. What is the opposite of every determinateness, that is, that which is alienated by existence, will then itself be alienated, "the alienated will alienate itself," and so on. This circular, not to say paradoxical, movement is the signature of Hegel's version of dialectics, and could be called "the restlessness of the negative," to preclude Jean-Luc Nancy's reading of Hegel, which I will touch on later. It is furthermore through the different moments within the movement of dialectics that existence comes to be as opposite moments of determinateness. However, these moments of determinateness are exactly that, moments on the verge of change, which means that the essence of existence is its restlessness, what Hegel calls "*Unruhe*." This, then, is the Notion (*Begriff*) of the whole, or, in other words, the continuous and restless process of perversion.

Bernhard's *Gargoyles*

At this point in my reading of the passage in Hegel's *Phenomenology* I want to turn to Thomas Bernhard's *Gargoyles*, his third major novel, published in 1968, with the German title *Verstörung*. However, before giving the passage from

Gargoyles which is the focus of my reading, I would like to point to the possibility of reading *Gargoyles* as well as Hegel's *Phenomenology* as a *Bildungsroman*, that is, as a journey of learning and experience (see, e.g. Gitta Honegger (2001)[1] on *Gargoyles* and Jean Hyppolite (1979)[2] on Hegel's *Phenomenology*).[3] And it is this possibility of a relation to education (*Bildung*) which I want to highlight, together with the movement of dialectics in Hegel, in my reading of the passage from Bernhard's novel. When it comes to *Gargoyles*, it tells the story of a boy who comes home to a small countryside village in Austria for a weekend break from his studies, and how his father, who is a country doctor in the area, takes him along on his rounds. Each patient they meet is somehow deranged, alienated from reality, or is living a marginalized and secluded life. The second half of the novel is entirely devoted to the boy and his father's meeting with the insane prince Saurau, who lives with his sisters, his wife, and daughters in a local castle. With the introduction of prince Saurau, the novel turns from bodily to metal sickness. Now, in terms of viewing the novel as a *Bildungsroman*, Saurau turns out to be the boy's mentor, guide, or teacher, or rather anti-teacher, given the views of education he communicates. Thus, in the passage I have chosen to read, prince Saurau addresses life and education, and how education is nothing but the education of death:

> "The world actually is, as has so often been said, a stage on which roles are forever being rehearsed. Wherever we look it is a perpetual learning to speak and learning to walk and learning to think and learning by heart, learning to cheat, learning to die, learning to be dead. This is what takes up all our time. Men are nothing but actors putting on a show all too familiar to us. Learners of roles," the prince said. "Each of us is forever learning one (his) or several or all imaginable [*Denkbaren*, italics in the original] roles, without knowing why he is learning them (or for whom). This stage is an unending torment and no one feels that the events on it are a pleasure. But everything that happens on this stage happens naturally. A critic [*Dramaturg*] to explain the play is constantly being sought. When the curtain rises, everything is over." Life, he went on, changing his image, was a school in which death was being taught. It was filled with millions and billions of pupils and teachers.

---

[1] In her book *Thomas Bernhard: The Making of an Austrian*, Honegger notes that *Gargoyles* "is a Bildungsroman of sorts [and] features a young man in the process of distancing himself from his parents" (p. 39).

[2] In *The Genesis and Structure of Hegel's Phenomenology of Spirit*, Hyppolite states: "The *Phenomenology*, then, is the itinerary of the soul which rises to spirit through the intermediary of *consciousness*. The idea of such an itinerary was undoubtedly suggested to Hegel by the philosophic works mentioned above [i.e. the works of Kant, Fichte, and Schelling], but the influence of the *Bildungsromanen* of the time seems to us to have been just as important" (p. 11).

[3] In his first footnote in *The Hegel Variations*, Fredric Jameson (2010) relates the following rumor about the *Phenomenology* as a *Bildungsroman*: "It has been rumored that the formal paradigm for Hegel's *Bildungsroman* was *La Vie de Marianne of Marivaux* (1731–1745): see Jacques d'Hondt, 'Hegel et Marivaux', in *Europe*, vol. 44, December 1966, 323–337. For d'Hondt, however, the kinship lies less in the sequence of episodes than in Marianne's achievement of a truly divided self-consciousness" (note 1, p. 1). For a discussion of the *Phenomenology* and its place in Hegel's own teaching, see Terry Pinkard's (2000) *Hegel: A Biography*.

The world was a school of death. "First the world is the elementary school of death, then the secondary school of death, then, for the very few, the university of death," the prince said. People alternate as teachers or pupils in these schools. "The only attainable goal of study is death," he said. (Bernhard, 2006, pp. 145–146)[4]

As a side note, there is an intertext to the cited passage that deserves to be highlighted, namely the allusion to Act 5, Scene 5 in Shakespeare's (1997) *Macbeth*, and especially to the lines:

Life's but a walking shadow, a poor player
    That struts and frets his hour on the stage
    And then is heard no more: it is a tale
    Told by an idiot, full of sound and fury,
    Signifying nothing. (p. 229)

Both *Macbeth* and *Gargoyles* have insanity and the futility of life as their major themes. And in Saurau's monologue in *Gargoyles* we hear the echo of Macbeth's lament against life and the comparison of life to an actor on a stage. One could without too much difficulty perceive of a reading of *Gargoyles* in which each character would be a variation of Macbeth's soliloquy. However, my interest in the passage has to do with a recurrent theme in Bernhard's work, namely the destructive force of education,[5] of which prince Saurau's monologue is a clear example. He views learning of different kinds as rehearsing a role or roles – life consists, according to Saurau, in learning to play one or more roles, including learning to die and learning to be dead. As he says: "The only attainable goal of study is death" [*Das einzige erreichbare Lernziel … ist der Tot*]. This statement is particularly interesting since is it ambiguous, either it means that the only thing we can learn about is death, or it means that the only achievable outcome of education is death, that is, that we (can) die from it. The second possible meaning is supported by Saurau's insistence on seeing life as a perpetual rehearsal which ends when the curtain rises. The final goal is unattainable, no matter how much we strive and rehearse for the grand opening to stage the actual finished play, to finally disclose the finished outcome of our studies, it ends before it has even begun. Or, to put it differently, the perfected and finished goal ends up as death, which means by extension that education is death. It is a nothingness and complete failure, and the process is a ruse. In *Gargoyles*, as in many other novels of Bernhard's, Absolute Knowledge and Absolute Freedom, to invoke Hegel, are nothing but pure negativity, empty death, without significance.

---

[4] For the German edition used, see Bernhard (2015).

[5] The critique of education in Bernhard's work should be viewed as part of, or parallel to, his critique of Austrian society, and the repression of the past after the second world war, which Bernhard saw at work in Austrian society. But, the negative opinion of education also had deeply personal reasons for Bernhard, as evidenced by how he portrays education in his autobiographies, translated as *Gathering Evidence*, a volume which collects the texts *Die Ursache: Eine Andeutung*, *Der Keller: Eine Entziehung*, *Der Atem: Eine Entscheidung*, *Die Kälte: Eine Isolation*, and *Ein Kind*.

Irony: Education and Dialectics

This bleak idea of life and education, and the search for knowledge and truth, is also echoed by Bernhard himself, as in the following excerpt from a speech he gave on receiving the Wildgans Prize in 1968:

> When we are searching for the truth … it is failure, death that we are searching for, our own failure, our own death, as far back as our thoughts or feelings go, or our imagination, or as far into the future as we *were to look*, it is death, the absence of repose, or repose as a sign of weakness, of failure (qtd, in Porcell 334). (Cousineau, 2008, p. 24)

This statement quite clearly reflects a similar perspective on life and knowledge as the monologue of prince Saurau in *Gargoyles*. The search for truth, whatever that might mean, is in Bernhard's world (the fictional as well as the real) bound to end in failure and death. The kind of education that life still provides, then, to put it more positively, is learning how to die. Learning how to die is a theme we can find in, for example, Plato and Montaigne. In Plato's (1892) *Phaedo*, Socrates says: "And, as I was saying at first, there would be a ridiculous contradiction in men studying to live as nearly as they can in a state of death, and yet repining when it comes upon them. Clearly. And the true philosophers, Simmias, are always occupied in the practice of dying, wherefore also to them least of all men is death terrible" (pp. 194–195). Later, this is picked up by Montaigne (2014), by way of Cicero, in his essay "That to Philosophize Is to Learn How to Die." Montaigne argues that learning how to die has the aim of alleviating the agony of the thought of death, and of giving us comfort when faced with our own as well as others' mortality: "For who would give ear unto him that for its end would establish our pain and disturbance" (p. 13). The answer to Montagne's question could be: The readers of Thomas Bernhard, as reflected in many of the protagonists in his novels, for "pain and disturbance" is the outcome, one could argue, of what has been called the nihilism of Thomas Bernhard's work.[6] However, something which becomes more obvious in Bernhard's later work is that this nihilism is countered by irony and self-parody (Martin, 205–206). Just like Kafka,[7] Bernhard finds his own dismal, agonizing description of the human condition to be humorous. And, importantly, humor, irony, and parody function as the leverage used to battle the absurdity and cruelty of the world. Thus, even in his early works (e.g. *Gargoyles* and *Frost*), works shrouded in an atmosphere of pending doom, failure, insanity, and death, there is an undercurrent of irony and dark humor, which, even if hard to detect, is present in the constant exaggerations, monotony and repetitiveness, and the use of a language bordering on derangement and insanity.

---

[6] See, e.g., Martin, C. W. (1995). *The Nihilism of Thomas Bernhard: The portrayal of existential and social problems in his prose work.* Amsterdam and Atlanta, GA: Editions Rodopi, B. V.

[7] As Jean Collignon (1955) suggests concerning Kafka's humor, which could be compared to Bernhard's, "it is the humor of a man both oppressed and depressed who smiles not in order to forget but to assert his independence, and makes plain his determination not to be overwhelmed by hardships: he will be defeated, he knows it, there is no hope; he will be murdered 'like a dog'; but he can keep smiling at the whole procedure and at himself into the bargain" (pp. 53–54).

Such language, and with it the absurd humor and irony, characterizes the rants of prince Saurau in *Gargoyles*, as can be noted in the quoted passage on death and education.

If we identify irony as a major trope in Bernhard's work, it is then possible to read it through my rendition of Hegelian dialectics, which suggests that it does not succeed in reaching the end point of Absolute Knowledge or Absolute Spirit. Instead we must conceive of this dialectic as a circle without an identifiable beginning or end. This kind of dialectics, I suggest, can be compared to the figure of irony, if we take irony as it is defined by Paul de Man, namely as "the permanent parabasis of the allegory of tropes."[8] Irony is, from this Hegelian/de Manian perspective, the perversion or derangement, the continuous reversal, of that which is determined into its opposite. We recognize this movement form the passage in Hegel's *Phenomenology of Spirit* which I cited at the outset. Irony, then, if one were to apply to it my reading of Hegelian dialectics, is the *Verkehrung* which makes existence (*das Dasein*) come to its own. Inherent in the figure of irony, similarly, is what Hegel calls alienation (*Entfremdung*), and the necessary movement of how "the alienation will alienate itself" [*die Entfremdung wird sich selbst entfremden*]. This way of thinking the movement of irony is quite different from Socratic irony, which is more commonly associated with education. That is, how Socrates pretend to be ignorant of a certain topic in order to challenge his pupil's or opponent's arguments. The Socratic maieutic method of teaching is still relevant and has been developed in modern educational theory, especially in relation to critical thinking, as a way to develop reasoning skills in pupils and students.[9] But, since this is far from the "teaching" that is going on in Bernhard's *Gargoyles* or Hegel's *Phenomenology of Spirit*, I will not go deeper into the Socratic version of irony. The relevance to education that rather applies to these two works is, as noted, to read them as (perhaps ironic) variations of the *Bildungsroman* genre.

How, then, can we approach the topic of death and education, even the death of education, given the ironic movement (as defined by de Man), in Bernhard's *Gargoyles* and Hegel's *Phenomenology of Spirit*? If we are to identify irony as a disruption of the narrative (i.e. disruption as parabasis, which de Man borrows from Schlegel, who picked it up from classical Greek tragedy) in the passage from *Gargoyles*, in which prince Saurau declares his views on life, the world, death and

---

[8] The figure of irony I am invoking takes its cue, as noted above, from Paul de Man's (1996) definition of irony in the essay "The Concept of Irony," in his *Aesthetic Ideology*, which is in itself an ironic title, it could be argued, since de Man uses the same title as Kierkegaard's work *The Concept of Irony*. To repeat de Man's definition, it reads as follows: "irony is the permanent parabasis of the allegory of tropes" (p. 179), which means that there is, in consequence, a constant indeterminateness to irony, which in turn means that as soon as something is determined as ironic, irony is suspended, put on hold, making it literal or at least non-ironic, giving us the possibility of reading that which is ironic as literal, which, paradoxically, is necessary in the first place, in order to identify something as ironic. "The Concept of Irony" was first given as a lecture by Paul de Man at Ohio State University in 1977, and was transcribed by Tom Keenan. For an historic overview of the concept of irony, see Behler (1990).

[9] See, e.g., Copeland (2005), and Tredway (1995).

education, we must act as that intermediary which prince Saurau says is constantly being sought, namely, the dramaturg (which is something different from a critic, with which the German *dramaturg* is translated in Bernhard's novel). Prince Saurau's remark that a dramaturg is needed for the roles we as humans are rehearsing is a comment on the inadequacy of the actors. Consequently, someone who can work as an interpreter for the actors and translate the play into an understandable language is necessary, which will make it easier for the actors to successfully perform the play. What is required, then, is a translation which would point to the parabasis in the narrative; in other words, a translation that would disrupt the narrative in order to reflect on the movement of irony in the text. But such a translation, I claim, would itself have to follow the movement of irony, which is to say it would have to follow the movement of the reversal of alienation. Translation, on this view, can be defined as the irony of dialectics, in which each determined term or word is decided on by the movement of reversal, which is a perversion of the determined term or word into its opposite, while still remaining, we could even say becoming, itself by being what it is not. This is how we must approach prince Saurau's assertion that "The only attainable goal of study is death" [*Das einzige erreichbare Lernziel … ist der Tot*].

The key word that I want to pay particular attention to in this sentence is the word death. Death is what we constantly rehearse, and when we finally reach the point where we can "perform" death, and the curtain rises, everything ends, because death is a play that cannot be played or performed as such, only rehearsed. This is why, furthermore, we can only learn *about* death, but never know it in itself. However, we can attain death, that is, we can die, but even if we reach death and die, learning is meaningless, since all knowledge is lost in death. This is why prince Saurau views death as a learning goal – death provides the end of derangement, ambiguity, and suffering, which is something the world, life, and formal education can never promise to offer. However, "in the face of death" we are confronted with the same movement that we have seen characterizes Hegel's dialectics, irony, and translation, that is, we are faced with an impossibility, or aporia, which can, again, only be rehearsed, never resolved, since death is the emptying out of all signification - there is no meaning in death, only of death.

Nancy's Hegel and "The Death of Signification Itself"

At this point I would like to refer to Jean-Luc Nancy's reading of Hegel in order to contextualize my position. In his short book titled *Hegel: The Restlessness of the Negative*, Nancy (2002) puts forward an interesting and compelling interpretation of the impact of Hegel's philosophy, which includes a quote from §590 of the *Phenomenology*: "Never again can this displacement [i.e. the dialectical movement of a determined term into its opposite] regain the movement of a transcendence that would raise it toward a supreme signification. It knows the possibility of a 'death which has no inner signification', that is, the possibility of the death of signification itself" (p. 3). In Nancy's (1997) original French these sentences run as follows: *"Jamais plus ce déplacement ne rejoint le movement d'une transcendence qui le soulèvera vers un signification suprême. Il connaît la possibilité du «la mort privée de signification», c'est-à-dire de la mort de la signification elle-même"* (p. 6). From this we could infer that, on Nancy's view, philosophy with Hegel came to an end as a transcendental project with a teleological ultimate goal and meaning. Or, if we consider the place in the *Phenomenology* from which this quote is taken ("Absolute Freedom and Terror"), we must infer that Nancy is pointing to the transcendence of revolution and terror, which Hegel identifies with a destructive force that leads to a death without meaning, that is, a death with no inherent fulfillment.[10] However, no matter which interpretation we choose to rely on, there is, first of all, reason to look closer at how Nancy is using the Hegel quote. The quote is, in fact, I would like to suggest, a perversion of what Hegel writes in §590. In Hegel's German the phrase stands as: *"ein Tot, der keinen innern Umfang und Erfüllung hat,"*[11] which in Miller's translation reads: "a death too which has no inner significance or filling,"[12] and which finally in Nancy's version becomes: *"la mort privée de signification* [death which has no signification]." The problem here is how we can reconcile Nancy's use of the word "signification," where Miller has "significance and filling," to translate

---

[10] Hegel's point of reference here is the French revolution and the Reign of Terror between September 1793 and July 1794. For a reading of Hegel by way of the themes of revolt and revolution, see Albert Camus's (1991) *The Rebel: And Essay on Man in Revolt.* For example, Camus states that "German nineteenth-century thinkers, particularly Hegel, wanted to continue the work of the French Revolution while suppressing the causes of its failure. Hegel thought that he discerned the seeds of the Terror contained in the abstract principles of the Jacobins. According to him, absolute and abstract freedom must inevitably lead to terrorism; the rule of abstract law is identical with the rule of oppression," and further that "Actually, in one sense, his work exudes an absolute horror of dissidence: he wanted to be the very essence of reconciliation. But this is only one aspect of a system which, by its very method, is the most ambiguous in all philosophic literature" (p. 68). Incidentally, Camus views *The Phenomenology of Spirit* as having in part a didactic purpose, and in *The Rebel* states that "it depicts, in its successive stages, the education of the mind as it pursues its way toward absolute truth" (p. 70). On death, freedom, Hegel, and the Reign of Terror, see also Maurice Blanchot's (1995) "Literature and the Right to Death."

[11] It can be clarifying to know the textual context in Hegel's *Phänomenologie* from which Nancy picks the statement under discussion: "–Das Verhältnis also dieser beiden, da sie unteilbar absolut für sich sind, und also keinen Teil in die Mitte schicken können, wodurch sie sich verknüpften, ist die ganz *unvermittelte* reine Negation; und zwar die Negation des Einzelnen als *Seienden* in dem Allgemeinen. Das einzige Werk und Tat der allgemeinen Freiheit ist daher der *Tod*, und zwar ein Tod, der keinen innern Umfang und Erfüllung hat, denn was negiert wird, ist der unerfüllte Punkt des absolut freien Selbsts; er ist also der kälteste, platteste Tod, ohne mehr Bedeutung als das Durchhauen eines Kohlhaupts oder ein Schluck Wassers" (p. 798).

[12] For context, I also provide the same excerpt from Miller's translation of §590: "The relation, then, of these two, since each exists indivisibly and absolutely for itself, and thus cannot dispose of a middle term which would link them together, is one of wholly unmediated pure negation, a negation, moreover, of the individual as a being existing in the universal. The sole work and deed of universal freedom is therefore death, a death too which has no inner significance or filling, for what is negated is the empty point of the absolutely free self. It is thus the coldest and meanest of all deaths, with no more significance than cutting off a head of cabbage or swallowing a mouthful of water" (p. 360).

Hegel's "*Umfang und Erfüllung.*"[13] Not even Hegel's use of the word "*Bedeutung*" a little later in the same paragraph comes close enough to warrant the use of the word signification. Moreover, Miller translates *Bedeutung* with "significance," which does not imply signification as the meaning, or representation, of a sign, but must rather be understood as meaning "importance," in this context. To complicate things further Nancy's translators have added the word "inner" to the Hegel quote in Nancy's text – a word which in the original French is lacking, but is present in Hegel's original German and in Miller's English translation of the *Phenomenology*. Nevertheless, one could argue, with Nancy and his translators, that the implication of Hegel's notion of a death "*der keinen innern Umfang und Erfüllung hat*" is exactly the possibility of a complete cessation of signification, that philosophy with Hegel faces the death of meaning as/of Absolute Knowledge, as a possibility that must always be taken into account.[14] There is no certainty in a transcendent Absolute, since when the curtain rises everything ends. However, to return to Nancy's rendition of Hegel, what is obvious here is that the inner extent, or scope and self-fulfillment, or realization (that is, the *innern Umfang und Erfüllung*) of Nancy's translation of Hegel is a rehearsal of his own argument. Just as with prince Saurau's language, Nancy's translation of Hegel here is deranged so that signification does not signify – it is in need of constant and continuous correction.[15] Again, we come up against what prince Saurau holds as the only achievable learning goal, death, that is, "unmediated pure negation," [unvermittelte *reine Negation* (emphasis in the original)] as Hegel calls it in §590. In death, to put it differently, the movement of dialectics ends, there is no mediation, no translation, no irony; there is, in short, no dramaturg interceding on behalf of the actors' need to signify.

Given this exegesis of death in Hegel and Bernhard, in which we are faced with the possibility as well as the impossibility of death, and the death of signification, a death which Hegel calls, in §590, "the coldest and meanest of all deaths, with no more significance [*Bedeutung*] than cutting off a head of cabbage or swallowing a

---

[13] An alternative translation of Hegel's characterization of this kind of death, suggested by Danko Grlić, could be "without inner *dimension* or *fulfillment.*" This translation is perhaps easier to grapple with than Miller's somewhat cumbersome "no inner significance or filling." See Crlić (1979).

[14] Catherine Malabou (2005), in *The Future of Hegel: Plasticity, Temporality, and Dialectic*, performs an in-depth analysis of Hegel and signification, drawing on the apparent ambiguity she finds in Hegel's use of the dichotomy between interiority and exteriority. As she writes, for Hegel "Man appears as the being who must come to experience the nonreferentiality of expression, or, in other words, signification's impossible state of nature. Through this experience he recognizes the lack of any ontological guarantee outside of the play of signification" (p. 68). Thus, Nancy and Malabou are close in their respective assessment of signification in Hegel. However, as opposed to Nancy, the section in the *Phenomenology* that Malabou has chosen for her analysis is "Observing Reason" which explicitly deals with signification and meaning.

[15] *Correction* (*Korrektur*) is the title of Bernhard's perhaps most well-known novel, published in 1975, which stages the idea of an unending need for correction and self-correction of what one does, thinks, and writes. The ultimate (existential) correction being death by suicide. One could, perhaps, within a Hegelian reading of *Correction*, conceive of the movement of dialectics as continuous corrections, with the final move of dialectics as correction being death instead of Hegel's Absolute Knowledge.

mouthful of water," we can return to the passage from *Gargoyles*, and read it from the perspective of death, as such. Now, prince Saurau's statement on education and death, that "the only attainable goal of study is death," appears to us in the light of the possibility of the death of signification as the parabasis that is the difference between signification and significance, the ambiguity which disrupts our reading of prince Saurau's rambling monologue, and addresses us by calling us to consider death as "unmediated pure negativity." At the same time, his statement stages death as such; it is a warning that study, education, causes death, which amounts to an absolute reversal, a perversion, of what education is. Education has no significance in death, since in death there is no signification. However, what must not be forgotten when we read these statements on death is the word that Nancy omits in his citation of Hegel, but that his English translators re-install into the quote, namely the word "inner" (*innern*), as in a death that has no inner significance/signification, which means a death without relation to affect another self, since what is implied is, as Hegel maintains, an absolutely free self, alone and unrelated, even to itself. It has no essence and is, Hegel states, an "empty point" (*unerfüllte Punkt*), an unfulfilled and unrealized moment, already lost in death.

Freud and the Return to Death

In order to mediate between Hegel and Bernhard, by considering the presence and absence of the word "inner," and also by developing the thought of death as the only goal of study in Bernhard's *Gargoyles*, we could look to Freud as a potential mediator – as a way to achieve a possible sublation (*Aufhebung*) of Hegel and Bernhard. I am thinking of Freud's (1961) *Beyond the Pleasure Principle*, which, I would like to suggest, connects and intertwines with Hegel's and Bernhard's texts that we have engaged with so far. The passage from *Beyond the Pleasure Principle* I have in mind is the following: "If we are to take it as a truth that knows no exception that everything living dies for *internal* reasons – becomes inorganic once again – then we shall be compelled to say that '*the aim of all life is death*' and, looking backwards, that '*inanimate things existed before living ones*'" (p. 32); ["*Wenn wir es als ausnahmslose Erfahrung annehmen dürfen, daß alles Lebende aus* inneren *Gründen stirbt, ins Anorganische zurückkehrt, so können wir nur sagen:* Das Ziel alles Lebens ist der Tod, *und zurückgreifend:* Das Leblose war früher da als das Lebende." (p. 40)]. The purpose and aim of the death drive, according to Freud, is for the living organic entity to return to a more originary inanimate state.[16] And, of pertinence to

---

[16] Malabou (2009) suggests an interesting movement of temporality in relation to Freud's theory, in which all living things strive to return to its inanimate, organic state before life (and death): "The tendency to go beyond the pleasure principle which Freud examines here is not exactly a tendency towards death but, as we just said, a tendency to go back to a time before death, to the temporal mode of being of the non-living and of the non-dying. This mode of being goes both beyond and below the pleasure principle, as a more primitive, more originary instance. [...] In 'Beyond the

our reading here, Freud's statement, without doubt, brings to mind the passage from *Gargoyles* in which Saurau states that "The only attainable goal of study is death" [*Das einzige erreichbare Lernziel ... ist der Tot*]. The goal of all living things, Freud says, is death, while Saurau in *Gargoyles* holds that the only learning goal (to put it literally) that we can hope to reach is death. Saurau, it could be said, is the verbalization of the death drive. Thus, death is both a biological and teleological end goal, and an abstraction, that is, a goal of study without immediate practical consequences, which means death viewed as something about which we can attain knowledge of and learn about, but not experience, as such. We moreover find in Freud's text a hint of dialectics in the words "*zurückkerht*" and "*zurückgreifend*," that is, a re-turn and looking back to the inorganic from its organic opposite. The inorganic, Freud is suggesting, signifies death, a death to which the organic inevitably must return. It is a purely external death, just like Hegel's death without inner significance – a death without meaning or importance, an empty death to which one attaches no interest or significance. This is the death of a stone or, as in the example Hegel gives, the empty death of cutting off the head of a cabbage. Pure exteriority in Hegel amounts to Absolute Freedom, which means that death, this death of "unmediated pure negativity," has no interiority; it is the inorganic out of which we came and to which we will return. It is worth repeating here Hegel's articulation of the dialectic movement that we started out with, namely how "existence is really the perversion [*Verkehrung*] of every determinateness into its opposite, and it is only this alienation that is the essential nature and support of the whole." To exist means to become in the oscillating movement of all that is determined. And within this becoming there resides the death drive, as the non-origin of existence. Death is the force of this dialectics. There is, then, a double movement of death itself: death as an unreachable abstract (mental) concept, and death as the physical re-turn (*zurückkehrt*) to the inorganic.[17] Death is not only the "cancellation of difference," that is,

---

Pleasure Principle', Freud articulates the first and unique concept of time in all Western thought in which the very notions of origin and end, past, present and future, are merely referred to inorganic matter. The temporality of the soul, the temporality of finitude, of existence, life and death themselves, would derive from this primitive material time" (pp. 42–43). Although interesting in and of itself, Malabou's reading of Freud's text is not entirely relevant to my argument in this chapter, since I am not trying to analyze a temporality beyond death (or life), or attempting to prove the existence of a beyond of the pleasure principle as manifested in the death drive, but rather how death as ultimate possibility/impossibility can be understood in relation to Bernhard's *Gargoyles* and education.

[17] It is worth referring at this point to Deleuze's (2001) *Difference and Repetition*, in which he states: "Every death is double, and represents the cancellation of large differences in extension as well as the liberation and swarming of little differences in intensity. Freud suggested the following hypothesis: the organism wants to die, but to die in its own way, so that real death always presents itself as a foreshortening, as possessing an accidental, violent and external character which is anathema to the internal will-to-die. There is a necessary non-correspondence between death as an empirical event and death as an 'instinct' or transcendental instance. Freud and Spinoza are both right: one with regard to the instinct, the other with regard to the event. Desired from within, death always comes from without in a passive and accidental form. Suicide is an attempt to make the two incommensurable faces coincide or correspond. However, the two sides do not meet, and every

of dialectics, but also the inception of difference. Death is thus simultaneously signification and non-signification, what we could perhaps call re-signation.[18] It is both
the most saturated and the emptiest of concepts.

Aporias, Impossibility, Death

Now, to avoid ending up with the somewhat trivial and disappointing conclusion
that death is nothing more than an abstract noun, just like words such as "life,"
"love," and "faith," and natural science's insistence on death as an empirical inevitability, and also to introduce Kant into my argument, I would like, very briefly, to
draw a line to Kant's notions of ontotheology and cosmotheology.[19] By the neologism ontotheology, Kant wanted to indicate that mode of transcendental theology
which attempts to understand God by the means of concepts alone, without recourse
to experience; Kant calls cosmotheology, conversely, the form of theology which
tries to understand the highest power by means of experience. What I am suggesting, in effect, is that the *ambiguity* of death that we find in Saurau's monologue can
be compared to Kant's notions of transcendental theology, rather than being a vacant
abstract noun. It is, accordingly, in the oscillation between knowledge gained by
reflection on the abstract concept of death, and a knowledge that through experience
(in and of life) attempts to know death, that we find ourselves closing in on the
notion of education, and, in relation to Bernhard's *Gargoyles*, death as the goal of
education. However, I am not suggesting that the doubleness of death resolves the
apparent aporia at the origin of the thinking of death which we have examined up
until now; instead, I would argue that it highlights, precisely, its irresolvable character. Even if only mentioned sketchily, Kant's notion of ontotheology provides a
bridge to Jacques Derrida (2004) and his reading of Kant in "Vacant Chair:
Censorship, Mastery, Magisteriality," the third essay in *Eyes of the University: Right
to Philosophy 2*. Moreover, Derrida (1993a) provides an extensive discussion, in his

---

death remains double" (p. 259). In other words, death, according to Deleuze, is both necessarily
interior and exterior.

[18] As Blanchot (1993) notes on the book as work: "the work [...] requires resignation, requires that
whosoever claims to write it renounce himself as a self and cease designating himself" (p. 429). In
other words, resignation is the death of the author, the one who claims the work as his/her own.
This, too, is the paradox of death and the death drive in Freud.

[19] A lucid account of Kant's ontotheology is given by Iain Thomson (2005) in his book *Heidegger
on Ontotheology: Technology and the Politics of Education*, in which he states: "Kant coined
'ontotheology' and 'cosmotheology' in order to distinguish between two opposing kinds of 'transcendental theology'. 'Ontotheology' is his name for that kind of transcendental theology exempli-
fied by St. Anselm's famous 'ontological argument' for the existence of God, which 'believes it
can know the existence of an [original being, *Urwesen*] through mere concepts, without the help of
any experience whatsoever' (*Critique of Pure Reason/Kritik der reinen Vernunft*, A632/B660).
Heidegger may have appropriated the term 'ontotheology' from Kant, but his use of it, as we will
see, is quite different" (p. 7, note 1).

book *Aporias*, of death and aporia, and death as aporia, to which I will refer in what follows. But to continue to trace the double movement of death, and extend it to the question of education, we must ask again what can actually be learned from and about death? Can death be learned at all? Can death be taught? Can it be the object of teaching? As we know from the passage in *Gargoyles*, Bernhard lets Saurau state that death is, in fact, the *only* goal of learning (*lernziel*); "Life," Bernhard has Saurau say "was a school in which death was being taught." Learning to die thus misses the point, since learning to die, just as with learning to walk, think, and live, are just the learning of roles to play on the stage which is the world. It is learning *death* that is at issue, Bernhard makes Saurau insist. To contrast and possibly complicate the notion of death and teaching/learning death I want, as a comparison, to acknowledge Derrida's reading of Kant concerning Kant's idea of teaching and learning philosophy as an activity of pure reason. In "Vacant Chair," Derrida (2004) refers to the section "The Transcendental Doctrine of Method" in Kant's *Critique of Pure Reason* in which Kant states that, to paraphrase, one cannot learn philosophy, but only learn to philosophize. That one can only "learn to philosophize" is repeated twice in Kant's text. Since, as Derrida also notes, the passage is of importance to understand Kant's statement, it is worth citing a longer segment from the section in question:

> In this way philosophy is a mere idea of a possible science, which is nowhere given *in concreto*, but which one seeks to approach in various ways until the only footpath, much overgrown by sensibility, is discovered, and the hitherto unsuccessful ectype, so far as it has been granted to humans, is made equal to the archetype. Until then one cannot learn any philosophy; for where is it, who has possession of it, and by what can it be recognized? One can only learn to philosophize, i.e., to exercise the talent of reason in prosecuting its general principles in certain experiments that come to hand, but always with the reservation of the right of reason to investigate the sources of these principles themselves and to confirm or reject them. (Immanuel Kant, 1998, *Critique of Pure Reason*, p. 694).
>
> Auf diese Weise ist Philosophie eine bloße Idee von einer möglichen Wissenschaft, die nirgend in concreto gegeben ist, welcher man sich aber auf mancherlei Wegen zu nähern sucht, so lange, bis der einzige, sehr durch Sinnlichkeit verwachsene Fußsteig entdeckt wird, und das bisher verfehlte Nachbild, so weit als es Menschen vergönnt ist, dem Urbilde gleich zu machen gelingt. Bis dahin kann man keine Philosophie lernen; denn, wo ist sie, wer hat sie im Besitze, und woran läßt sie sich erkennen? Man kann nur philosophieren lernen, d. i. das Talent der Vernunft in der Befolgung ihrer allgemeinen Prinzipien an gewissen vorhandenen Versuchen üben, doch immer mit Vorbehalt des Rechts der Vernunft, jene selbst in ihren Quellen zu untersuchen und zu bestätigen, oder zu verwerfen. (Immanuel Kant, *Kritik der reinen Vernunft*, 1956, p. 753).

"In this way" here refers to Kant's argument, in the same paragraph as the just cited passage, that there are many minor philosophies which make up the over-arching concept or discipline of philosophy, against which all, as he states, "attempts to philosophize" should be measured. What Kant says in the cited passage, in effect, is that as long as one has not been able to unearth and make manifest the archetype of philosophy it is only an idea (of a science) which one has to analyze in different ways until one finds its right and ideal path of philosophy which will replace the copy or imitation (*Nachbild*) of philosophy with philosophy as an original (*Urbild*) science or discipline. What Derrida centers on is the aporia of the statement that one cannot learn philosophy, but only learn to philosophize. As he notes, what Kant says is that we can never learn philosophy, or rather the idea or archetype (*Urbild*) of philosophy, but only learn how to philosophize about philosophy. The path, or as Kant calls it, *Fußsteig*, of philosophy never reaches its goal, even though the goal (*lernziel*, *telos*), the *only* goal, might very well be to learn the idea of philosophy. Interestingly, the path, Kant states, is overgrown by sensibility, which is one reason we cannot find the right way to the ideal philosophy. Sensibility, Kant seems to be implying, clouds philosophy as pure reason. Moreover, as Derrida points out, there is a problematic of translation here. The first time the statement "learn to philosophize" is made, Kant underlines *philosophieren*, while the second time the statement occurs, the emphasis, according to Derrida, lies on the word learn: "One can only *learn* to philosophize." Of the first instance the statement occurs, Derrida (2004) states:

> It is a question of translation: in French, the syntactic displacement of the "ne ... que" (one can learn *only*...; one can *only* learn... [on *ne* peut apprendre *que*, on *ne* peut *qu'*apprendre]) allows one to mark the difference clearly. Since in German the sentence retains the same syntax, *philosophieren* had to be underlined ("to philosophize") in the first statement – and the ambiguity remains. It is not out of the question that these two occurrences retained almost the same meaning for Kant. (pp. 61–62)
>
> Question de traduction : en français le déplacement syntaxique du ne que (on *ne* peut apprendre *que*, on *ne* peut *qu'*apprendre...) permet de bien marquer la différence. En allemand, la phrase restant la même dans sa syntaxe, il a fallu souligner *philosophieren* dans le premier énoncé – et l'équivoque demeure, il n'est pas exclu que les deux occurrences aient gardé à peu près le même sens pour Kant. (p. 368)

The problem of translation is one between French and German (and English, since the English language also retains the syntax of the statement). In German (and English) the statement is ambiguous, while in French the statement marks the difference in meaning between the two instances where it occurs in Kant's text. However, Kant only emphasizes *philosophieren* in the statement's first occurrence, but not *lernen* in its second occurrence, as we can see in the quoted passage from *Critique of Pure Reason*; that is: "*Man kann nur philosophieren lernen*" as opposed to "*Man kann also unter allen Vernunftwissenschaften (a priori) nur allein Mathematik, niemals aber Philosophie (es sei denn historisch), sondern, was die Vernunft betrifft, höchstens nur* philosophieren *lernen*" to quote the whole sentence in which the statement is made the first time. How, then, do we know that *lernen* is emphasized and not *philsophieren* in the statement's second occurrence? Even though Derrida admits to the fact that Kant explicitly emphasizes *philosophieren*, but only by implication emphasizes *lernen*, the sentence remains fundamentally ambiguous. We cannot with absolute certainty say where the emphasis should lie in the second occurrence of the statement, not even the qualifying clause can help us: "i.e., to exercise the talent of reason in prosecuting its general principles in certain experiments that come to hand, but always with the reservation of the right of reason to investigate the sources of these principles themselves and to confirm or reject them." This qualifying clause can equally well refer to *lernen* as to *philosophieren*. There is, then, a moment in Kant's text that not even Derrida's intricate and detailed analysis manages to capture and explain; he is right in that the ambiguity remains, for it remains also, as I have pointed out, in his reading of the two occurrences of Kant's statement "only learn to philosophize." This impasse or aproia of philosophy (similar to the aporia of death) must remain unresolved. To learn how to philosophize or to learn the history of philosophy are two modes of learning, and in consequence of education, which are dependent on a question of emphasis and an aporia of translation, with the important outcome that we are faced with a double bind within which philosophy as idea and the history of philosophy are both impossible and necessary. To *learn* how to philosophize or to learn how to *philosophize* is thus, Derrida suggests, the impasse or aporia of a philosophizing as pure reason, which is described by Kant as "to exercise the talent of reason in prosecuting its general principles in certain experiments that come to hand, but always with the reservation of the right of reason to investigate the sources of these principles themselves and to confirm or reject them." The education of philosophy can in this way be compared to the education of death – both are caught up in an unresolvable aporia.

To sum up, we find the same movement toward the moment of impossibility, that is to say aporia, which we have identified in Derrida's reading of Kant, in a number of instances throughout the chapter: in the passage from Hegel's *Phenomenology* that started out this chapter, in de Man's notion of the concept of irony, in Nancy's (mis)reading of Hegel, in Freud's idea of a return to the inorganic in *Beyond the Pleasure Principle*, and most importantly in Bernhard's *Gargoyles*. This brings me to my last example of how to conceive of death, and the impasse that an education of death poses in *Gargoyles*, which is Derrida's analysis of aporia and/as death in his book *Aporias*. Derrida takes as a starting point for his analysis Heidegger's (1962, 1977) well-known definition of death in *Being and Time*: "Death is the possibility of the absolute impossibility of Da-sein" (p. 250) ["*Der Tod ist die Möglichkeit der schlechthinnigen Daseinsunmöglichkeit*" (p. 250)]. It is necessary, however, to pause before setting out to follow Derrida's line of argument, in order to come to grips with Heidegger's understanding of possibility [*Möglichkeit*], which is needed to put Derrida's use of the notion of possibility and impossibility into context. Heidegger explains what he means by possibility in his "Letter on Humanism" in relation to how thinking is lost when it is left out of its element. The element, says Heidegger, is for thinking what is truly enabling and enriching [*Vermögende*], that is, it is "the enabling"[20] [*das Vermögen*] (but also an element as wealth, or a fortune, or an asset). Heidegger then goes on to draw on the etymology of *mögen*, meaning to like, to care for, to be fond of, to favor, in order to arrive at *Möglichkeit* which corresponds to possibility. This gives Heidegger reason to tie the three words *Vermögen*, *Mögen*, and *Mögliche* together, which he does in the following manner: "This enabling is what is properly 'possible' [*das 'Mögliche'*], whose essence resides in favoring. From this favoring Being enables thinking. The former makes the latter possible. Being is the enabling-favoring, the 'may be' [*das*

---

[20] In Heidegger's (1995) *Aristotle's* Metaphysics Θ 1–3, *Vermögen* is translated as capability. This text is furthermore essential for understanding Heidegger's reading of Aristotle's terms potentiality (δύναμις) and actuality (ἐνεργέω).

'*Mög-liche*']. As the element, Being is the 'quiet power' of the favoring-enabling, that is, of the possible."[21] The "favoring-enabling" could, and perhaps should, be translated, it must be pointed out, as "the giving wealth" of Being which gives out of a "quiet power" (*stille Kraft*). Thus, Heidegger's analysis of the etymology of "*Mögen*" uncovers what the possible "is," which means, for Heidegger, that the possible is the giving wealth of Being, which also favors and enables, as a silent power. Heidegger (1993) consequently distances himself from Aristotle and St. Thomas of Aquinas when he states: "When I speak of the 'quiet power of the possible' I do not mean the *possibile* of a merely represented *possibilitas*, nor *potentia* as the *essentia* of an *actus* of *existentia*; rather, I mean Being itself, which in its favoring presides over thinking and hence over the essence of humanity, and that means over its relation to Being" (p. 220). It is clear form Heidegger's thinking concerning the notion of possibility that the possible, just like Being, cannot be determined or defined in a single way, but has to be put into relation with what it hides or does not show, and what remains undisclosed, in order to articulate its possible meanings, that is, what Heidegger (2012) calls inapparent (*Unscheinbar*).[22] From this follows that possibility is understood as belonging to the impasse inherent in difference, which means a notion of difference as possibility. Difference here should not be understood as a difference that only separates, breaks up, and divorces, but difference as a movement that is both, and at the same time, diremptive and unifying. We can then say that out of the difference of wealth as abundance, which is the silent power of this kind of difference, comes the possible. As will be clear in what follows, what Derrida calls aporia points to the impossibility of this possibility, but it is through the moment of aporia, Derrida proposes, that we can come closer to understanding death.

As stated, Derrida's (1993a) point of departure for his reflections on death and aporia is Heidegger's definition of death: "Death is the possibility of the absolute impossibility of Da-sein." And the apparent paradox or aporia in Heidegger's definition lies in the combination of the terms possible and impossible. Now, an important aspect to consider in Derrida's analysis is his use of markers throughout the text, with which he engages the language of death and lets language expose death as the end, for example in repeating the phrase "*en somme*," that is "in sum," which he extracts form a quote from Cicero's treatise on ethics *De finibus bonum et malorum* (On the ends of good and evil), more precisely Cicero's justification, in that work, for his translation of the Greek word for "the end." Derrida's text can thus be read as a continual postponement of death and the end, the "*en somme*," while at the same time staging the end as a death to come. "*En somme*," then, is one instance of Derrida's invocation of the vocabulary of death or the end. And, importantly, this

---

[21] For a better understanding of the way in which Heidegger utilizes the possibilities of etymology I give the passage in German: "Dieses Vermögen ist das eigentlich »Mögliche«, jenes, dessen Wesen im Mögen beruht. Aus diesem Mögen vermag das Sein das Denken. Jenes ermöglicht dieses. Das Sein als das Vermögend-Mögende ist das »Mög-liche«. Das Sein als das Element ist die »stille Kraft« des mögenden Vermögens, das heißt des Möglichen" (Heidegger, 1976, p. 319).

[22] For an analysis of Heidegger's notion of a phenomenology of the inapparent, see Alvis (2018).

whole vocabulary of death and the end that Derrida opens up by relating to the aporia of translation, as for example by referencing Cicero's difficulties in translating the Greek τέλος (*telos*),[23] installs an aporia in his own text. Nevertheless, Derrida (1993a) provides a summary explanation and definition of how he thinks aporia in relation to "crossing the ultimate border," that is, death:

> What, then, is it to cross the ultimate border? What is it to pass the term of one's life (*terma tou biou*)? Is it possible? Who has ever done it and who can testify to it? The 'I enter', crossing the threshold, this 'I pass' (*perao*) puts us on the path, if I may say, of the *aporos* or of the *aporia*: the difficult or the impracticable, here the impossible, passage, the refused, denied, or prohibited passage, indeed the nonpassage, which can in fact be something else, the event of a coming or of a future advent [*événement de venue ou d'avenir*], which no longer has the form of the movement that consists in passing, traversing, or transiting. It would be the 'coming to pass' of an event that would no longer have the form or the appearance of a *pas*: in sum, a coming without *pas*. (p. 8)

As Derrida insists there is no movement in an aporia; hence, there is in an aporia no time and space. The aporia is the place without place, in which movement, κίνησις (*kinesis*), (as indicated in such notions as, for example, the English word path, the German words *weg*, *steig*, *holtzwege*, and the French word *pas*), as well as in the concepts time and space, ceases to be an intelligible notion to reckon and reason with in order to gain knowledge and understanding. An aporia is, Derrida suggest, "in sum, a coming without *pas*" (*en somme, une venu sans pas*). Derrida's analysis of death and aporia, it should be said, is an extended reflection on the indeterminacy, untranslatability, and, indeed, the aporia of *pas* (step/not), that is to say, a movement and suspension of movement, that is, what Derrida calls the nonpassage, which can open up toward an event to come, or as Derrida states: "*un événement de venue ou d'avenir*." Moreover, the aporia, Derrida suggests, involves paradox, as is seen in the following sentence that he repeats throughout the text: "*Il y va d'un certain pas.* [It involves a certain step/not; he goes along at a certain pace.]" (p. 6). The ambiguity and paradox of this untranslatable sentence thus stages what is at stake in an aporia. As related to death, the word *pas* signals the impossibility to step beyond it, that is, the movement toward death ends in pure impossibility, which is to say aporia. The implication being that death cannot be made phenomenologically present; no matter how much *epoché* or reduction, death cannot be given to present itself to consciousness, but remains always and already inaccessible according to the aporia of the *pas*, which means *pas* as prohibition, an imperative No!, and *pas* as step, as in going along (at a certain pace) – death is the aporetic non-passage that prohibits the gift of death as presence.[24]

The aporia, then, is impossible – that which cannot be, not even *pas*, or as Derrida puts it: the aporia "is not even the *non-pas*, the non-step, but rather the deprivation of the *pas* (the privative form would be a kind of *a-pas*)" (p. 23). And thus, what Derrida's notion of aporia entails is the impossibility of Heidegger's possibility, that

---

[23] Cicero is confronting Aristotle's use of τέλος in the *Nicomachean Ethics*.

[24] See Derrida's (2011) essay "*Pace* Not(s)" in *Parages* for an analysis of the complex logic of the *pas* in relation to Blanchot's writing.

is to say, the possible as the giving wealth of Being, and also the impossibility of any phenomenology. To put it differently, according to Derrida, Heidegger insists on the primacy of an existential analysis, and the presupposition of the meaning of death in any metaphysics, as well as any psychology (including psychoanalysis), anthropology, theology, and biology, of death. These discourses in consequence lack the possibility of coming to an understanding of the meaning of death as such, while Heidegger's existential analysis has the aim to uncover these ontological presuppositions (Derrida, 1993a, p. 27). In other words, without an existential analysis, there is no possibility of the impossibility of death, only the impossibility which a presupposed meaning of death runs up against. In contrast, the giving wealth of Being, which in an existential analysis gives rise to the possibility of impossibility, is death, paradoxically enough.[25] Now, Derrida's reading takes this reasoning a step further by claiming that even Heidegger's existential analysis presupposes the meanings of death identified in biology, theology, and anthropology, *et cetera*. And what is more, as Derrida asserts, "the existential analysis of *Dasein* (that is, the 'as such' of death) is also what ruins the very possibility of the analysis form within" (77–78).[26] The existential analysis of death in *Being and Time* is accordingly deconstructed in three movements: (1) The movement of aporia, which Derrida claims can never be an aporia as such, that is, reduced to aporia as aporia, or Being as Being, or death as death. As Derrida states: "Death, as the possibility of the impossible *as such*, is a figure of the *aporia* in which 'death' and death can replace ... all that is possible only as impossible, if there is such a thing: love, the gift, the other, testimony, and so forth" (78–79). Consequently, in death, as a figure of aporia, there is no possibility of impossibility, but only impossibility. (2) The second movement goes to show how the presupposition of breaking out of the discourses of metaphysics, theology, anthropo-thanatology, and biology is itself the impossible. To limit and reduce, to circumscribe, in order to arrive at a more original way of thinking death is, precisely, impossible: "this fundamentalist dimension is untenable and ... cannot even claim to have any coherence or rigorous specificity" (p. 79), Derrida claims. And this applies also to Heidegger's existential analysis of death. (3) The third, and final, deconstructive movement Derrida identifies concerns the existential analysis of death: "Despite all the distance taken from anthropo-theology, indeed, from Christian onto-theology, the analysis of death in *Being and Time* nonetheless repeats all the essential motifs of such onto-theology that bores into its originarity right down to its ontological foundation" (p. 80). In other words, Heidegger's existential analysis of death uncovers the pre-understanding of the meaning of death in biology, psychology, theology, anthropology, theology, and all other onto-theological

---

[25] This contradictory logic can also be found in, for example, Heidegger's short lecture on "Poverty" (*"Die Armut"*) from 1945, (GA 73.1), in which he juxtaposes the concepts rich and poor which he borrows from Hölderlin. In an essay draft, Hölderlin states: "For us everything is concentrated upon the spiritual, we have become poor in order to become rich" [*"Es koncentrirt sich bei unsalles auf's Geistige, wir sind arm geworden, um reich zu warden."*] (Qtd in Heidegger, 2013, p. 873).

[26] See Chap. 6 for a continued discussion of the notion "as such" and its relation to the Kantian "as if."

discourses, while at the same time inscribing itself within it. The phenomenological methodology of the "as such" of death which, within the existential analysis, aims to reach or step back, away from and ahead of, onto-theology, remains contaminated by that from which it tries to escape, Derrida insists.[27]

What can be gathered from Derrida's analysis of death, aporia, and Heidegger's existential analysis, is that the aporia remains, the inaccessibility of death remains, it remains as the impossible. We thus have to remain in and endure the aporia of death, which is how we perhaps must come to understand death, as an impassable impasse which holds us back to wait within that form which there is no way out, not even as *auf dem holzweg sein*, as the German saying goes. Or as Derrida puts it within parentheses: "When someone suggests to you a solution for escaping an impasse, you can be almost sure that he is ceasing to understand, assuming that he had understood anything up to that point" (p. 32). We should be careful, then, to find ourselves having escaped, or perhaps cheated, death. To be cheating death, it seems, is what Saurau is accusing his fellow human beings of doing. But, what must be taken into consideration when it comes to Saurau's monologuing, and *Gargoyles* as a whole, is the radical unreliability that constitutes the precondition of the text. Everything Saurau says must be taken as recorded statements without any discerning of its truth value or correlation to any rational ground, since he must be considered deranged, and thus his language has no stable signification or meaning. We are

---

[27]What remains to be worked through in Derrida's analysis of death is, as he himself admits, Blanchot's work as it relates to death, which, one might argue, is almost his entire *oeuvre*. In a footnote, Derrida (1993a) states of Blanchot's work, specifically referring to *L'Attente l'oubli, Le pas au-delà*, and *L'Écriture du désastre*: "It would now be necessary to re-read and cite these texts from beginning to end" (p. 87, note 18), hinting once again at the impossibility of circumscribing death, even in, or perhaps especially in, a deconstructive reading of death. For a critique not only of Derrida's notion of *aporia*, but his entire deconstructive project, one could mention François Laruelle's chapter on Derrida in *Philosophies of Difference: A Critical Introduction to Non-Philosophy*, in which Laruelle writes: "Derrida, even more than Heidegger: (1) avows what there is of inconsistency, and accentuates what there is of latent self-dislocation in Greco-Occidental philosophical decision, whose originary dehiscence, its primitive incapacity to assure its real and rigorous unity with itself, he points out; (2) refuses to unknot this decision and conserves it despite everything as aporia that does not resolve itself except through sheer movement as an unreal. Wished for, hallucinated unity: this headlong flight is the very essence of incoherence, of impossible Unity, and so wished for all the more. Derrida is the thinker who carries philosophical decision to the limit of aporetic dislocation pure and simple and who yet, through a virtuosity of the endangered tightrope-walker, undertakes to seize decision again one last time and to maintain its possibility and truth, refusing to take the final step" (p.104). It is beyond the scope of this chapter to analyze Laruelle's claims against Derrida's "refusal" to solve the impasse of the notion of aporia; however, for a problematization of Laruelle's reading of Derrida, see McGettigan (2012). Moreover, one would, I believe, be amiss, within this context, not to mention Jean-Luc Marion's (2002) phenomenological analysis of death in his *In Excess: Studies of Saturated Phenomena*, which should be compared to and contrasted with Derrida's reading of death in *Aporias*, not least because of the focus on death as a passage and event. Marion states: "death: a phenomenon that can only be phenomenalized in happening [se passant], because, save this passage, it cannot strictly be; it is not, therefore it only appears inasmuch as it happens [se passe]; if it were not happening [s'il ne se passait pas], it would pass immediately and would never be. Death only shows itself, therefore, in giving itself by way of event" (p. 39).

faced with words that are simultaneously completely empty and excessive of meaning. In other words, we are faced with an aporia. There is no way out of Saurau's entangled narrative other than to document what is said, which is precisely what the narrator does. The narrator makes no attempt at interpretation or explanation of what Saurau says, but only engages in the straight forward documenting of Saurau's contradictory speech. Saurau's way of communicating oscillates between extremes reminiscent of the movement of Hegel's dialectics, as in the passage quoted at the beginning of the chapter. As Bernhard (2006) has Saurau say: "A depth is always a height, the deeper the depth of the height, the higher the height of the depth, and vice versa [*umgekehrt*]" (p. 148). However, Saurau's dialectics is an impossible one: "'Impossibility [*Unmöglichkeit*] is a ghastly foundation', he said. 'Everything is based on impossibility'" (p. 148). And the closest we come to unraveling the impossibility of the narrative is precisely by taking it as impossible, in the sense we have tried to pinpoint throughout the chapter, culminating in the notion of aporia and the impossibility of death in Derrida.

How, then, given this analysis, are we to approach an education of death? First of all, we must return to and acknowledge the impossibility latent in Hegel's statement which concludes that "existence is really the perversion [*Verkehrung*] of every determinateness into its opposite," which must then be related to Saurau's contradictory dialectics, including the passage in which he posits death as the only attainable goal of study, echoing Freud's claim in *Beyond the Pleasure Principle*, which states that the goal of all living things is death ["*Das Ziel alles Lebens ist der Tod*"]. We must also consider, through Derrida's reading of Kant, the aporia of approaching an education of death as the history/culture of death and/or death as a pure concept. Finally, we must take into account Derrida's notion of death as impossibility and aporia which insists on our inability to escape the culture and history of death, even within an existential analysis such as Heidegger's in *Being and Time*. And, we cannot escape the biology of death, but as Derrida suggests of the aporia, death "would be the 'coming to pass' of an event that would no longer have the form or the appearance of a *pas*: in sum, a coming without *pas*" (p. 8). This polysemous sentence itself being an aporia, and virtually untranslatable, warrants it to be rendered in French, and I quote a longer passage: "le difficile ou l'impracticable, ici le passage impossible, refusé, dénié ou interdit, voire, ce qui peut être encore autre chose, le non-passage, un événement de venue ou d'avenir qui n'a plus la forme du mouvement consistant à passer, traverser, transiter, le « se passer » d'un événemet qui n'aurait plus la forme ou l'allure du pas : en somme une venue sans pas" (1993b, p. 312). We find this notion of the aporia, I suggest, at work in the education of death, as we have analyzed it here, including through de Man's notion of the rhetorical trope irony, and the precariousness of translation pointed to in Nancy's reading of Hegel.

Concluding Remarks

What is clear, toward the end of Bernhard's (2006) novel, is that the boy narrator's journey through the Austrian countryside with his father is a *Bildungsreise* to become a writer, as an outcome of the informal education that the journey provides. The novel, moreover, turns out to be a record of his experiences of going on visits to patients with his father, which amounts to an education that is very different from the boy's formal studies in mining in Loeben. In fact, it seems that the boy views this *Bildungsreise* as more relevant and important to him than his studies at university. Having returned to his father's house, lying in bed, he begins writing a letter to a friend who has invited him to visit his farm; he writes to turn down the offer: "My studies did not allow for any interruptions, I had written, and then tore up the letter I had begun. In bed I thought: *What did the prince say?*" (p. 203). The studies referred to, we can assume, are not those in mining, but rather the study of gargoyles, of *Verstörung*, that is to say, derangement, which the Austrian countryside breeds. For the boy, the only attainable goal of study is death, just as Saurau claims, and what the boy studies is the existence [*das Dasein*] of the people in the area, where his father works as a doctor. To study the derangement of these people makes more sense to the boy than his university studies, since the existence of the people in the area is one full of aporias, irony, restless dialectics, perversion [*Verkehrung*], untranslatability, impossibility, and death. If we assume that *Gargoyles* is the outcome of the boy's *Bildungsreise*, then the unreliability of the text, indeed, its founding aporia, relates to the impossibility to disentangle which thoughts are the boy's, which are Saurau's, or even Bernhard's, given his extremely ironic stance toward public life and his writer persona, indeed, toward life, and existence itself. These voices seem to blend together into what becomes, through what we now dare to call, an education of death; that is, the work of art with the title *Gargoyles/Verstörung*. As Bernhard has Saurau say: "No matter how we look at things, we can feel that the tendency is directed entirely toward death. Our teachers are dead and by always dying very early have escaped from responsibility. Our teachers have left us alone. There are no future teachers and the ones of the past are dead" (pp. 178–179). Formal education with its rigid instrumentalism cannot give the boy what he needs. Instead, he turns to the ambiguity and restlessness of existence to provide him with education. In its indeterminateness, its untranslatability, and thus its impossibility, the novel, as a record of the absurdity of existence, stages an education of death, within which the only attainable goal of study is, precisely, that which cannot be learned, namely, death as such.

References

Alvis, J. W. (2018). Making sense of Heidegger's 'phenomenology of the inconspicuous' or inapparent (*Phänomenologie des Unscheinbaren*). *Continental Philosophy Review, 51*, 211–238.
Behler, E. (1990). *Irony and the discourse of modernity*. University of Washington Press.

Bernhard, T. (2006). *Gargoyles* (R. Winston & C. Winston, Trans.). Vintage International.
Bernhard, T. (2015). *Verstörung (Werke 2)*. Suhrkamp.
Blanchot, M. (1993). *The infinite conversation* (S. Hanson, Trans.). University of Minnesota Press.
Blanchot, M. (1995). Literature and the right to death (L. Davis, Trans.) In M. Blanchot, *The work of fire* (pp. 300–344). Stanford University Press.
Camus, A. (1991). *The rebel: An essay on man in revolt* (A. Bower, Trans.). Vintage International.
Collignon, J. (1955). Kafka's humor. *Yale. French Studies, 16*, 53–62.
Copeland, M. (2005). *Socratic circles: Fostering critical and creative thinking*. Stenhouse Publishers.
Cousineau, T. J. (2008). *Three-part inventions: The novels of Thomas Bernhard*. University of Delaware Press.
Crlić, D. (1979). Revolution and terror. In M. Marković & G. Petrović (Eds.), *Praxis. Boston studies in the philosophy of science* (Vol. 36). Springer.
de Man, P. (1996). The concept of irony. In *Aesthetic ideology* (pp. 163–184). University of Minnesota Press.
Deleuze, G. (2001). *Difference and repetition* (P. Patton, Trans.). Continuum.
Derrida, J. (1993a). *Aporias* (T. Dutoit, Trans.). Stanford University Press.
Derrida, J. (1993b). *Apories:Mourir – s'attendre aux limites de la vérité*. Galilée.
Derrida, J. (2004). Vacant chair: Censorship, mastery, magisteriality (B. Havercrof). In *Eyes of the university: Right to philosophy 2* (pp. 43–63). Stanford University Press.
Derrida, J. (2011). *Pace* not(s) (J. P. Leavey, Trans.). In J. Derrida, *Parages* (J. P. Leavey, Ed.) (pp. 11–102). Stanford University Press.
Freud, S. (1961). *Beyond the pleasure principle* (J. Strachey, Trans.). Norton.
Hegel, G. W. F. (1977). *The phenomenology of spirit* (A. V. Miller, Trans.). Oxford University Press.
Heidegger, M. (1962). *Being and time* (J. Macquarrie & E. Robinson, Trans.). Harper.
Heidegger, M. (1976). Brief über den Humanismus. In M. Heidegger (Ed.), *Wegmarken* (GA 9) (pp. 313–364). Vittorio Klostermann.
Heidegger, M. (1977). *Sein und Zeit* (GA 2). Vittorio Klostermann.
Heidegger, M. (1993). Letter on humanism (A. Hofstadter, Trans.). In M. Heidegger, *Basic writings* (D. F. Krell, Ed.) (pp. 217–265). HarperCollins.
Heidegger, M. (1995). *Aristotle's* metaphysics Θ 1–3: *On the essence and actuality of force* (W. Brogan & P. Warnek, Trans.). Indiana University Press.
Heidegger, M. (2012). *Four seminars* (A. Mitchell & F. Raffoul, Trans.). Indiana University Press.
Heidegger, M. (2013). Die Armut. In M. Heidegger (Ed.), *Zum Ereignis-Denken* (GA 73.1) (pp. 873–881). Vittorio Klostermann.
Honegger, G. (2001). *Thomas Bernhard: The making of an Austrian*. Yale University Press.
Hyppolite, J. (1979). *The genesis and structure of Hegel's* phenomenology of spirit (S. Cherniak & J. Heckman, Trans.). Northwestern University Press.
Jameson, F. (2010). *The Hegel variations: On the phenomenology of spirit*. Verso.
Kant, I. (1956). *Kritik der reinen Vernunft*. Felix Meiner.
Kant, I. (1998). *Critique of pure reason* (P. Guyer & A. W. Wood, Trans.). Cambridge University Press.
Malabou, C. (2005). *The future of Hegel: Plasticity, temporality, and dialectic* (L. During, Trans.). Routledge.
Malabou, C. (2009). Plasticity and elasticity in Freud's 'beyond the pleasure principle'. *Parallax, 15*(2), 41–52.
Marion, J-L. (2002). *In excess: Studies of saturated phenomena* (R. Horner & V. Berraud, Trans.). Fordham University Press.
McGettigan, A. (2012). Fabrication defect: Françoise Laruelle's philosophical materials. *Radical Philosophy, 175*, 33–42.
Montaigne, M. (2014). *Shakespeare's Montaigne: The Florio translation of the essays* (J. Florio, Trans.). New York Review Books.
Nancy, J.-L. (1997). *Hegel: L'inquietude du négatif*. Hachette Littératures.

Nancy, J-L. (2002). *Hegel: The restlessness of the negative* (J. Smith & S. Miller, Trans.). University of Minnesota Press.

Pinkard, T. (2000). *Hegel: A biography*. Cambridge University Press.

Plato. (1892) *Phaedo*. In B. Jowett (Trans.), *Dialogues* (Vol. 2). Oxford University Press.

Shakespeare, W. (1997). *Macbeth* (A. R. Braunmuller, Ed.). Cambridge University Press.

Thomson, I. (2005). *Heidegger on ontotheology: Technology and the politics of education*. Cambridge University Press.

Tredway, L. (1995). Socratic seminars: Engaging students in intellectual discourse. *Educational Leadership, 53*(1), 26–29.

Chapter 3
"The Supreme Exertion of Thinking": Censorship, Critique, and Education

Introduction

Each of the three concepts censorship, critique, and education implies a confrontation in some form. There can be no censorship without a confrontation between two opposed parties; for example, a state or government censor and a work of art, or any other form of (free) expression. Similarly, we could say that there is no critique without a confrontation between different ways of thinking, or between ideas about judging and evaluating. Likewise, there can be no education without a confrontation between a teacher and a student, a teacher and a curriculum, or a student and an object of study. These different confrontations thus involve a force or, as we will see, an act of violence, which necessarily works to suppress whatever is confronted. This is a further example of the effect of the aporia of translation, that is, a translation which, I argue, is an unavoidable part of a confrontation. In a translation something always remains untranslated or left out and leaves the translation contaminated by the act of translation. The inexorable force of translation installs an aporia precisely in the founding act of making sense and assigning meaning to that which was hitherto incomprehensible, so that when we come to understand, our understanding is based on the estrangement of meaning. In Hegel's language, we could say that alienation alienates itself, which is an act that both makes sense and, once again, alienates us form meaning.

The three concepts censorship, critique, and education, taken together, make it possible to trace their potential interrelatedness, which will, in turn, elucidate our understanding of each of the three concepts under scrutiny, while also exposing their aporetic character. This will, to anticipate the final step in my reading, lead me to consider a perspective on ethics set forth by Rodolphe Gasché in the chapter "Toward an Ethics of *Auseinandersetzung*" in his *The Honor of Thinking: Critique, Theory, Philosophy*. However, the point of departure for my reflections on the three concepts is a work of literature, namely what I hold to be the key text in Dostoevsky's novel *Demons* (Бесы [*Bésy*]). This key text, which is the censored chapter "At

© Springer Nature Switzerland AG 2022

E. Schwieler, *Aporias of Translation*, Contemporary Philosophies and Theories in Education 18, https://doi.org/10.1007/978-3-030-97895-2_3

Tikhon's" (first translated by S.S. Koteliansky and Virginia Woolf under the title "Stavrogin's Confession"),[1] will serve to open up for my reading of censorship, critique, and education. Next, I will reference Derrida's consideration of censorship in Kant, in the text "Vacant Chair," which, importantly, broaches the subject of academic disciplines in relation to censorship. I will then read passages form Hegel's *Phemenology of Spirit* and *Science of Logic*, Novalis on translation, Benjamin on critique, and especially Heidegger on *Auseinandersetzung* (traditionally translated as confrontation) and his notion of *aletheia* as unconcealment, to work out, or rather confront a possible ethics of critique, and what consequences such a critique might entail for education. These themes and concepts all share an affinity with what I call the aporia of translation.

Confronting Dostoevsky's "at Tikhon's"

Fyodor Dostoevsky's novel *Demons* was first published in the journal *The Russian Messenger* in 1871–1872. The publisher and editor of *The Russian Messenger* at this time was a man named Mikhail Katkov, who published and served as editor of several of Dostoevsky's major novels, for example *Crime and Punishment* and *The Brothers Karamazov*. My primary interest in Dostoevsky's *Demons* is the chapter "At Tikhon's," often included as an appendix to the novel, since it was censored and suppressed by the editor Katkov. The reason for Katkov's refusing to publish the chapter was most certainly the description of Stavrogin's (one of the main protagonists in the novel) molestation of a 10-year-old girl, confessed to in a letter, which he lets the monk Tikhon read. Even after Dostoevsky's many attempts to rewrite the chapter, Katkov did not allow it to be published, and Dostoevsky finally revised the novel so that the chapter could be excluded. The chapter was not published until 1922, translated the same year by S. S. Kotelinasky and Virginia Woolf.[2]

The theme of the molested girl is recurring throughout Dostoevsky's novels, and besides in *Demons*, it can be found, for example, in *The Brothers Karamazov* and

---

[1] I use this edition since it provides footnotes with the scratched passages that Dostoevsky did not include in the text, instead of grafting these scratches onto the text without making the reader aware of it. This also highlights the way Dostoevsky revised the chapter in order to get it published.

[2] For a discussion of the publishing history of the chapter, see Joseph Frank, *Dostoevsky: A Writer in his Time* (2010), p. 622. As Frank states concerning the chapter's absence from the text published in book form: "Dostoevsky himself did not include this chapter in later editions, but both internal and external reasons provide a plausible answer for his failure to reinstate it. For one thing, he had altered the published text as much as possible before magazine publication to meet the crisis he had not foreseen; the work thus no longer represented his original conception, and extensive rewriting would have been required to transform it once again. Also, he would then have had to face the formidable hurdle of the official censorship, and perhaps fail" (625). In other words, even if Katkov's suppression of the chapter was not an act of *official* censorship, this would have been then next step. All practical consequences considered, Katkov's suppression of the chapter undoubtedly constitutes a form of censorship.

Crime and Punishment.[3] The possible origin of the theme is documented in *The Dostoevsky Encyklopedia*, where it is recorded that when Dostoevsky was visiting his friend Anna Filosofova's salon, the question of the greatest sin was raised, to which Dostoevsky responded by recounting how he as a child had witnessed a nine-year-old girl being brutally raped. He had rushed to bring his father, who was a doctor, but the girl died before they could get back to help her. This crime was, Dostoevsky said, unforgivable, and also, notably, the crime he had punished Stavrogin for in *Demons*; importantly, Stavrogin being arguably the main character in *Demons*[4] makes the exclusion of the chapter "At Tikhon's" even more significant, since it includes the most extensive explication of Stavrogin's almost exaggerated Byronic character, and also a description of the nature of his crime.[5] What are the implications, then, of this defining chapter being censored and withheld, and subsequently omitted from the novel altogether, a chapter which reveals a good deal about Stavrogin, and informs the reader of his nature and personality, and not least introduces the recurring theme of the molested girl? First of all, the irony of the matter is that the fictional character Stavrogin himself wants his confession to be published and has 300 copies of it made to be sent to the police and the newspapers. He even planned to have it published abroad in translation. It is as if he wants to get found out and arrested, charged, judged, and sentenced, and so able to officially and publicly pay for his crime. But this he is denied; even the one confession Stavrogin makes, the one to Tikhon, in the chapter "At Tikhon's," is denied, this time by Katkov, who refused, as noted, to have the confession published, and the chapter was repeatedly censored, despite Dostoevsky's revisions and pleas to have the it included, first as an installment in the journal, and later in the novel.

Importantly, when it comes to the confession in "At Tikhon's," Dostoevsky portrays Stavrogin as a student and Tikhon as a teacher correcting and commenting on the confession as if it were an essay assignment for school. Thus, in his analysis of the chapter, Mikhail Bakhtin (1984) points to the inter-relationship between style and content in Stavrogin's written confession at which Tikhon's critique is first aimed:

> In actual fact the style of Stavrogin's Confession is determined above all by its internally dialogic orientation vis-á-vis the other person. Precisely this sideward glance at the other person determines the breaks in its style and its whole specific profile. Tikhon had precisely this in mind when he began directly with an "aesthetic critique" of the confession. (p. 243)

This contributes to making Tikhon's critique of Stavrogin's written confession take on the shape of a teacher commenting on a student essay, which means that he questions the style of it (what Bakhtin calls Tikhon's "aesthetic critique"), as well as the

---

[3] For a discussion of this theme in Dostoevsky, see Melvin Seiden (1972), "Nabokov and Dostoevsky", p. 425.

[4] K. A. Lantz, *The Dostoevsky Encyclopedia* (Westport, CT and London, UK: Greenwood Press, 2004), p. 61.

[5] There is an anecdote, or rumor, about how Dostoevsky confessed to a similar crime to Turgenev; see Seiden (1972), p. 425.

tone, and so by implication, also the actual matter or case, what Bakhtin calls the profile, of the confession, and in consequence the sincerity and truthfulness of Stavrogin's revelations. As Bakhtin asserts: "Tikhon's critique is very important, for it doubtless expresses the artistic intention of Dostoevsky himself" (p. 243). This goes to show that the comments on style have profound existential consequences, not only for Stavrogin, but also for the reader, and for Dostoevsky, since Tikhon's critique takes on a meta-character in that it becomes a statement on Dostoevsky's style in composing the confession, and also how it reflects his existential, religious, and ideological concerns. As Tikhon says, Stavrogin's crime, and by implication his confession, is "inelegant" (79).[6] The passage of the dialogue leading up to Tikhon's characterization of Stavrogin's confession and his crime as being "inelegant" deserves detailed attention. I will quote the passage at length:

> "Enough. Tell me, then, where exactly am I ridiculous in my manuscript? I know myself, but I want you to put your finger on it. And tell it as cynically as possible, tell me with all the sincerity of which you are capable. And I repeat to you again that you are a terribly queer fellow.
>
> "In the very form [форме (forme)] of this great penance [покаяния (pokayaniye)] there is something ridiculous. Oh, don't let yourself think that you won't conquer!" he suddenly exclaimed, almost in ecstasy. "Even this form will conquer" (he pointed to the pages), "if only you sincerely accept the blows and the spitting. It always ended in the most ignominious cross becoming a great glory and a great strength, if the humility of the deed was sincere. Perhaps even in your lifetime you will be comforted!..."
>
> "So you find something ridiculous in the form itself? [Editors' note: "After 'form' is struck out 'In the style'."][7] Stavrogin insisted.
>
> "And in the substance [сущности (sushchnosti)].[8] The ugliness of it will kill it," Tikhon said in a whisper, looking down.

---

[6] The Russian phrase Dostoevsky uses is "не изящные" (ne izyashchnyye) which literally means not graceful; Pevear and Volokhonsky translate it as ungracious, while Woolf renders it as "inelegant."

[7] Dostoevsky uses the phrase "в слоге" which is translated as "style" by Woolf as well as Pevear and Volokhonsky, but as "diction," with "style" within parentheses, in F. D. Reeve's translation used by Caryl Emerson, the translator of Bakhtin's *Problems of Dostoevsky's Poetics*: "The English version used here (and elsewhere) is by F. D. Reeve, and appears as an appendix to the Garnett translation" (note 5, p. 76). The bibliographical entry for the standard translation of *Demons* given by Emerson runs as follows: "*The Possessed* [*Besy*], trans. Constance Garnett (New York: Dell, 1961). This edition contains a translation of "Stavrogin's Confession" (the chapter "At Tikhon's") by F. D. Reeve. His text differs significantly in detail – although not in tone – from the variant Bakhtin cites. I have adjusted the Reeve translation to approximate more closely the Russian, and noted the major discrepancies" (xii). The general complexity of translation, although specifically translations of *Demons*, is evident here.

[8] Сущности (sushchnosti), translated here as substance (the word could also be translated as essence, which thus carries with it the whole problematic of translating the Greek οὐσία, including its designation as Being and presence), and so has interesting implications, as we will see later on when we come to the analysis of Hegel's refutation of Spinoza's system of philosophy. Moreover, Tikhon's opinion of Stavrogin's text has the consequence that it becomes less important whether Stavrogin committed the crime or not, since it is almost equally damning in his own opinion, if it was only imagined. It becomes a question, rather, of the way of presentation, that is, of method and style, with the aim of confronting another person. Cf. Seiden (1972): "Apparently Dostoevsky

"Ugliness! What ugliness?"

"Of the crime. There are truly ugly crimes. Crimes, whatever they be, the more blood, the more horror in them, the more imposing they are, so to say, more picturesque. But there are crimes shameful, disgraceful, past all horror, they are, so to say, almost too inelegant..."

Tikhon did not finish.

"You mean to say," Stavrogin caught him up in agitation, "you find me a very ridiculous figure when I kissed the hands [legs, feet] of the dirty little girl... [Editors' note: "After 'dirty little girl' is struck out: 'and all that I said about my temperament and, well, all the rest.. I see'."] I understand you very well, and that is why you despair for me, that it is ugly, revolting – not precisely revolting, but shameful, ridiculous, and you think that this is what I shall least of all be able to bear."

Tikhon was silent. [Editors' note: "After 'Tikhon was silent' is struck out: 'Yes, you know people, that is, you know that I shan't bear this'."] (417)

One of the main issues in Stavrogin's dialogue with Tikhon centers on whether to publish or not to publish the confession. Tikhon is in favor of not publishing it and tries to persuade Stavrogin not to. As for the chapter "At Tikhon's," Katkov censored it, we can assume, because it broke with the law of decorum, which correlates to Tikhon's use of the word "ugliness" to describe Stavrogin's crime. Bakhtin points to the paradoxical bond between Stavrogin and Tikhon, and how Stravrogin is dependent on another person for his confession, but also despises this other person for being willing to listen: "Without recognition, and affirmation by another person Stavrogin is incapable of accepting himself, but at the same time he does not want to accept the other's judgment of him" (p. 244). Stavrogin wants his confession to be made public for all to read so that he can be judged, but he at the same time feels nothing but contempt for the potential readers of his confession and their judgment of him. It is not hard to, in the same way, imagine Dostoevsky's struggle to write and compose Stavrogin's confession of the unforgivable crime he has committed, and his fear of, or repulsion by, how it might be received by his readers. As we know, Katkov reacted by refusing to publish the chapter, and in a way, one could say that both Dostoevsky and Stavrogin are confronting Tikhon with the confession to see what reaction it entices and to get a sense of how it might be received. Also, Tikhon reprimands Stavrogin not only on the form and style of the confession, but also, as noted, on its "essence" or "substance," which amounts to a denunciation of Stavrogin's intention for it to serve as repentance and a way to redemption. What Tikhon in fact declares is that the crime's "ugliness will kill it" which is why his first comment after hearing the confession is if Stavrogin can revise the manuscript: "Can't certain corrections be made in this document?" (p. 70) Tikhon asks. To put it crudely, what Tikhon is asking for is Stavrogin to self-censor his text, which is exactly what Dostoevsky ended up doing, to no avail. For Dostoevsky, the chapter was necessary, because he wanted to present more than Stavrogin's appalling crime,

could not decide whether to make Stavrogin guilty of physical or mental rape – though the latter, as Stavrogin's confessions show, is neither less culpable nor less tormenting to him; nor could Dostoevsky, in this novel in which politics looms so large, justify, if only to himself, insisting on the inclusion of this lurid sexual material, even in the ambiguous form of the first version cited above" (426).

namely its consequences and how to, possibly, atone for it by turning to religion. In other words, Dostoevsky wanted to explore the question: What could a possible response to Stavrogin's crime be? Tikhon suggests a form of penance, which would entail Stavrogin, if not becoming a monk, then at least living like one, but under the guidance of a monk that Tikhon is acquainted with:

> Make a vow to yourself, and by this great sacrifice you will acquire all that you long for and don't even expect, for you cannot possibly realize now what you will obtain.
> Stavrogin listened gravely.
> You suggest that I enter the monastery as a monk? [Editors' note. "After the word 'monk' is struck out: 'However much I respect you, I ought to have expected this. Well, I must confess to you, that in moments of cowardice this idea has occurred to me – once having made these pages universally known, to hide from people in a monastery, be it only for a time. But I blushed at the meanness of it. But to take orders as a monk, that did not occur to me even in moments of most cowardly fear'.]
> You must not be in a monastery, nor take orders as a monk; be only a lay-brother, a secret, not an open one; it may be that, even living altogether in society... (p. 81)

Now, what I would like to suggest is that the penance that Tikhon proposes can be likened to a movement from what we can call λήθη (*lethe*) to ἀλήθεια (*alethea*),[9] that is, from ignorance about the reason of the crime and a blindness to its consequences, to insight and revelation into the reason and consequences of the crime. However, the knowledge that such a revelation brings with it is still hidden, since as Tikhon tells Stavrogin: "[F]or you cannot possibly realize now what you will obtain." The issue here is not forgiveness; what Stavrogin represents is rather a movement toward imago Christi – a person who carries on his shoulders an unforgivable sin, caused by his committing a crime against, not only the law, but against God. One could say that Stavrogin, given the severity of his crime, represents the extreme human sinner whose crime and sin are also those of all humanity. In the end, Stavrogin does not take Tikhon up on his suggestion, but takes his leave from Tikhon, and eventually ends up committing suicide. Thus, from a religious point of view, the movement of penance, going from λήθη to ἀλήθεια, was something that

---

[9] It would be possible to trace a whole history of philosophy related to oblivion, ignorance, and blindness being opposed to revelation, knowledge, and insight. For example, one could invoke Heidegger's thinking concerning Λήθη and ἀλήθεια as the hiddenness and unhiddenness of the truth of Being. See, e.g. Martin Heidegger's (1998) "Plato's Doctrine of Truth" in *Pathmarks* and (2002) *The Essence of Truth: On Plato's Cave Allegory and* Theaetetus. Moreover, one should keep in mind the importance of the definition of truth as ἀλήθεια in the New Testament. Pertinent to my discussion of the religious themes in *Demons* and specifically in "At Tikhon's," see the informative discussion of truth (ἀλήθεια) in the New Testament, and also in philosophy more generally, under the entry on "Truth" in (1978) *The New International Dictionary of New Testament Theology, Vol. 3: Pri-Z*, ed. Colin Brown, Grand Rapids, MI: The Zondervan Corporation, 874–902. For an analysis of the connection between ἀλήθεια and παιδεία in Plato and Heidegger, see Paulina Sosnowska, (2019), *Hannah Arendt and Martin Heidegger: Philosophy, Modernity, and Education*, Washington DC: Lexington Books.

Stavrogin could not accede to and go through with. After all, as Dostoevsky made clear at Anna Filosofova's salon, Stavrogin's crime is unforgivable.[10]

To develop the above, the movement from λήθη to ἀλήθεια, which amounts to exposing the crime and showing the way to atonement, provides an opportunity to pose, as an experiment, the transfer of this movement of λήθη to ἀλήθεια from a religious to an educational-pedagogical situation, in which the student goes from blindness-ignorance to insight-knowledge. This is how Tikhon first engaged with Stavrogin's confession – as a teacher giving comments on a student paper. (The λήθη-ἀλήθεια, or ἀ-λήθεια (*a-letheia*), figuration is haunted, as noted, by Heidegger's deep involvement with these notions, which for him signifies, in his later thinking, the clearing which makes way for the possibility of the event (*Ereignis*) of the truth of Being.[11] This clearing, moreover, involves both λήθη and ἀλήθεια, concealment and unconcealment (*Verborgenheit-Unverborgenheit*) darkness and light, blindness and insight, ignorance and knowledge, hiddenness and revelation.) But, to get to the point, what I suggest is that there is a form of censorship implied in the pedagogical confrontation represented in the scene that Dostoevsky lets Stavrogin and Tikhon stage. What Tikhon wants his advice to achieve is the "correction" of Stavrogin's written account, and that it be altered and covered over (λήθη), because of its ugly, even ridiculous, form and style; so, Tikhon's aim to guide Stavrogin to ἀλήθεια as redemption goes through λήθη as censorship. In Dostoevsky's *Demons*, enlightenment, reason, and atonement are, in consequence, closely connected to a form of censorship and repression. Tikhon's advice is for Stavrogin to take the vows, if not publicly as a monk, then as a lay brother taking the vows in secret, and not publish the manuscript. Even though Stavrogin could, as Tikhon suggests, live in society as a lay brother, in secret, he would still have to abide by the vows he has taken. This instead of the penance involved in publishing his manuscript and exposing himself to endure public humiliation. What Tikhon's advice amounts to is, in other words, to cover up the crime, to not make it public, not submit himself to secular law, and impose a form of forgetting on Stavrogin's crime, and instead work on his repentance under the cover of religious vows. To sum up the case, Tikhon's critique guides Stavrogin by confronting him without offering the promise of forgiveness, and Stavrogin is left alone to find his own way, since forgiveness cannot be given. Tikhon, as a pedagogue and

---

[10] P. H. Brazier comments on the eschatological perspective in Dostoevsky's novels: "At any given moment the most deprived and evil persons in Dostoevsky's novels can turn and, through personal sacrifice, re-establish allegiance to Christ-God. (Or they may not: perceiving the *potential* for repentance and salvation in a depraved sinner does not guarantee an eventual redemption, but merely the possibility). […] Such is the eschatological view that underpins Dostoevsky [sic] novels: the reality of the eschaton is being worked out minute-by-minute in the here-and-now; when we die it will be obvious what we have become and where we are bound for. The 'classic' model of atonement defines the characters and their relation to God in Christ … or to Satan" (Brazier, P. H. *Dostoevsky: A Theological Engagement*. Eugene, OR: Pickwick Publications, 2016, p. 39).

[11] I will attend to the question of the event of the truth of Being in relation to ἀλήθεια in detail later in the chapter. For a chronological treatment of how ἀλήθεια as unconcealment (*Unverborgenheit*) figures in Heidegger's thinking, see Wrathall (2010).

religious guide, in consequence, confronts and censors Stavrogin's confession on moral religious premises, but also for formal and stylistic reasons, that is, strictly speaking on educational grounds.

Now, from my initial reading of the chapter "At Tikhon's" in Dostoevsky's *Demons*, one of the questions that can be raised is the following: Given the pedagogical situation that the censored chapter "At Tikhon's" stages, and the connection between critique, forgiveness, and censorship in it, how can we analyze the concept of censorship in relation to education more generally? This will be the guiding question in what follows.

Exploring the Notion of Censorship

In the chapter "Vacant Chair: Censorship, Mastery, Magisteriality," in *Eyes of the University: Rights to Philosophy 2*, Jacques Derrida (2004) touches on the question of education and censorship. More precisely, Derrida asks: *"What is censorship as a question of reason?"* (emphasis in original, p. 44). He turns to Kant in order to answer this question, whose definition of censorship Derrida finds in *Religion within the Limits of Reason Alone* (*Die Religion innerhalb der Grenzen der bloßen Vernunft*), book two of which was itself censored by the censorship commission established in Germany in 1792. In this text, Kant's definition of censorship runs as follows (in three different languages): "critique qui dispose de la force [Derrida's translation]" (2009, p. 347), "criticism which has coercive power [trans. Wood and di Giovanni]" (1998, p. 36), "criticism that has power [trans. Pluhar]" (2009, p. 6), and "critique that has power [trans. Greene and Hudson]" (1960, p. 7) These translations are renderings of Kant's (1922) "einer Kritik, die Gewalt hat" (p. 7). Given Kant's definition of censorship, Derrida turns to its "essential features": "The possibility of censorship – its necessity also and its legitimacy – appears in that place where an institution simultaneously intervenes and assures the mediation between pure reason (here in its highest form, pure practical reason) and the disposal of force, force at the disposal of the State" (p. 48). These essential features of censorship could without too much force or violence (*Gewalt*) be translated so that they could equally well apply to education. An academic discipline, for example, has the power to decide what belongs to its body of knowledge, that is, what counts as acceptable knowledge and representation of that knowledge. This amounts to the reason of the discipline. The teacher, in consequence, is one who enforces this disciplinary reason, which necessarily also includes censoring that which cannot be accepted as disciplinary knowledge or an acceptable method for conducting research as the pursuit of knowledge. The teacher's critique, in other words, his or her teaching, is a "critique that has power," which, as we have seen, is the very definition of censorship. In addition, as Derrida insists, the effects of censorship cannot be limited to the action of State power, but must be acknowledged as an unavoidable effect of reason. As Derrida makes clear, the censoring effect is part of any prohibition to express oneself:

Censorship exists as soon as certain forces (linked to powers of evaluation and to symbolic structures) simply limit the extent of a field of study, the resonance or the propagation of a discourse. [...] The moment a discourse, even if it is not forbidden, cannot find the conditions for an exposition or for an unlimited public discussion, one can speak of an effect of censorship, no matter how excessive this may seem. The analysis of this is more necessary and more difficult than ever. (p. 46)

There is, then, in education and instruction, for example as translation or critique, a censoring force, which amounts to a necessary suppression of what, consciously or unconsciously, is deemed as not belonging to a certain discipline or discourse. We also noticed it in the double censoring effect in "At Tikhon's," which exposed both the censoring force of Katkov, and also the administrative censoring effect of religious dogma, together with the same censoring effect conducted by the individual teacher personified by Tikhon. At the same time, if we follow Derrida's line of argument, the teacher (he is talking about the teacher of pure reason) is conspicuously absent. Derrida points to how the teacher, as Kant conceives of it, takes on the shape of a phantom, a ghost. But, we are obliged to ask, what is the nature and essence of this absence of the teacher? Before Kant, one should remember, Derrida notes at the outset of his lecture (linking to his previous lecture on Descartes) that Descartes was not a teacher and professor in the service of the State, and was consequently without the power to censor (in Kant's sense). Descartes, writes Derrida,

while explaining himself and struggling with all sorts of institutional authorities, never did so as a teaching philosopher, as a professor and civil servant in a State university. He no doubt posed pedagogical questions and analyzed the rhetoric and language of "exposition," but he did so without having to deal with a teaching of philosophy organized by the State and entrusted to teachers who are also servants of the State. (p. 43)

This situation changed at the end of the eighteenth century and the beginning of the nineteenth century, when teaching became a concern of the State – the university teacher became a civil servant. However, even if it could be argued that the teacher in the formal sense of a civil servant was not invented yet when Descartes was an active philosopher, and thus the teacher-philosopher could be viewed as being absent, Derrida is invoking the absent teacher in the time of Kant. How, then, is the teacher-philosopher absent in Kant's thinking? The teacher-philosopher is an ideal whose absence is likened to that of a ghost or phantom. This absence is an absence that in essence is a present absence, in other words, it is a haunting presence, and so inscribes itself in Derrida's notion of a hauntology.[12] What is important here,

---

[12] The ghost returns from the past to haunt the present, but the ghost isn't really there, it is neither present, nor absent. The aporia governing the haunting of the ghost is that it returns for the first time, the first time it shows itself is a return, which is true of any concept, be it history, identity, speech, language, or the Being of beings. This return of a singular appearance for the first time is what Derrida calls a hauntology (importantly, in French, hauntology is a homophone to ontology). In *Specters of Marx*, Derrida (2006) discusses what he terms hauntology in relation to the formation of concepts: "To haunt does not mean to be present, and it is necessary to introduce haunting into the very construction of a concept. Of every concept, beginning with the concepts of being and time. That is what we would be calling here a hauntology. Ontology opposes it only in a movement of exorcism. Ontology is a conjuration" (p. 202). The formation of concepts thus has its origin in

however, is that in Kant the teacher is not an artist, but a legislator, as opposed to the situation for someone like Descartes who was, as noted, not a formal teacher-philosopher belonging to an administrative body, but, importantly, in whose time French was elevated to the language of the State, which in turn can be related to the linguistic force of censorship.

In consequence, we are presented with a situation in which the teacher is one who enforces the discipline of reason, that is, acts as a censor, but who is conspicuously absent, and only conceivable as an archetype and an ideal. In the example of Dostoevsky's *Demons* the discipline of reason is religion, the supreme administrative authority, and Tikhon, following the curriculum of religion and Christianity, the absent-present teacher (he avoids direct teaching and instruction, but only engages in teaching Savrogin in a circumspect way), and censor of Stavrogin's case, while Katkov takes on the role in Dostoevsky's case. However, to relate in a more tangible way to the current situation in education, one could claim that the censoring power today is New Public Management with the implementation of its command-and-control concept onto education with the aim of achieving social efficiency through an instrumental use of learning outcomes and assessment procedures resembling corporate RoIs (Return on Investment). Thinking, and indeed critique, play an exceedingly subordinate role, if at all, in this kind of education. Instead there has developed a mode of critical thinking developed out of a scientism that values what is called "rationality" above any kind of reflective and speculative knowledge. Within this hegemony, the censoring effect manifests itself in how learning is streamlined and optimized according to predetermined criteria of social efficiency under the guises of entrepreneurship and employability, which means that alternative paths to knowledge and other kinds of knowledge are deemed useless, that is, without practical value, and irrelevant to the course of study.[13] This can be seen also in the way critical thinking has come to take on a vulgar rationality; and, moreover, education is not the only place where this kind of thinking governs, it also rules the entire university organization, as well as the political mirco-management of education. In literature studies we can see a similar stance in the Darwinism and evolutionary perspectives on literary theory that have developed since the mid 1990s. As for philosophy as a discipline, Derrida (2004), in "If There is Cause to Translate I: Philosophy in its National Language (Toward a 'licterature en françois')," describes a similar movement beginning already in the seventeenth century, where he focuses on Descartes' *Discourse on Method*. More precisely, as Derrida points out, this movement started as a question of language and of writing in one's mother tongue,

---

language, and the arbitrariness of the sign, which means that every concept is haunted by the non-presence of language; in other words, it is haunted by translation and its aporetic character. This temporal-spacial character of haunting is also a trait belonging to the date and the signature in Derrida's thinking, see, e.g. his essay "Schibboleth: For Paul Celan" (2005).

[13] For a critique of education on similar grounds, see Magrini (2014). I will revisit this issue in more detail in Chap. 4.

rather than Latin, in order to reduce ambiguity. This was decreed and made into law in all matters concerning justice.[14]

However, I suggest further that the same movement, that is, the movement of the censoring effect, can be compared to the movement of virtually all systematic categorizations of knowledge (that is, any curriculum of, for example, knowledge or religion, leading up to a method of onto-theological thought), and thus to what is called reason and rationality. This censoring effect is also an effect of translation, and it belongs properly to the moment of the aporia of translation, which I am trying to uncover. In translation – any translation – there is, as we have witnessed, always a moment of repression, in which there is no way out, or rather no passage through, over, or beyond – there is no *method* to be used to resolve or sublate the aporia. In the final paragraphs of "If There is Cause to Translate I: Philosophy in its National Language (Toward a 'licterature en françois')," Derrida (2004) broaches the issue of the aporetic character of translation in relation to the idiom and to method as path:

> Thus, when an "original" speaks about its language by speaking its language, it prepares a kind of *suicide by translation*, as one says suicide by gas or suicide by fire. Suicide by fire, rather, for it lets itself be destroyed almost without remainder, without apparent remainder *inside* the corpus.
>
> This tells us a great deal about the status and function of what one could call the self-referential signs of an idiom in general, of a discourse or a writing in its relationship to the linguistic idiom, for instance, but also in its relationship to all idiomaticity. The (metalinguistic and linguistic) *event* is then doomed to be erased in the translating structure. Now, this translating structure does not begin, as you know, with what is commonly called translation. It begins as soon as a certain type of reading of the "original" text is instituted. It erases but also exposes that which it resists and which resists it. It offers up language to be read in its very erasure: the erased traces of a path (*odos*), of a track, the path of erasure. The *translatio*, the translation, *die Übersetzung* is a path that passes over or beyond the path of language, passing its path.[15]
>
> Translation is passing its path, right here. (p. 19)

Is Derrida here in fact proposing a way to read what is censored, that is, a "language to be read in its very erasure"? This would mean that translation and censure is always already there, as soon as we start to read or write, it would mean that there is an aporia on the way (*odos*) toward any pure method, always contaminated by the impossible, the impasse, which nevertheless makes it possible to read. We start out, in consequence, with an aporia of translation. We could say that the effect of censorship, translation, erasure, and λήθη is the unavoidable but already erased beginning of reading. I will give the crucial last three sentences of the passage just quotes in Derrida's French: "Elle donne à lire la langue dans son effacement même: traces effacées d'un chemin (*odos*), d'une piste, chemin d'effacement. La *translatio*, la

---

[14] See especially pp. 11–19 of Derrida's essay.

[15] Jan Plug, the translator of the chapter, points out that Derrida is "no doubt" referring here to Heidegger's *Unterwegs zur Sprache* (*On the Way to Language*) and that "the German *Weg* is translated in French as *chemin*, path" (note 16, p. 284). However, it should be noted that one could invoke Heidegger's entire motif of Weg in his work, such as *Holtzwege, Wegmarken*, to name two of his titles, not to mention his motto for the *Gesamtausgabe* "*Wege, nicht Werke*" as, precisely, the *method* of arranging the *Gesamtausgabe*.

traduction, *die Übersetzung* est un chemin passant au-dessus ou au-delà du chemin de la langue, passant son chemin. La traduction passe son chemin, ici même" (p. 309). "The path of erasure" the λήθη of ἀλήθεια – this is how we should approach translation as aporia. It furthermore means that critique and method always involve erasure, censorship, and repression, in the very event of their happening. These paragraphs hint at the complexity of the notion of translation, and they also provide us with the possibility to connect translation to aporia. This is possible by way of Derrida's invocation of a way or path and the passing of translation. As noted in the previous chapter, Derrida's understanding of aporia entails a necessary reflection on the passage and the non-passage, the impossible passage of what makes up an aporia; in other words, the aporetic character of translation censors any and all discourses, or methods, by its movement of simultaneous erasure and exposure, as Derrida makes evident in the cited passage above, or his invocation of *pas*, the no-step, of aporia, as we saw in the last chapter.

Now, in education, we are faced with the same situation: there is an unavoidable censoring effect which works through the translational character of teaching and learning, that is to say, in disciplinary critical thinking as a general academic and scientific method to discover the truth, founded on an idea and an ideal of what constitutes rationality and rational thought and knowledge. Education is, in other words, intertwined with a method founded on a censoring movement of erasure and exposure, of λήθη and ἀλήθεια, the simultaneous absence and presence that I compared to haunting. And, as we noted in the case of Dostoevsky's "At Tikhon's," what is censored has a tendency to come back and haunt us.[16]

Given my exposition so far, the next step will be to explore the concept of critique in light of the preceding examination of censorship, which will then be related to the guiding thought of translation and aporia.

Toward a Notion of Critique

In his *The Honor of Thinking: Critique, Theory, Philosophy*, Rodolphe Gasché (2007) conducts a thorough reading of the concept of critique and its history. My examination of Gasché's reading of the concept of critique will serve as the basis for my analysis of Heidegger's notion of *Ausenandersetzung* and how it can open up for a possible ethics of critique, and by extension an ethics of education. Critique, as we will see, has a strong affinity with method – critique as a way or path to investigate, for example, a work of art or another person's thinking. I will begin with an

---

[16] Here it is impossible not to mention the return of the repressed within psychoanalysis; in particular, Nicolas Abraham and Maria Torok's thinking concerning the phantom, trauma, and the return of the repressed is relevant. See for example Nicolas Abraham and Maria Torok (1994), *The Shell and the Kernel: Renewals of Psychoanalysis*. Of importance is also Nicolas Abraham and Maria Torok (1986), *The Wolfman's Magic Word: A Cryptonomy*. Especially Derrida's foreword ("*Fors*: The Anglish Words of Nicolas Abraham and Maria Torok") is of interest.

exposition of method, and its etymological meaning as signifying a way or passage, as Derrida's reference to *odos* in the above quotes makes evident. In what follows, I address Hegel's analysis of method in the Preface to his *Phenomenology of Spirit*, and his refutation of Spinoza's philosophical method in *Science of Logic*, which leads up to Gasché's analysis of critique, and his reading of Heidegger's notion of *Ausenandersetsung*.

In the Preface to the *Phenomenology of Spirit*, Hegel (1977) states: "True thoughts and scientific insight are only to be won through the labour of the Notion." (p.73) [Wahre Gedanken und wissenschaftliche Einsicht ist nur in der Arbeit des Begriffs zu gewinnen (1986a, p. 65)]. This labor or work points to a way to develop one's thinking, which amounts to following the Hegelian dialectics or speculative thinking. However, Hegel specifically states that is it the work of the notion that accomplishes true thinking. But what does he mean by the Notion (*Begriff*)? In the *Science of Logic*, Hegel (2010) formulates the birth of the concept in the following way:

> The dialectical movement of substance through causality and reciprocal affection is thus the immediate genesis of the concept by virtue of which its becoming is displayed. But the meaning of its becoming, like that of all becoming, is that it is the reflection of something which passes over into its ground, and that the at first apparent other into which this something has passed over constitutes the truth of the latter. Thus the concept is the truth of substance, and since necessity is the determining relational mode of substance, freedom reveals itself to be the truth of necessity and the relational mode of the concept. (p. 509)
>
> Die *dialektische Bewegung der Substanz* durch die Kausalität und Wechselwirkung hindurch ist daher die unmittelbare *Genesis* des *Begriffes,* durch welche sein *Werden* dargestellt wird. Aber sein *Werden* hat, wie das Werden überall, die Bedeutung, daß es die Reflexion des Übergehenden in seinen *Grund* ist und daß das zunächst anscheinend *Andere,* in welches das erstere übergegangen, dessen *Wahrheit* ausmacht. So ist der Begriff die *Wahrheit* der Substanz, und indem die bestimmte Verhältnisweise der Substanz die *Notwendigkeit* ist, zeigt sich die *Freiheit* als die *Wahrheit der Notwendigkeit* und als die *Verhältnisweise des Begriffs.* (1986b, p. 246)

To paraphrase, the mediated but instantaneous birth of the concept is the absolute foundation that is represented by and reflected in the dialectics of substance as the subject as simple negativity which amounts to the causality and oscillating movement of becoming that is the freedom of truth. Even when we make an attempt at paraphrasing, we recognize Hegel's oscillating language, which seems to swing back and forth in a movement similar to what it describes. This laboring of language and, importantly, of thought, brings forth, one could even venture to say gives birth to, the concept, and thus to the true thoughts and scientific insight that Hegel mentions. After summing up the development or work of the genesis of the concept, Hegel refers to the refutation of a philosophical system, and the system of philosophy in question is Spinoza's. Already in the *Phenomenology*, Hegel addresses the critique and method of philosophy within the context of systems of philosophy generally, and in the *Logic* he goes on to exemplify the refutation of a philosophical system by addressing Spinoza. I will not go into the validity of Hegel's critique of Spinoza, but rather consider it from the perspective of a method of critique, which will give context to Heidegger's use of *Auseinandersetzung*.[17] Now, as part of Hegel's critique of Spinoza, he addresses the method necessary to refute Spinoza's system of philosophy, more precisely his thinking on substance. Hegel (2010) states:

> Effective refutation must infiltrate the opponent's stronghold and meet him on his own ground; there is no point in attacking him outside his territory and claiming jurisdiction where he is not. The only possible refutation of Spinozism can only consist, therefore, in first acknowledging its standpoint as essential and necessary and then raising it to a higher standpoint on the strength of its own resources. The relation of substantiality, considered simply on its own, leads to its opposite: it passes over into the concept. The exposition in the preceding Book of substance as leading to the concept is, therefore, the one and only true refutation of Spinozism. It is the unveiling of substance, and this is the genesis of the concept the principal moments of which we have documented above. (p. 512)
>
> Die wahrhafte Widerlegung muß in die Kraft des Gegners eingehen und sich in den Umkreis seiner Stärke stellen; ihn außerhalb seiner selbst anzugreifen und da Recht zu behalten, wo er nicht ist, fördert die Sache nicht. Die einzige Widerlegung des Spinozismus kann daher nur darin bestehen, daß sein Standpunkt zuerst als wesentlich und notwendig anerkannt werde, daß aber zweitens dieser Standpunkt *aus sich selbst* auf den höheren gehoben werde. Das Substantialitätsverhältnis, ganz nur *an und für sich selbst* betrachtet, führt sich zu seinem Gegenteil, dem *Begriffe*, über. Die im letzten Buch enthaltene Exposition der Substanz, welche zum *Begriffe* überführt, ist daher die einzige und wahrhafte Widerlegung des Spinozismus. Sie ist die *Enthüllung* der Substanz, und diese ist die *Genesis des Begriffs*, deren Hauptmomente oben zusammengestellt worden. (1986b, pp. 250–251)

Hegel's focus is on Spinoza's notion of substance, which, as we have just determined, is a concept that is crucial to Hegel's own notion of concept. Thus, Hegel's choice of Spinoza is not arbitrary, but chosen because Hegel considers Spinoza's system of philosophy to be the most urgent and challenging system to refute.[18] For Hegel, then, Spinoza is the most worthy opponent, which makes it imperative for him to address Spinoza's system of philosophy; hence Hegel's discussion of methods of refutation. The preferred method of refutation consists in acknowledging the importance and value of the system, to recognize how the system is necessary for one's own thinking, which entails using the system's strengths to develop and raise it "to a higher standpoint," as Hegel's suggests. It is not a question of simply and crudely tearing down and destroying a system of philosophy and replace it with another, but to engage with the opponent's system of philosophy in order to develop it, given its own merits, into an evolved system that has thus been raised to a higher standpoint. In fact, this insistence on the need to acknowledge the value, not to say necessity, of Spinoza's philosophy contributes to bringing Hegel's philosophy in

---

[17] For a thorough analysis of the relationship between Hegel and Spinoza, and the debates between Hegelianism and Spinozism, see Gregor Moder (2017).

[18] See Hegel's (1895) *Lectures on the History of Philosophy*, Vol. 3, where he states: "It is therefore worthy of note that thought must begin by placing itself at the standpoint of Spinozism; to be a follower of Spinoza is the essential commencement of all Philosophy" (p. 257) and "But the fact is that Spinoza is made a testing-point in modern philosophy, so that it may really be said: You are either a Spinozist or not a philosopher at all" (p. 283).

close proximity to Spinoza's – the very system Hegel sets out to refute.[19] In the *Phenomenology* we get a further hint at what Hegel (1977) sees as the challenge of this method of refutation when he discusses the laziness of only passing judgment on other thinkers without actually confronting "the real issue (*die Sache selbts*)" (p. 2): "To judge a thing that has substance and solid worth is quite easy, to comprehend it is much harder, and to blend judgement and comprehension in a definitive description is the hardest thing of all" (p. 3) [Das leichteste ist, was Gehalt und Gediegenheit hat, zu beurteilen, schwerer, es zu fassen, das schwerste, was beides vereinigt, seine Darstellung hervorzubringen (1986a, p. 13)]. What, in sum, is demanded of a serious refutation is "to blend judgement and comprehension in a definitive description" which amounts to an affirmation of the other person's thinking to be able to raise it to a higher level.

Now, the concept in Spinoza's philosophy that Hegel centers on in his refutation is Spinoza's understanding of substance. According to Hegel, substance in Spinoza lacks the dialectical movement necessary for it to become as Notion, that is, what Hegel calls the genesis of the concept (*Begriff*). In other words, the negative is absent form Spinoza's notion of substance: the unity of the One, which is substance, is not dialectically negated.[20] So, for Hegel, Spinoza's substance is "lifeless" and too abstract, as it does not account for the necessary movement that constitutes what Hegel calls becoming. This movement of raising a notion and also an entire system of philosophy to a "higher standpoint" is the sublation (*Aufhebung*) of dialectics and also what amounts to what I will provisionally call critique in Hegel.

To briefly revisit Dostoevsky, we are reminded of Tikhon's critique of Stavrogin's confession in how Hegel refutes Spinoza. The passage I would like to reconsider in "At Tikhon's" is the following:

> "In the very form [форме (forme)] of this great penance [покаяния (pokayaniye)] there is something ridiculous. Oh, don't let yourself think that you won't conquer!" he suddenly exclaimed, almost in ecstasy. "Even this form will conquer" (he pointed to the pages), "if only you sincerely accept the blows and the spitting. It always ended in the most ignominious

---

[19] As Pierre Macherey (2011) states in his seminal work on Hegel and Spinoza: "Hegel is never so close to Spinoza as in the moments when he distances himself from him, because this refusal has the value of a symptom and indicates the obstinate presence of a common object, if not a common project, that links these two philosophers inseparably without conflating them" (p. 11). See Pierre Macherey, *Hegel or Spinoza*, trans. Susan M. Ruddick (Minneapolis: University of Minnesota Press, 2011).

[20] Again, Macherey (2011) provides a thorough and important reading of what he considers Hegel's misreading of Spinoza, specifically as relates to the Absolute, substance, and the negative. See, specifically, Macherey's chapter "*Omnis Determinatio Est Negatio*" in *Hegel or Spinoza*. See also Efraim Shmueli (1970) for an interesting take on the One in Hegel and Spinoza, Shmueli states: "Underlying both systems was the mystical Neoplatonic idea of the 'One', conceived as a natural power. Instead of creation of the world and the soul, they offer the emanation as physically and logically necessitated; instead of revelation both propose intuitive cognition to which the soul is capable, by its own natural power, although ultimately this power has its source in the "One." The redemption of man through love of God is replaced by the climbing of the mind upwards, by which the way of descendence is reversed on the ascendence, through a series of logical operations in Hegel, and through the *amor dei intellectualis* in Spinoza" (p. 191).

cross becoming a great glory and a great strength, if the humility of the deed was sincere. Perhaps even in your lifetime you will be comforted!..."

"So you find something ridiculous in the form itself? [Editors' note: "After 'form' is struck out 'In the style'."] Stavrogin insisted.

"And in the substance [сущности (sushchnosti)]. The ugliness of it will kill it," Tikhon said in a whisper, looking down. (p. 417)

As with Hegel's method of critique, Tikhon's strategy is to "infiltrate the opponent's stronghold" and raise Stavrogin's confession to a "higher standpoint." Stavrogin's crime provides the foundation for penance, but, as Tikhon tries to relate to Stavrogin, the substance and form of its representation are ugly and will not serve as a way to forgiveness. Tikhon's way of approaching Stavrogin thus echoes Hegel's suggestion of how to refute a philosophical system: "Effective refutation must infiltrate the opponent's stronghold and meet him on his own ground. [...] The only possible refutation of Spinozism can only consist, therefore, in first acknowledging its standpoint as essential and necessary and then raising it to a higher standpoint on the strength of its own resources" (p. 512). And as Hegel, Dostoevsky's Tikhon centers on substance, but, of course, substance here means something quite different form the way Hegel and Spinoza use this concept. Nevertheless, it is not impossible to discern a critique of the one-sidedness, not to say pathological subjectivity, of Stavrogin's confession, which Tikhon is subtly, perhaps too subtly, trying to confront (by calling it ugly and inelegant), so that the confession can be sublated into proper Christian repentance. Be that as it may, and even if I am stretching the interpretation of Tikhon's reading of Stavrogin's confession too far by comparing substance in Hegel and Spinoza, there is undoubtedly an instance of refutation present in Tikhon's approach to Stavrogin's confession. This is a method of refutation, moreover, which builds on the resources of what is refuted, namely Stavrogin's confession of his crime.

How then can we continue to develop the notion of refutation in Hegel, as well as in Dostoevsky's "At Tikhon's"? In what way is refutation as a method related to critique? In *The Honor of Thinking: Critique, Theory, Philosophy*, Rodolphe Gasché (2007) traces the history of the concept of critique and compares it to what he calls "theory" and Derrida's notion of deconstruction. Pure Derridean deconstruction, Gasché argues, should not be confused with the deconstruction as it is used in literary criticism, which is a distortion of deconstruction, a false deconstruction, which does not adhere to what Derrida actually states about what deconstruction is. As Gasché (2007) writes:

Deconstruction demands demarcation that proceeds without a criteriology, or that is not critical. And yet, it is precisely as critique – in the sense of literary criticism – or as a critique of philosophy understood either as an antiphilosophy or as a Kantian investigation of the transcendental condition of possibility of knowledge, if not of philosophizing, that deconstruction has often been presented. This misjudgment of its thrust could have easily been avoided by a more careful scrutiny of Derrida's texts. (p. 21)

What Gasché calls a "misjudgment" of Derrida's work within literary criticism is countered, or rather refuted, by J. Hillis Miller (1995) in his book *Topographies*, where, in the chapter "Derrida's Topographies," Miller contests Gasché's argument:

Rodolphe Gasché was the first to argue in detail that Derrida is a technical philosopher in the wake of Husserlian phenomenology and that de Man, myself, and other American "deconstructionists" have falsified his work by using it in literary criticism. We have made it, so the story goes, into nothing more than a new New Criticism. In fact, the Yale group were more influenced by William Empson and Kenneth Burke than by John Crowe Ransom or Allen Tate. And they were by no means ignorant of Continental phenomenology. Derrida's teaching at Yale was spectacularly forceful and original, but it entered a context there that was far from foreign to it. (pp. 291–292)

Moreover, in commenting on Gasché's (1986) argumentation in the book *The Tain of the Mirror: Derrida and the Philosophy of Reflection*,[21] Miller states that Gasché "ignores that fact that the influence of phenomenology on American literary criticism, including, among many others, three members of the so-called Yale School (de Man, Hartman, and myself), had already made a decisive break in the continuity of American New Criticism in the 1950s, prior to any influence of Derrida in America" (note 3, pp. 362–363). As regards literary criticism's alignment with, rather than appropriation of, deconstruction, Gasché's understanding of literary criticism and deconstruction is certainly problematized by Miller, and there are compelling reasons to conclude that the misjudgment resides with Gasché.[22] However, a more pressing question given the aim of the present study is how Gasché's reading of Heidegger's notion of *Auseinandersetzung* can provide alternative ways to think the concept of critique, specifically as an ethics of critique in relation to translation and education.

In order to answer this question two steps are necessary. First, an outline of the exposition of critique that Gasché undertakes in *The Honor of Thinking* is required; second, an examination of Gasché's reading of Heidegger's notion of critique as *Auseinandersetzung* in relation to Gasché's overall analysis of critique is needed. It is, indeed, through Heidegger's notion of *Auseinandersetzung* that I want to suggest an alternative understanding of critique to the ones presented so far by Hegel and Dostoevsky. But before taking on the task of suggesting an alternative, we must attend to Gasché's discussion of critique, which consists in an extensive confrontation with Walter Benjamin's critique of critique. Gasché's point of departure is Benjamin's essay "A Critique of Violence" and Derrida's reading of Benjamin's essay in "The Force of Law." Gasché sets out to describe Benjamin's argument in detail and he ends his reading with a description of Derrida's deconstruction of Benjamin's essay. However, and more importantly, as part of his analysis of Benjamin's "Critique of Violence," Gasché conducts a reading of Benjamin's doctoral thesis "The Concept of Criticism in German Romanticism," and in the course of his reading Gasché broaches the theme of translation. More specifically, it is Benjamin's rendering of Novalis' conception of translation that Gasché addresses.

---

[21] In *The Tain of the Mirror* Gasché asserts the following: "So-called deconstructive criticism, which, however important, is but an offspring of New Criticism, has not, to my knowledge, undertaken the preparatory steps and has done little more than apply what it takes to be a method for reading literary texts to the unproblematized horizon of its discipline" (p. 255).

[22] For an in-depth personal account of the relationship between Miller and Derrida, see J. Hillis Miller (2009), *For Derrida*, especially Chap. 1, "A Profession of Faith."

In line with the theme of the present study, it will be fruitful to take a closer look at the context of what Gasché (2007) asserts about translation and critique in his reading of Benjamin, which is the following: "Criticism, indeed, is 'perfecting, positive', in that it is an *Übersetzung*, a translation of the necessarily incomplete work into its own absolute idea. For Benjamin, this idea of critique as translation hinges on the Romantics' conception of the artwork in terms of form understood as self-limited reflection" (p. 49). Now, when Gasché quotes Benjamin saying "'perfecting, positive'" (*vollendenden, positiven*), this is, we should be aware, Benjamin quoting and paraphrasing Novalis' description of what he calls the mythical form of translation, which is one of three different forms of translation identified by Novalis (the two other forms of translation being the grammatical form and the modifying form). In Fragment 68 of his "Miscellaneous Observations," Novalis (1997) states: "Mythical translations are translations of the highest kind. They represent the pure, perfected [*reinen, vollendeten*] character of the work of art" (p. 33). Commenting on Novalis' description of the mythical form of translation Benjamin states: "It may be that, in bringing criticism and translation close to each other, Novalis was thinking of a medial, continuous transposition of the work from one language into another – a conception which, given the infinitely riddling nature of translation, is from the start as admissible as any other" (p. 154). However, for Novalis, translation is more than "the medial, continuous transposition of the work from one language into another," as he makes evident in the last sentence of Fragment 68: "Not only books but everything can be translated in these three ways" (p. 34) ["*Nicht bloß Bücher, alles kann auf diese drei Arten übersetzt werden*" (GW, Band 2, 1945, p. 25)]. In other words, any event, any action, any phenomenon can be translated, which means that, for Novalis, translation takes on a character of critique as onto-theo-logical, that is, a founding act striving to express (the idea of) the Absolute.[23] Moreover, Novalis' idea of translation is relevant to Gasché's exposition of Benjamin's celebrated reading of Goethe's *Elective Affinities*, which is his next step in the analysis of the concept of critique in Benjamin. With this final step of his reading of Benjamin, Gasché introduces ethics into the analysis and points to its importance in Benjamin's treatment of Goethe's novel. A more detailed treatment of this part is warranted, since it points forward to the ethical in Gasché's reading of Heidegger's

---

[23] In Chap. 2, I referred to Kant's neologism ontotheology. What is meant here with this concept is more in line with Heidegger's development of it. He explains the concept in the 1961 essay "Kant's Thesis about Being" in *Pathmarks* (1998): "But if we recall once again the history of Occidental-European thought, then we see that the question about being, taken as a question about the being of beings, is double in form. It asks on the one hand: What are beings, in general, as beings? Considerations within the province of this question come, in the course of the history of philosophy, under the heading of ontology. The question 'What are beings?' includes also the question, 'Which being is the highest and in what way is it?' The question is about the divine and God. The province of this question is called theology. The duality of the question about the being of beings can be brought together in the title 'onto-theo-logy'. The twofold question, What are beings? Asks on the one hand, What are (in general) beings? The question asks on the other hand, What (which one) is the (ultimate) being?" (p. 340).

notion of *Auseinandersetzung*. In the following, Gasché connects Benjamin's idea of critique, its relation to truth, and how it is necessarily ethical:

> Thus, if Benjamin concludes that the truth content of artworks, which is the prime concern of critique, cannot be reached in the questioning mode (in Kantian terms, theoretically cognized) but can be known only "as something that is demanded" – more precisely, as something required, called for, or exacted – the truth content of a work is, in holding to Kantian terminology, clearly of the order of a practical, or moral, idea. Distinct from commentary, critique would, therefore, be practical in essence. As criticism's intent, the truth to which everything beautiful is connected, and whose virtuality can be determined in philosophy, is of an order akin to ethical truth. (p. 67)

According to Gasché, then, for Benjamin critique is the practice which lays bare the truth of art, and this truth is necessarily ethical. But what does ethical mean here? Gasché points to a passage in Bejamin's essay which, Gasché holds, sums up Benjamin's theory of art, and also introduces the important notion of the "expressionless" (*das Ausdruckslose*). In this key passage, Benjamin (1996) writes:

> The expressionless is the critical violence which, while unable to separate semblance [*Schein*] from essence [*Wesen*] in art, prevents them from mingling. It possesses this violence as a moral dictum. In the expressionless, the sublime violence of the true appears [*erscheint*] as that which determines the language of the real world according to the laws of the moral world. [...] Only the expressionless completes the work, by shattering it into a thing of shards, into a fragment of the true world, into the torso of a symbol. (p. 340)

Benjamin goes on to compare the expressionless to Hölderlin's idea of the caesura, developed in *Anmerkungen zum Ödipus*. In Greek tragedy, the force or power (*Gewalt*) of the expressionless is, Benjamin (1996) states, "the falling silent of the hero" (*Verstummen des Helden*) (p. 341; GW 1, 1974, p. 182). The silence is what "speaks" in the expressionless, which relates to the silence of the catastrophe in tragedy, its caesura, which critique puts into words. Thus, by invoking the silence of the tragic hero, Benjamin connects the expressionless and his idea of ethics to the tragic movement. When the tragic hero comes face to face with fate, that is, that which is unavoidable and bound by necessity to happen, but of which the hero is completely unaware, the ethical is staged. The ethical is that for which there is no formal guidance, no code of conduct or commandments, but which happens as a consequence of the inevitable, the unavoidable decision, which in tragedy leads to the hero's downfall in ἄτη (*atê*), catastrophe, which forces the hero, as well as the spectators, who become exposed to, and involved in, the ethical decision, to contemplate the crime, ἁμαρτία (*hamartia*),[24] which stages the ethical, and for a

---

[24] For example, in Sophocles' *Oedipus Rex* the crime is incest, a crime which Oedipus unknowingly commits; in *Antigone*, (to simplify) committing the crime is Antigone's conscious choice, and consists in going against Creon's edict (representing human law) prohibiting the mourning and burial of Antigone's brother Polyneices, whom Creon considers a traitor; however, Antigone is caught in an aporia, since not burying her brother would go against divine law. Antigone chooses to adhere to divine law, and is in consequence sentenced to death by Creon for breaking his edict. In Aristotle's *Poetics* the crime in tragedy is termed ἁμαρτία (*hamartia*) and signifies a tragic flaw or error on the hero's part. There have been debates about the precise meaning of ἁμαρτία, see for example van Braam (1912) and Golden (1978).

moment the beautiful and the ethical coincide in κάθαρσις (*catharsis*). This very condensed description of the dramatic movement in Greek tragedy, as related to the silence of the tragic hero, is what Benjamin calls the "sublime violence of the true" (*die erhabne Gewalt des Wahren*) (1974, p. 181; 1996, p. 340). As for the notion of an ethics without formal guidelines or rules, Benjamin puts forth the idea, as paraphrased by Gasché, that "[i]n an ethical relation, the individual is not to have advance knowledge of the rule according to which he or she will have to act. In this manner alone will the individual achieve the 'moral uniqueness of responsibility' (322) without which there exists, strictly speaking, no morality" (p. 94).[25] What is interesting here is how our reading of Kant's and Derrida's ideas of censorship converge in Benjamin's notion of critique as "critical violence" (p. 140) expressed as a "moral dictum" (*moralische Wort*) (p. 140, 181). In effect, Benjamin (perhaps unwittingly) reformulates Kant's definition of censorship, "critique that has force (*Gewalt*)," so that the emphasis lies on how its disruption of the whole is a moral dictum that reveals the truth. Again, in Gasché's paraphrase: "This violence (*Gewalt*) shatters the work, but by preventing semblance and essence to mingle, the critical intervention of the expressionless also completes the work, as it were. It completes it precisely as a fragment of the true world" (p. 85).

What Gasché is describing here, in his paraphrase of Benjamin, we could connect to our reading of the censored chapter "At Tikhon's" in Dostoevsky's *Demons*. One could argue that the censoring of the chapter disrupts and fragments the novel, but at the same time the chapter "At Tikhon's" viewed as a fragment, in Benjamin's sense, highlights its significance for any reading of the novel, something which Dostoevsky insisted on and which is evident from his repeated rewritings and entreaties to include the chapter in the novel. In other words, the censorship of "At Tikhon's" completes the novel precisely because it turns it into a fragment formed out of the shattering movement of censorship as critique, a "critique that has force" (*einer Kritik, die Gewalt hat*) in Kant's terms, or as Benjamin has it, the critical violence of the expressionless, that is, "the sublime violence of the true." As Gasché writes of Benjamin's notion of critique: "Critique interrupts the work, and breaks it up into shards, with the effect of showing it as a fragment of truth. Furthermore, critique can have this power only as a moral dictum of sorts," and he continues: "Made possible by the expressionless, which prevents the mingling of essence and semblance in the work, critique is therefore ethical through and through" (p. 86).

---

[25] In *The Gift of Death*, Derrida (1995) develops a similar argument about ethics, which culminates in the ambiguous statement "*tout autre est tout autre*." As Derrida insists "I cannot respond to the call, the request, the obligation, or even the love of another without sacrificing the other other, the other others. *Every other (one) is every (bit) other [tout autre est tout autre]* [emphasis in original], everyone is completely or wholly other. [...] As a result, the concepts of responsibility, of decision, or of duty, are condemned a priori to paradox, scandal, and aporia. Paradox, scandal, and aporia are themselves nothing other than sacrifice, the revelation of conceptual thinking at its limits, at its death and finitude" (p. 68). Derrida's deconstruction of ethics and responsibility here corresponds to my development of aporias of translation. It also shares affinities with Heidegger's revision of ἀλήθεια (*aletheia*) as being not yet truth (which I will attend to later in the chapter). I will return to Derrida's *The Gift of Death* in Chap. 7.

The chapter "At Tikhon's" could thus be viewed as a "fragment of truth" and is made so, paradoxically, by the movement of censorship which had the intention of suppressing the chapter, and so limit its significance.

I have as yet to comment on two of the words that have figured recurrently in my citations of Benjamin and Gasché, and their use of these words in relation to critique. The words in question, translated into English, reads "semblance" and "essence" in Benjamin's and Gasché's texts; in German they read, "*Schein*" and "*Wesen*," respectively. These words have an intricate history in German philosophy and have, depending on context, additional possible translations; for *Schein*: "shine," "glow," "appearance;" and for *Wesen*: "essence," "substance," "nature," "creature," "being." As noted, this cluster of words includes the word substance, which we found translated the Russian сущности (sushchnosti) in Dostoevskly's *Demons*. Furthermore, the whole problematic of translation indicated by these words stems back to the Greek οὐσία (*ousia*), including its meaning as Being, and παρουσία (*parousia*), designating the appearance of the idea of a thing or being, that is, presence. Heidegger (2000) traces the meaning of οὐσία in *Introducation to Metaphysics* in the following way:

> The main term for the Being of beings – that is, its definitive interpretation – is *ousia*. As a philosophical concept, the word means constant presence. Even at the time when this word had already become the dominant conceptual term in philosophy, it still retained its original meaning: *hê huparchousa ousia* (Isocrates) is present-at-hand assets. But even this fundamental meaning of *ousia* and the track it lays out for the interpretation of Being could not maintain itself. *Ousia* immediately began to be reinterpreted as *substantia*. This meaning remains current in the Middle Ages and in modernity up to now. (p. 207)

Consequently, the interrelationship between substance, essence and semblance, being and appearance, stems from the οὐσία-παρουσία coupling.[26] And this coupling is what Benjamin holds that critique cannot keep separated but, nevertheless, can hinder from merging. The work of critique, then, in Benjamin's sense, is to use force or violence to uncover what is true in the coupling between οὐσία-παρουσία. The aim of critique is to confront essence and semblance, substance and

---

[26] Concerning the development of παρουσία, Norman Cheadle gives the flowing exposition in his book *The Ironic Apocalypse in the Novels of Leopoldo Marechal* (2000): "This term was originally used by Plato to denote the relation obtaining between the ideal form or Idea and the particulars which depend upon it. A particular concrete thing is beautiful, for example, because the Idea of beauty is present in it. *Parousia* means literally "presence," i.e. the presence of the Idea in the particular (Ross 29). In Hellenism, *parousia* meant the epiphany of a god or goddess, and secondly, the visit of an emperor or a king to a province (Hastings 728). When John the Evangelist (or some posterior interloper) identified the Logos with Christ, all three of these meanings converged and were heightened by the eschatological expectancy of the primitive Christians. Thus was created the apocalyptic concept of the Parousia as Christ's second coming, the resurrection of all Christians, the definitive redemption" (p. 131). Cheadle, N. (2000). *The Ironic Apocalypse in the Novels of Leopoldo Marechal*. London: Tamesis. For further discussions of οὐσία-παρουσία as related to the metaphysics of presence, see Marin Heidegger, *Being and Time*, section 2, § 6, p. 47; Marin Heidegger, *Kant and the Problem of Metaphysics*; and Jacques Derrida (1982), "*Ousia* and *Grammê*: Note on a Note from *Being and Time*" in *Margins of Philsophy*.

appearance, *Wesen* and *Schein*, οὐσία-παρουσία, with each other, so that each is, what we could call, the other's Other, to speak with Hegel's dialectics in mind.

This critical confrontation, moreover, is the sublime violence of the true which is an ethical movement and a moral dictum, since, as Gasché states at the very end of his reading of Benjamin, "critique is eminently ethical, in that its aim is to save – to save a life as a human life, by demonstrating that, however inconspicuously, it manifests a relation to truth. By doing so, critique cherishes hope – the hope of redemption – for this life" (p. 102). This hope of redemption which the confrontation of οὐσία-παρουσία stages for Benjamin corresponds to the pedagogical situation between Stavrogin and Tikhon. What is in question in "At Tikhon's" is the possible redemption of Stavrogin, which the two protagonists try to negotiate in the censored chapter. What is more, Stavrogin and his crime personifies an idea, namely the foreign ideologies and "isms" that Dostoevsky viewed as a major threat to the traditional Russian values of orthodox Christianity. In the novel, Stavrogin's appearance on the social scene in a small town turns out catastrophic, which the novel stages as a confrontation of the conflicting values represented by Stavrogin on the one hand, and Christianity on the other hand. This is the conflict that comes to its zenith and is played out in the chapter "At Tikhon's." It is a confrontation of ideas, as much as it is a struggle between two characters, and at the center of the discussion between Stavrogin and Tikhon is Stavrogin's sin, and so the crime, ἁμαρτία (*hamartia*), which in essence is unforgivable. The crime represents the destructive consequences of the ideologies that Stavrogin personifies, and his downfall and the ἄτη (*atê*), catastrophe, consists in the act of suicide – an act, which in itself is extensively discussed and enacted by Dostoevsky with the character Kirillov in the novel.[27] However, the educational-pedagogical thrust of the novel, together with the confrontation of ideas, resides, as has already been pointed out, in the encounter between Stavrogin and Tikhon. It is in the censored chapter that the confrontation is staged as an example of critique, that is, as Tikhon's questioning of Stavrogin's crime and also the letter in which Stavrogin has documented his confession of the crime. As has been indicated, Tikhon's pedagogic strategy and his suggestion that Stavrogin redeem himself by taking the vows fail because of Stavrogin's resistance to seriously reflect on Tikhon's critique.[28] The question becomes, then, how a confrontation, pedagogical and philosophical, can be developed which would be both ethical and inclusive of the other?

---

[27] There have been many attempts to explain Kirillov's idea of suicide as well as the act itself. Perhaps the most well-known and arguably the most important discussion of Kirillov is Albert Camus' analysis in *The Myth of Sisyphus*. For a balanced analysis of Kirillov that includes a thorough assessment of prior scholarship on the issue, see Allan (2014).

[28] In a thorough analysis of Stavrogin, Joseph Frank (1969) states that in Tikhon's assessment "Stavrogin's egoism […] has taken on its subtlest form of all as a carefully staged martyrdom of contempt" (p. 671). Hence Stavrogin's urge to publicly confess and have his confession published in the newspapers.

Confronting Ethics: "The Supreme Exertion of Thinking"

From Benjamin's, as well as Dostoevsky's Tikhon's, religious notion of critique as a redemptive confrontation, a "sublime violence of the true," which, however, cannot be entirely separated from censorship in the Kantian sense, we move on to Heidegger's development of the concept *Auseinandersetzung*. I suggest that by building on the notion of *Auseinandersetzung* we can find a way to discuss the pedagogical implications inherent in the idea of critique, both taken as a philosophical-theoretical concept, and as a pedagogical-educational practice. I will do so by, again, turning to Gasché, and the reading he performs of *Auseinandersetzung* in Heidegger, since he suggests that *Auseinandersetzung* is a critique that is ethical, as the title of his analysis indicates: "Toward an Ethics of *Auseinandersetzung*".

But first it is necessary to attend to how Heidegger invokes *Auseinandersetzung* as a critique or criticism. In the "Author's Foreword to All Volumes" of his Nietzsche lectures, Heidegger (1991) states: "The matter [*die Sache*], the point in question, is in itself a confrontation [*Aus-einander-setzung*]. To let our thinking enter into the matter, to prepare our thinking for it – these goals determine the contents of the present publication" (p. xxxviii). Thus, Heidegger indicates that we have to confront Nietzsche's thought by letting our thinking into the case (*die Sache*), a move that will prepare us for Nietzsche's thought. As Heidegger (1991) insists: "The confrontation with Nietzsche has not yet begun, nor have the prerequisites for it been established. [...] Nietzsche's thought and speech are still too contemporary for us" (p. 4). However, if we follow the path of Heidegger's confrontation with Nietzsche, which makes up the text of the published Nietzsche lectures, we may, Heidegger suggests, come closer to an understanding of Nietzsche's thought. This is what Heidegger aims for, and by invoking the case (*die Sache*) of Nietzsche's thinking he also implies the legal meaning of *Auseinandersetzing*, that is, to give each other what each is due or what belongs to each as the result of a legal a dispute. Already here we recognize the difficulty of translating *Auseinandersetzung*, since apparently it is not a straight forward confrontation, but can also relate to a legal dispute between two parties. What is more, and as both Gasché and David Farrell Krell (the translator of the Nietzsche lectures) point out, Heidegger ties *Auseinandersetzung* to Heraclitus' notion of πόλεμος (*polemos*).[29] However, not to its violent connotations such as battle, fight, and war, but rather with the meaning "to separate" and "set apart." Importantly, Krell (1991), in his analysis of Volume I of the Nietzsche lectures, "The Will to Power as Art," emphasizes the paradoxical character of *Auseinandersetzung* as πόλεμος: "In Heidegger's view *polemos* is a name for the lighting or clearing of Being in which beings become present to one another and so can be distinguished from one another. Heraclitus speaks of *ton polemon xynon*, a setting apart from one another that serves essentially to bring together, a contest that unites" (p. 231). In fact, Heidegger (2000) quotes and translates Heraclitus' Fragment 80 in *Introduction to Metaphysics*, in relation to his discussion of δίκη

---

[29] For an extensive treatment of πόλεμος in Heidegger, see Fried (2000).

(*dikê*), as follows: "Heraclitus, likewise, names *dikê* at a point where he determines something essential about Being. Fragment 80 begins: *eidenai de chrê ton polemon eonta xunon kai dikê erin, . . .* 'but it is necessary to keep in view confrontation, setting-apart-from-each-other (*Aus-einander-setzung*) essentially unfolding as bringing-together, and fittingness as the opposed . . .'" (p. 177).[30] What is of interest here is that Heidegger associates *Auseinandersetzung* with justice, δίκη (*dikê*), which will be of importance to my discussion of critique and ethics in relation to *Auseinandersetzung*. Heraclitus's Fragment 80, and Heidegger's translation of it, along with the more conventional translations of the fragment, highlight the relation between justice, force, violence, and critique that we also found in Kant's definition of censorship and in Benjamin's notion of critique.

It is in the Nietzsche lectures, however, that Heidegger defines and signals the importance of *Ausenandersetzung* as criticism or critique (*Kritik*). Echoing the way Hegel conceives of genuine critique in relation to Spinoza, Heidegger states: "Confrontation is genuine criticism. It is the supreme way, the only way, to a true estimation of a thinker. In confrontation we undertake to reflect on his thinking and to trace it in its effective force, not in its weakness. To what purpose? In order that through the confrontation we ourselves may become free for the supreme exertion of thinking" (pp. 4–5).[31] As we remember, Hegel (2010) takes a similar stance in confronting Spinoza's philosophy: "Effective refutation must infiltrate the opponent's stronghold and meet him on his own ground; there is no point in attacking him outside his territory and claiming jurisdiction where he is not. The only possible refutation of Spinozism can only consist, therefore, in first acknowledging its standpoint as essential and necessary and then raising it to a higher standpoint on the strength of its own resources" (p. 512). The similarity, then, lies in Hegel's and Heidegger's mutual aim to highlight and emphasize the preeminent aspects of a thinker's philosophy as a necessary step toward overcoming or developing the philosophy under discussion. Genuine confrontation, for both Hegel and Heidegger, consists in a focus on the most essential in Spinoza's and Nietzsche's philosophies, respectively, which will liberate and so develop one's own thinking. Importantly, as

---

[30] It should be noted that Heidegger's translation differs from how the fragment is translated in what is considered standard translations, as the note to Heidegger's translation makes clear: "'But it is necessary to know that war is common to all and justice is strife.'" (note 69; p. 177). In Heidegger's (1983) German the quotation reads: "Im Blick aber zu be-halten, not ist, die Aus-einander-setzung wesend als zusammen-bringend und Fug als Gegenwendiges . . ." (p. 175). In their *Die Fragmente der Vorsokratiker*, Diels and Kranz's (1960) standard German translation of the fragment reads: "Man soll aber wissen, daß der Krieg gemeinsam (allgemein) ist und das Recht der Zwist und daß alles geschieht auf Grund von Zwist und Schuldigkeit" (p. 169). One of the standard English translations is that of Charles H. Kahn (1979), which reads: "One must realize that war is shared and Conflict is Justice, and that all things come to pass (and are ordained?) in accordance with conflict" (p. 67).

[31] The passage, in Heidegger's (1996) German, reads: "Auseinandersetzung ist echte Kritik. Sie ist die höchste und einzige Weise der wahren Schätzung eines Denkers. Denn sie übernimmt es, seinem Denken nachzudenken und es in seine wirkende Kraft, nicht in die Schwächen, zu verfolgen. Und wozu dieses? Damit wir selbst durch die Auseinandersetzung für die höchste Anstrengung des Denkens frei werden" (p. 3).

Heidegger explicitly states, and what is implicit in Hegel, is that we are obliged to engage with the "effective force" (*wirkende Kraft*) of a thinker's philosophy to do justice both to the other's thinking and to our own. There is, then, an affinity between justice, censorship, critique, and violence, which should be recognized and, precisely, confronted.

But how is such a confrontation ethical? How can *Auseinandersetzung* be an ethical activity? Especially if we consider Heidegger's view of ethics as fundamentally grounded in metaphysical thinking; that is, ethics was developed, on Heidegger's view, as a discipline of philosophy beginning with Plato. In fact, it is with the school of Plato that philosophy itself first becomes a discipline.[32] It thus becomes urgent to inquire as to how ethics as a concept and as a discipline can be reconciled with Heidegger's notion of *Auseinandersetzung*. Now, as I mentioned, someone who has attempted to elaborate on ethics and *Auseinandersetzung* is Rudolph Gasché. But, what kind of ethics does Gasché find at work in Heidegger's notion of *Auseinandersetzung*? It should, first of all, be emphasized that Gasché's reading of Heidegger's *Auseinandersetzung* is thorough and highly informative, and he accounts for the concept's etymology and dictionary meanings, in order to explain its complex position within Heidegger's thinking. Gasché (2007) at the outset of the chapter conveys what he sees as the promise of the concept, which is that it might be easier to relate to and employ than traditional critical theory and deconstruction. And, as he makes clear, the Heideggerian *Auseinanderstezung* has a different aim than traditional notions of critique, which in Gasché's Heideggerian reading centers on the decision – *krinein*[33]:

> The critical operation thrives on the dream of a pure difference guaranteeing that the separated suffers no contamination by that from which it is cut off and allowing the determination of essence to proceed in a realm free of all intrusions and within which decision is clear and without ambiguity. This is the philosophical meaning and thrust of critique established by the tradition out of the original meaning of *krinein*. (p. 108)

So how then does Heidegger's genuine or authentic critique differ from traditional critique? Gasché formulates the difference in the following manner:

> Rather than a severing of one thing from another in pure difference and free of all contamination, critique, in the authentic sense, serves to raise what is separated into its proper rank

---

[32] In "Letter on Humanism," Heidegger (1993) states: "Along with 'logic' and 'physics', 'ethics' appeared for the first time in the school of Plato. These disciplines arose at a time when thinking was becoming 'philosophy', philosophy *epistēmē* (science), and science itself a matter for schools and academic pursuits. In the course of a philosophy so understood, science waxed and thinking waned. Thinkers prior to this period knew neither a 'logic' nor an 'ethics' nor a 'physics'. Yet their thinking was neither illogical nor immoral. But they did think *physis* in a depth and breadth that no subsequent 'physics' was ever again able to attain. The tragedies of Sophocles – provided such a comparison is at all permissible – preserve the *êthos* in their sagas more primordially than Aristotle's lectures on 'ethics'" (p. 256).

[33] Κρίνειν (*krinein*) is the present active infinitive of κρίνω (*krino*) which contains a conglomerate of meanings, among them the following: to separate, part, divide, distinguish, order, arrange, inquire, investigate, select, choose, prefer, decide, judge, discern, bring to court, accuse, pass sentence on, condemn, criticize.

precisely by contrasting it to what it is separated from. Critique secures propriety and property as it locates its possibility in the other. Critique allows particularity to arise on both sides of the divide; indeed, it is the very condition through which something can come into its most proper own. In this sense, critique is the same as *Auseinandersetzung*. (p. 109)

This difference from traditional critique,[34] as characterized in Gasché's reading of Heidegger, is also where we intimate the ethical dimension of *Auseinandersetzung*. Specifically, the suggestion that genuine/authentic critique "secures propriety and property as it locates its possibility in the other" points to a possible ethical dimension. In other words, it is in an open recognition of the strengths and merits of an other; these strengths and merits are then engaged with in order to develop one's own thinking. Thus, in confronting the other, one is putting one's own thinking under the most thorough and strict scrutiny. It is a recognition of the necessity of the Other to become more than the One. This means that there will always remain, what Gasché calls (echoing Derrida) some form of contamination in genuine/authentic critique, which, as we will see, has implications for any possibility of ethics of *Auseinandersetzung* as genuine/authentic critique. Now, when it comes to the ethical dimension of *Auseinandersetzung*, Gasché (2007) states: "In *Auseinandersetzung*, the critic comes face to face in a direct confrontation with the thought of an Other. [...] In confrontation as *Auseinandersetzung*, opponents meet stripped of ideological masquerade. It is a debate that suggests honesty, responsibility, and a shared commitment to things that truly matter" (p. 103). The ethical force of the concept, Gasché suggests here, is its direct confrontation with an other's thought, uncontaminated (to invoke the Derridean notion of contamination again) by ideology and presupposition, it is a form of debate, characterized by honesty and responsibility, about what is genuinely worthy of question.

---

[34] An interesting discussion of the limits and shortcomings of traditional critique is Rita Felski's (2015) *The Limits of Critique*, which takes its cue from Ricoeur's analysis of a "hermeneutics of suspicion" in discussing Marx, Freud, and Nietzsche. Speaking of literary critique, Felski states that "the idea of critique contains varying hues and shades of meaning, but its key elements include the following: a spirit of skeptical questioning or outright condemnation, an emphasis on its precarious position vis-à-vis overbearing and oppressive social forces, the claim to be engaged in some kind of radical intellectual and/or political work, and the assumption that whatever is not critical must therefore be uncritical" (p. 2). Instead, Felski proposes what she calls a form of "postcritical reading": "Rather than looking behind the text – for its hidden causes, determining conditions, and noxious motives – we might place ourselves in front of the text, reflecting on what it unfurls, calls forth, makes possible. This is not idealism, aestheticism, or magical thinking but a recognition – long overdue – of the text's status as coactor: as something that makes a difference, that helps makes things happen" (p. 12). Felski's notion of postcritical readings certainly shares some aspects with the genuine or authentic critique proposed by both Hegel and Heidegger. However, Felski attends to neither Hegel's nor Heidegger's thinking on critique, nor does she mention Benjamin's notion of the critique of violence and the violence of critique in her study. It is, in consequence, clear that Felski takes a different perspective in her analysis of critique than I do in the present study.

Moreover, Gasché relates the ethics of the other, and thus of confrontation as *Auseinandersetzung*, to the notion, in Heidegger, of *Befremdung*.[35] *Befremdung* signifies the event of intimacy which holds apart and at the same time gathers together, that is, as signifying the meanings Heidegger assigns to πόλεμος (*polemos*) and λόγος (*logos*). In *Contributions to Philosophy (From Enowning)*, Heidegger (1999) even states that *Befremdung* constitutes Being itself: "Here, in the unavoidable ordinariness of beings, be-ing is the most non-ordinary; and this estranging of be-ing is not a *manner* of its appearing but rather is be-ing itself" (p. 163).[36] In line with Heidegger's characteristic insistence on the movement of simultaneous presencing and withdrawal to describe how Being comes to appear, *Befremdung* cannot be disconnected from the gathering intimacy which works in symphony with alienation or estrangement. Heidegger's claim is thus that Being "holds sway" as estranging alienation. This movement, which is different from Hegel's dialects,[37] also encompasses the ethics of *Ausenandersetzung* that Gasché proposes. As Gasché asserts:

> Undoubtedly, *Auseinandersetzung* has a clear advantage over critique, for rather than putting separation to work as a means to exclude the Other, or non-proper, in *Auseinandersetzung*, separation, as the space from which *Befremdung* occurs, is the very condition by which not only justice is done to Other, but in which the constitution of propriety shows itself to be a function of the Other's (dis)appropriating address. (p.111)

The movement here goes in two opposite directions: separating distance and appropriating nearness, so that in order to come close in thought to another's thinking we must separate ourselves from it; closeness, thus, depends on our separation from the other. In consequence, the movement of separation and appropriation carries with it the implication that justice is enacted as a singular event and is then disrupted by the contamination of the otherness necessarily posed by the movement. Gasché puts it thus: "In *Auseinandersetzung* as *polemos* – and as *logos*, which is the same thing – a harmonious ringing takes place in which there is no priority, neither of the One, nor of the Other. Indeed, One and the Other both presuppose *das Walten der Befremdung*" (p. 111). It means, furthermore, that the ethics of *Auseinandersetzung* is always provisional, it is in constant need of renegotiation by the parties involved.[38] This

---

[35] In *Contributions to Philosophy (From Enowning)*, Parvis Emad and Kenneth Maly translate *Befremdung* as estranging. Gasché renders "the happening of *Befremdung*" as "of being taken (aback) by the Other or alien" (p. 111).

[36] In *Beitrage zur Philosophie (Vom Ereignis)*, Heidegger (1989) writes: "Hier ist in der unumgänglichen Gewöhnlichkeit des Seienden das Seyn das Ungewöhnlichste; und diese Befremdung des Seyns ist nicht eine Erscheinungsweise desselben, sondern es selbst" (p. 230).

[37] In the Chap. 2 I pointed to Hegel's notion of how alienation alienates itself in the process of dialectics. The word Hegel makes use of to signify alienation is *Entfremdung*, and not, as we have seen in Heidegger, *Befremdung*. While Hegel's dialectics is a movement striving for development into higher levels of knowledge and insight, with its telos in Absolute Knowledge, we find in the movement Heidegger insists on a happening or event of reciprocal presencing and withdrawal which does not entail any development in the way Hegel envisioned it.

[38] The idea of ethics as provisional can be compared to Hegel's (1977) discussion of morality in the *Phenomenology of Spirit*: "[T]o advance in morality would really be to move towards its disap-

also relates to Gasché's insistence on a preliminary injustice inherent in the movement described. He notes: "Although Nietzsche's thought necessitates from within a certain injustice on Heidegger's part in order that it be recognized in its greatest strength, this necessary injustice, this limitation of justice to do justice, is at the same time the condition by which Heidegger will be able to exert the supreme task of thinking" (2007, p. 118). However, the question is if we can equate ethics with justice? Moreover, the question still lingers how an ethics of *Auseinandersetzung* is possible within Heidegger's thinking when he insists on breaking with ethics as part of metaphysics?

One way to approach these problems is the depart form Heidegger's way of thinking concerning ethics. Given Gasché's proposed notion of ethics, we would have to distance ourselves from Heidegger's view, which would mean, perhaps, to do an injustice to Heidegger's thinking, to contaminate it, in order to be able to do it, as well as ourselves, justice in the end. This critical violence, which could be seen as a censoring move, would nevertheless constitute a pedagogical-ethical engagement with the other (in this case Heidegger-Gasché) which would, one could argue, amount to critique as *Auseinandersetzung*. This would also open up possibilities for how to approach pedagogical situations in education, in which the ultimate goal would be to raise our students to what Heidegger calls "the supreme exertion of thinking." Regardless of discipline, to cultivate thinking as *Ausenandersetzung* in this way would also constitute an ethical response to our students and a recognition of them as human beings who challenge us and in whom we must strive to develop the strengths and uniqueness worthy of equals. That is, and to return to Heidegger's (1991) definition of *Auseinandersetzung* in his *Nietzsche*: "Confrontation is genuine criticism. It is the supreme way, the only way, to a true estimation of a thinker. In confrontation we undertake to reflect on his thinking and to trace it in its effective force, not in its weakness. To what purpose? In order that through the confrontation we ourselves may become free for the supreme exertion of thinking" (pp. 4–5). In confronting the Other's strengths, not his or her weaknesses, we become free to develop our own thinking, and the Other that also confronts us in return can be Heidegger, or Kant, or Dostoevsky's Stavrogin, or it can be our first-year students. This, I suggest, is where ethics and justice intersect as a matter (*Sache*) in and of education.

Finally, in order to pull together the different themes we have crossed paths with, I want to mention the revision of the meaning of ἀλήθεια (*aletheia*) which Heidegger conducts in the 1964 essay "The End of Philosophy and the Task of Thinking." Leading up to his reconsideration of his earlier insistence on rendering ἀλήθεια as truth, Heidegger once again broaches the matter or case (*Sache*) of thinking, which he now relates to Plato's notion of τὸ πρᾶγμα αὐτό (*to pragma auto*) in Epistle VII

---

pearance. That is to say, the goal would be the nothingness or the abolition [...] of morality and consciousness itself" (p. 378). Consequently, moral "perfection is never perfected" (p. 378).

(7.341c).[39] In the course of answering the question "What task is reserved for thinking at the end of philosophy?" Heidegger (1993) states:

> When we ask about the task of thinking, this means in the scope of philosophy to determine that which concerns thinking, is still controversial for thinking, and is the controversy. This is what the word *Sache* [matter] means in the German language. It designates that with which thinking has to do in the case at hand, in Plato's language *to pragma auto*. (p. 437)

As we can see, Heidegger's treatment of *die Sache* here converges with how he conceives of it within an *Auseinandersetzung* in the Nietzsche lectures. Now, the matter or case for Heidegger in "The End of Philosophy and the Task of Thinking" is to confront the inability in earlier philosophical thinking, including his own, to translate, and thus to think, ἀλήθεια as unconcealment rather than truth, and to stake out the consequences of this move.[40] Philosophy since Aristotle, Heidegger holds, has been defined by metaphysical thinking as ontotheology, which implies thinking ἀλήθεια as truth. But if we are to find what the matter (*Sache*) for thinking is, it is necessary to conceive of ἀλήθεια as unconcealment. Ἀλήθεια for Heidegger is not yet truth, but rather the openness of what he calls the clearing (*Lichtung*) in which beings come to presence: "*Alêtheia*, unconcealment thought as the clearing of presence, is not yet truth" (1993, p. 446). The openness which gives way to the clearing is the place for the simultaneous play of concealment and unconcealment, of what Heidegger calls ἀ-λήθεια (*a-letheia*), in which what presences withdraws while it at the same time reveals what is hidden in its retreat. This is the event or happening (two words that better describe what I have referred to as movement) which makes

---

[39] In the *Dictionary of Untranslatables* (2014), under the entry for "Res," the following is stated concerning "*pragma*": "*Pragma* designates the fact or affair that must be discussed, debated, and judged in a trial […], and not only the material and individual reality given or immediately present. That is why this same term can also characterize what is indicated by a word or proposition, the meaning or state of affairs in question. That is certainly how Plato uses it in letter 7.341.c: *to pragma auto* [πρᾶγμα αὐτό] does not signify the thing in itself, but rather the matter at issue, the 'problems' debated, or the 'subject' in dispute […]. And it is legitimate to see in this passage of Plato the final anchoring point of the phenomenological maxim – as Husserlian as it is Heideggerian: '*Zur Sache selbst*'" (p. 894). Giorgio Agamben (2000) has, if not a different, then certainly a more complex take on the issue: "The thing itself is not a thing; it is the very sayability, the very openness at issue in language, which, in language, we always presuppose and forget, perhaps because it is at bottom its own oblivion and abandonment. […] The presuppositional structure of language is the very structure of tradition; we presuppose, pass on, and thereby – according to the double sense of the word *traditio* – betray the thing itself in language, so that language may speak about something (*kata tinos*). The effacement of the of the thing itself is the sole foundation on which it is possible for something like tradition to be constituted" (p. 35). In other words, the thing itself is effaced by the necessary translation of language into what is sayable, that is, into some-thing. This act makes what is said enter into metaphysics as presence. This goes for every concept as well, such as ethics or education. The effacement of the thing itself is thus the withdrawal that unconceals the matter (*Sache*) for thinking. It is an act of the aporia of translation.

[40] For an important and in many respects complementary reading of thinking in Heidegger, see Emma Williams (2016), *The Way We Think*. Williams's reading does not, however, attend to Heidegger's *Nietzsche* or "The End of Philosophy and the Task of Thinking" which means she does not take *Auseinandersetzung* or the re-interpretation of ἀλήθεια translated as unconcealment and signifying "not yet truth" into account.

way for truth and meaning.[41] In other words, the aporetic moment before which no decision has been made makes truth and meaning possible.

The discussion of Heidegger's re-evaluation of ἀλήθεια as ἀ-λήθεια also serves to explain what the aporia of translation signifies in this study. Heidegger's struggle with the translation of ἀλήθεια and the controversy within philosophy about the word's translation are instances that show the aporetic character of the word. More importantly, the notion of translation that I suggest shares with the event of ἀ-λήθεια the simultaneous concealment and unconcealment that precisely makes up the aporetic character of translation. Moreover, when it comes to education, I suggested to compare it to λήθη-λήθεια, designating a movement from blindness to insight, ignorance to knowledge, hiddenness to revelation, etc. However, we should now be able to conceive of a more fundamental notion of education in which it consists in an enactment of aporias of translation that would, in a similar fashion to Heidegger's ἀ-λήθεια, be the opening up for genuine thinking to take place. To learn this kind of thinking, to attend to the task of thinking, would not be criticism, or so-called critical thinking. It would rather be critique as *Ausenandersetzung*, and would be an education which elevated one's own and others' thinking to a higher level. The task of thinking, after all, is dependent on education and education, in turn, is dependent on the task of thinking. As Heidegger (1993) concludes his essay "The End of Philosophy and the Task of Thinking": "We all still need an education in thinking, and first of all, before that, knowledge of what being educated and uneducated in thinking means" (p. 449). An education in thinking, I suggest, is a necessary foundation for thinking within any specific discipline. In literary studies, for example, the didacticism of Dostoevsky's "At Tikhon's," that is, what it wants to teach its readers about religion and culture is secondary, even Stavrogin's failed redemption is secondary, to a thinking of the text as staging the event of opening up for thinking. And to open up for thinking demands sensitive readings, which means enduring the impasse exposed in the notions of, for example, critique and censorship, and which calls for remaining concerned when faced with these aporias of translation.

References

Abraham, N., & Torok, M. (1986). *The Wolfman's magic word: A cryptonomy* (N. T. Rand, Trans.). University of Minnesota Press.

Abraham, N., & Torok, M. (1994). *The shell and the kernel: Renewals of psychoanalysis* (N. T. Rand, Ed. & Trans.). University of Chicago Press.

Allan, D. (2014). A logical redeemer: Kirillov in Dostoievskii's *demons*. *Journal of European Studies, 44*(2), 97–111.

---

[41] As John D. Caputo (1987) explains: "*A-letheia* means the process by which things (beings) emerge into presence (Being), the on-going happening of that process, from the Greeks to the medievals to the moderns. [...] Truth as the unconcealment of beings in their Being, the unconcealment of the Being of beings, is an intra-metaphysical event made possible by *a-letheia*. Indeed, far from getting beyond metaphysics, the truth of Being is what constitutes metaphysics" (pp. 176–177).

Bakhtin, M. (1984). Problems of Dostoevsky's poetics (C. Emerson, Ed. & Trans.). University of Minnesota Press.

Benjamin, W. (1974). Goethes Wahlverwandtschaften. *Band I*. Gesammelte Werke (pp. 123–201). Surkamp.

Benjamin, W. (1996). Goethe's elective affinities. In M. Bullock & M. W. Jennings (Eds.), *Selected writings, Vol. 1: 1913–1926* (pp. 297–360). Harvard University Press.

Caputo, J. D. (1987). *Radical hermeneutics: Repetition, deconstruction, and the Hermneutic project*. University of Indiana Press.

Cheadle, N. (2000). *The ironic apocalypse in the novels of Leopoldo Marechal*. Tamesis.

Derrida, J. (1982). *Ousa* and *Grammê*: Note on a note from being and time. In *Margins of philosophy* (A. Bass, Trans.) (pp. 29–67). The Harvester Press.

Derrida, J. (1995). *The gift of death* (D. Wills, Trans.). University of Chicago Press.

Derrida, J. (2004). *Eyes of the university: Rights to philosophy 2* (J. Plug, et. al., Trans.). University of Stanford Press.

Derrida, J. (2005). Shibboleth: For Paul Celan (J. Wilner & T. Dutoit, Trans.). In *Sovereignties in question: The poetics of Paul Celan* (T. Dutoit & O. Pasanen, Eds.) (pp. 1–64). Fordham University Press.

Derrida, J. (2006). *Spectres of Marx: The state of debt, the work of mourning and the new international* (P. Kamuf, Trans.). Routledge.

Diels, H., & Kranz, W. (1960). *Die Fragmente der Vorsokratiker*. Erster Band. Weidmannsche Verlagsbuchhandlung.

Dostoevsky, F. (1922). *Stavrogin's confession and the plan of the life of a great sinner* (S. S. Koteliansky & V. Woolf, Trans.). Hogarth Press.

Dostoevsky, F. (1995). *Demons* (R. Pevar & L. Volokhonsky, Trans.). Vintage.

Felski, R. (2015). *The limits of critique*. University of Chicago Press.

Frank, J. (1969). The masks of Stavrogin. *The Sewanee Review, 77*(4), 660–691.

Frank, J. (2010). *Dostoevsky: A writer in his time*. Princeton University Press.

Fried, G. (2000). *Heidegger's Polemos: From being to politics*. Yale University Press.

Gasché, R. (1986). *The Tain of the mirror: Derrida and the philosophy of reflection*. Harvard University Press.

Gasché, R. (2007). *The honor of thinking: Critique, theory, philosophy*. Stanford University Press.

Golden, L. (1978). Hamartia, ate, and Oedipus. *The Classical World, 72*(1), 3–12.

Hegel, G. W. F. (1895). *Lectures on the history of philosophy* (Vol. 3) (E. S. Haldane & F. H. Simons, Trans.). Kegan Paul, Trench, Trübner.

Hegel, G. W. F. (1977). *Phenomenology of spirit* (A. V. Miller, Trans.). Oxford University Press.

Hegel, G. W. F. (1986a). *Phänomenologie des Geistes*. (Werke 3). Surkamp.

Hegel, G. W. F. (1986b). *Wissenschaft der Logik. Erster Teil; Zweiter Teil*. (Werke 6). Surkamp.

Hegel, G. W. F. (2010). *Science of logic* (G. di Giovanni, Ed. & Trans.). Cambridge University Press.

Heidegger, M. (1983). *Einführung in die Metaphysik*. Gesamtausgabe. Band 40. Vittorio Klostermann.

Heidegger, M. (1989). *Beiträge zur Philosophie (Vom Ereignis)*. Gesamtausgabe. Band 65. Vittorio Klostermann.

Heidegger. (1991). *Nietzsche: Volumes I and II* (D. F. Krell, Trans.). HarperCollins.

Heidegger, M. (1993). Letter on humanism (F. A. Capuzzi & J. G. Gray, Trans.). In D. F. Krell (Ed.), *Basic writings* (pp. 213–265). HarperCollins.

Heidegger, M. (1996). *Nietzsche. Erste Band*. Gesamtausgabe. Band 6.1. Vittorio Klostermann.

Heidegger, M. (1998). Kant's thesis about being (T. E. Klein Jr & W. E. Pohl, Trans.). In *Pathmarks* (W. McNeill, Ed.) (pp. 337–363). Cambridge University Press.

Heidegger, M. (1999). *Contributions to philosophy (from enowning)* (P. Emad & K. Maly, Trans.). Indiana University Press.

Heidegger, M. (2000). *Introduction to metaphysics* (G. Fried & R. Polt, Trans.). Yale University Press.

Kahn, C. H. (1979). *The art and thought of Heraclitus: An edition of the fragments with translation and commentary*. Cambridge University Press.

Kant, I. (1922). *Die Religion innerhalb der Grenzen der bloßen Vernunft*. Verlag von Felix Meiner.

Kant, I. (1960). *Religion within the limits of reason alone* (T. M. Greene & H. H. Hudson, Trans.). Harper Torchbooks.

Kant, I. (1998). *Religion within the boundaries of mere reason, and other writings* (A. Wood & G. di Giovanni, Ed. and Trans.).

Kant, I. (2009). *Religion within the bounds of bare reason* (W. S. Pluhar, Trans.). Hackett Publishing.

Krell, D. F. (1991). Analysis. In M. Heidegger (Ed.), *Nietzsche: Volumes I and II* (D. F. Krell, Trans.) (pp. 230–257). HarperCollins.

Lantz, K. A. (2004). *The Dostoevsky encyclopedia*. Greenwood Press.

Macherey, P. (2011). *Hegel or Spinoza* (S. M. Ruddick, Trans.). University of Minnesota Press.

Magrini, J. M. (2014). *Social efficiency and instrumentalism in education: Critical essays in ontology, phenomenology, and philosophical hermeneutics*. Routledge.

Miller, J. H. (1995). *Topographies*. Stanford University Press.

Miller, J. H. (2009). *For Derrida*. Fordham University Press.

Moder, G. (2017). *Hegel and Spinoza: Substance and negativity*. Northwestern University Press.

Novalis. (1945). *Fragmente I*. Gesammelte Werke. Band 2. Bühl-Verlag.

Novalis. (1997). Miscellaneous observations. In *Philosophical writings* (M. M. Stoljar, Ed. & Trans.) (pp. 23–46). State University of New York Press.

Seiden, M. (1972). Nabokov and Dostoevsky. *Contemporary Literature, 13*(4), 423–444.

Shmueli, E. (1970). Hegel's interpretation of Spinoza's concept of substance. *International Journal for Philosophy of Religion, 1*(3), 176–191.

van Braam, P. (1912). Aristotle's use of Ἁμαρτία. *The Classical Quarterly, 6*(4), 266–272.

Williams, E. (2016). *The way we think: From the straits of reason to the possibilities of thought*. Wiley Blackwell.

Wrathall, M. A. (2010). *Heidegger and unconcealment: Truth, language, and history*. Cambridge University Press.

Chapter 4
Toward a Notion of Aporetic Thinking: Translation, Culture, and Critical Thinking

Introduction

The development of students' critical thinking skills is one of the general and major aims of higher education. However, the apparent difficulty in defining the concept and the continuing debates over how best to teach it permeate the scholarly discourses on it. Many of the skills and abilities that constitute signs of critical thinking are related to some of the most fundamental and generic concepts within higher education, such as judgment, logical reasoning, argumentation, analysis, interpretation, and evaluation, to name a few. Moreover, critical thinking is often associated with certain ways of being or dispositions, for example, being honest and open-minded. As what is called criticality, critical thinking furthermore aims to transform not only the individual student but society at large, which makes it a political and democratic endeavor. Nevertheless, tensions arise precisely in how one understands reason within critical thinking, that is, if reason is relative to the circumstances and contexts within which it is articulated or if reason is *semper idem*, absolute, and independent of the discipline and discourse one is engaged in. One of the main questions I will attempt to address in the following is how to reconcile or mediate between the opposing views of reason and reasoning. This will lead me to consider the notion of cultural translation and attempt a reading of one of its definitions,[1] namely Sarah Maitland's definition of it in her book *What is Cultural Translation?* My aim is to analyze Maitland's definition so as to explore its inherent limits.

---

[1] Kyle Conway (2012), in his article "A Conceptual and Empirical Approach to Cultural Translation," attempts to synthesize the different forms cultural translation has taken. And, as he states, cultural translation is "an idea – or, rather, a frequently messy collection of ideas – that has captured the imagination of scholars in fields ranging from anthropology to translation studies to cultural studies. The idea's popularity has had a strange consequence: discussion about it, especially across disciplinary lines, often moves in circles because scholars do not define what they mean by it, presuming that others share their definitions even when they do not" (p. 264). This situation is similar to how critical thinking is approached in higher education.

© Springer Nature Switzerland AG 2022

E. Schwieler, *Aporias of Translation*, Contemporary Philosophies and Theories in Education 18, https://doi.org/10.1007/978-3-030-97895-2_4

From cultural translation I will move on to an analysis of critical thinking as represented by the debate between its discipline specific and generic variants, that is, whether critical thinking as such is learned independent of its disciplinary context, or if it is necessarily tied to the specific discipline and its language the student is engaged in. I will then consider Jon Elster's critique of Edward Said's reading of Jane Austen's *Mansfield Park*. My analysis aims to show the inadequacy of generic logical reasoning to do justice to Said's reading of *Mansfield Park*, and to an analysis of *Mansfield Park* based on the novel's own merits. I conclude by pointing toward a possible third way, as indicated by Michel Foucault, Jacques Derrida, and Marin Heidegger, which emphasizes the priority of a way of thinking that remains faithful to the affirmative force of the aporetic nature of knowledge, culture, history, and education. That is, aporetic thinking involves a rethinking, in other words, a translation, of both cultural translation and critical thinking in Higher Education.

Translation and Culture

In a letter to A. W. Schlegel of July 23, 1796, Wilhelm von Humboldt (2017) raises his concerns regarding translation:

> Alles Uebersetzen scheint mir schlechterdings ein Versuch zur Auflösung einer unmöglichen Aufgabe. Denn jeder Uebersetzer muß immer an einer der beiden Klippen scheitern, sich entweder auf Kosten des Geschmacks u. der Sprache seiner Nation zu genau an sein Original, oder auf Kosten seines Originals zu sehr an die Eigenthümlichkeit seiner Nation zu halten. Das Mittel hierzwischen ist nicht bloß schwer, sondern geradezu unmöglich. Indem aber Uebersetzungen ihren eigentlichen End zweck verfehlen, erfüllen sie freilich einen andern, sehr wichtigen. Sie sind für die Sprachen, was der Umgang für die Menschen ist, sie bringen sie in Berührung u. machen sie gewandt u. vielseitig. (pp. 274–275)

This passage is given, in its English translation, in the section on cultural translation in the book *Introducing Translation Studies*, by G. Pierce (2018):

> All translation seems to me simply an attempt to solve an impossible task. Every translator is doomed to be done in by one of two stumbling blocks: he will either stay too close to the original, at the cost of taste and the language of his nation, or he will adhere too closely to the characteristics peculiar to his nation, at the cost of the original. The medium between the two is not only difficult, but downright impossible. [...] [D]espite the fact that translation brings cultures nearer, in each translation, there will be a definite deformation between cultures" (quoted in Pierce, 2018, p. 135).

Pierce does not provide any information as to where he borrowed the translation, or if he translated the passage himself, but only references it as addressing the challenges of cultural and anthropological translation. However, concerning the content of the letter, there can be little doubt, as the cited passage makes clear, that Humboldt was concerned about the possibilities of cultural as well as interlingual translation. He was, after all, a Sanskrit scholar and translator, and discussed Sanskrit translations with A. W. Schlegel.[2] Even though this particular letter is addressing the necessity of translating Shakespeare and not Sanskrit, there is, of course, a cultural hurdle to overcome also in translating Shakespeare into German. I will not pursue the problems which are evident in the translation of Humboldt's letter which Pierce is using, nor the question of translating Shakespeare into German,[3] but instead directly move on to address the somewhat controversial notion called cultural translation.

Sarah Maitland's study of cultural translation, with its title, asking precisely the question under scrutiny here, *What is Cultural Translation?*, gives us not only a valuable definition of the concept, but also provides the reader of her book with a succinct summary of the debate over what cultural translation is, or rather what it potentially can and cannot be, its possibilities and limitations, as well as its history.[4] In developing her version of cultural translation, she takes her cue from Paul Ricœur's hermeneutics and Walter Benjamin's work on language and translation, which informs her view of translation as an, in essence, interpretative endeavor. However, Maitland does not devalue the practice of interlingual translation, which is central to her notion of cultural translation. Importantly, she underscores the critical and emancipatory character of cultural translation, which means that she assigns a political dimension to it. Given these traits of cultural translation, her definition becomes the following:

> In my definition, cultural translation applies the interpretive methods by which philosophical hermeneutics attempts to understand the unknown and deploys them deliberately in order to effect change. Cultural translation is thus a gesture of interpretation – of contested understandings of the objects of human expression that suffuse the practice of everyday life in the social sphere and the attendant gestures of thoughtful reflection and analysis this entails. But this gesture of interpretation is also accompanied by a simultaneous gesture of desire – to occasion different behaviours and different ways of thinking and acting within an identified audience. As such, not everything in the world is cultural translation. To qualify as cultural translation a phenomenon of human expression in the social sphere must be shown to engage in a contemplative work of understanding addressed towards a particular

---

[2] For an analysis of Humboldt's and A. W. Schlegel's views on translation and the translation of Sanskrit, in particular, see Dorothy M. Figueira's (1994) study *The Exotic: A Decadent Quest.*

[3] In the essay "Sticky Transfers," Valentine Cunningham (1994) mentions Schlegel's translation of Shakespeare's *The Merchant of Venice*, and George Eliot's critique of it. Cunningham writes that Eliot "complains that Schlegel turns Lorenzo's words in *The Merchant of Venice*, 'Soft stillness and the night/Become the touches of sweet harmony', into 'Sanfte Still und Nacht/Sie warden Tasten süsser Harmonie': 'That is to say: "Soft stillness and the night *are* the *finger-board* of sweet harmony."' But, as Eliot's recent editors have pointed out, Schlegel is not far wrong, if he is wrong at all, since *touches* has much to do with the paying and fingering of the musical instruments that produce sweet harmony" (p. 328). I would argue that Schlegel's translation is as good as it gets and that "*tasten*" indeed can translate "touches." There is no need to invoke playing or fingering instruments, as Eliot's editors do, which would amount an interpretation of *tasten* that might overtranslate Schlegel's translation. Schlegel's translation, I would argue, is, as we will see, more in line with the notion of translation proposed by Walter Benjamin.

[4] For a somewhat argumentative, but clear and comprehensive, overview of translation studies, including summaries and explanations of different theories and methods of translation, including cultural translation, see Anthony Pym's (2010) *Exploring Translation Theories.*

substance, but it must also have as its primary objective nothing short of the transformation of human hearts and minds. (Maitland, 2017, p. 53)

As is evident from Maitland's definition, the practice of cultural translation extends the work of translation beyond the traditional notion of text to any "phenomenon of human expression" which can be interpreted, and so transformed, "in a contemplative work of understanding." To work toward an understanding of the foreign is thus, according to Maitland, an emancipatory act, that is, "to occasion different behaviours and different ways of thinking and acting within an identified audience." In other words, cultural translation is more than the literal translation of one language into another, and it also entails more than taking into consideration the different cultures of the source and target language. Cultural translation is, importantly, performative and transformational – it instigates some sort of change, not only of texts but of the human beings engaged in and with cultural translations.

In working her way toward a definition of cultural translation, Maitland provides the reader with several passages mainly from the work of Ricœur and Benjamin, the two thinkers whose work serve as her major theoretical inspiration. Interestingly, she does so in a manner which, at times, makes the reader wonder about the context of the passages she quotes. It is one of these instances that I aim to explore and, in a sense, translate further. The case that I wish to address concerns a passage from Benjamin's essay "On Language as Such and on the Language of Man" ("*Über Sprache überhaupt und über die Sprache des Menschen*") written in 1916, but not published in Benjamin's lifetime. The passage is the following:

> After the Fall, which, in making language mediate, laid the foundation for its multiplicity, linguistic confusion could only be a step away. Once men had injured the purity of name, the turning away from that contemplation of things in which their language passes into man needed only to be completed in order to deprive men of the common foundation of an already shaken spirit of language. Signs must become confused where things are entangled. The enslavement of language in prattle is joined by the enslavement of things in folly almost as its inevitable consequence. In this turning away from things, which was enslavement, the plan for the Tower of Babel came into being, and linguistic confusion with it. (Benjamin, 1991, p. 72, original emphasis)

Maitland rightly points to Benjamin's use of Biblical language and takes him up on the post-Babelian rise of a multitude of languages and by extension the plurivocity of language within language. Moreover, the confusion of languages has implications for interpretation and understanding, since interpreting an expression of whatever sort is comparable to facing a foreign language in order to interpret what is expressed and transfer and transform it into a, for the interpreter, known language. However, this act of translation is never complete, there always remains something untranslated and thus something unknown – which, Maitland holds, constitutes a part of the "mysteries of language" (p. 46).

What Maitland does not pay much attention to is the importance of Benjamin's use of theology in his work, and its significance to his thinking, especially when it comes to hermeneutics and language. His perhaps most well-known expression concerning his relationship to theology, can be found as an aphorism in the unfinished *The Arcades Project* and reads as follows: "My thinking is related to theology as blotting pad is related to ink. It is saturated with it. Were one to go by the blotter, however, nothing of what is written would remain" (1999, p. 470). Here Benjamin illustrates how theology saturates his thinking, but not necessarily his writing. However, when we read the early "On Language as Such and on the Language of Man," we cannot avoid being struck by the recurring references to theology.[5] Now, to address Benjamin's thinking regarding an aspect of his use of theology and language, I would like, first of all, to focus on a word in the passage Maitland quotes which might otherwise be passed by without further notice. The word in question is "prattle" which appears in the sentence "The enslavement of language in prattle is joined by the enslavement of things in folly almost as its inevitable consequence" (p. 72). Earlier in the essay, Benjamin reveals from where he borrows the word: "The knowledge of things resides in name, whereas that of good and evil is, in the profound sense in which Kierkegaard uses the word, 'prattle', and knows only one purification and elevation, to which the prattling man, the sinner, was there submitted: judgment" (p. 71). In this sentence, many of the keywords for understanding Benjamin's essay are found, while also pointing to his use of theological language. When it comes to the word prattle, it is the English translation of the German word Benjamin makes use of, namely *Geschwätz*, which in turn is a translation of the Danish word *snak*, as used by Kierkegaard.[6] That the origin of the word prattle is the Kierkegaardian *snak* makes it quite a complex matter from a philological, philosophical, theological, as well as translational perspective. It is intimately connected to Benjamin's use of theological discourse, which in turn is connected to Benjamin's theory of language.

Thus, given the translational complications of the word prattle, what are the consequences of Benjamin's theological linguistics in the 1916 essay for translation, and specifically for cultural translation? Moreover, given Maitland's use of Benjamin, and her overall theory of cultural translation, does Maitland's theory and practice of cultural translation require us to attend to what she leaves out of Benjamin's thinking by her choice of quotes? For example, what are the consequences of how we come understand Benjamin read in translation, for instance the translated word prattle, given the fact that the word is two translations away, not to mention the cultural implications of this?

Tracing the word prattle, it travels, in translation, from one context to another: cultural, epistemological, temporal, and historical, each time carrying its particularity and singularity, its otherness and foreignness, with it. We go from Danish to German to English, which is not a straight forward journey when it comes to translation, as Humboldt made clear in his letter to Schlegel about the translation of Shakespeare into German. For the word to carry over hermeneutically, that is, if we are to be given a chance to understand it, or at least be aware of its importance in Benjamin's work, we must be able to trace its history, its cultural, and theological

---

[5] Several studies have been written on Benjamin's relation to theology and religion, see for example Naishtat (2019), Dickinson and Symons (2016), Plate (2005), and Gibbs (1998).

[6] The Danish word *snak*, or derivatives thereof, is a word used in northern Germany (*schnack*), in Sweden (*snack*), and in Norway (*snakk*).

implications. And if interlingual translation is to be at the center of the practice of cultural translation, as Maitland holds, we must attend to those acts of translation that give rise to the use of the word prattle. To return to Benjamin's reference to Kierkegaard and his use of prattle in "On Language as Such and on the Language of Man": "The knowledge of things resides in name, whereas that of good and evil is, in the profound sense in which Kierkegaard uses the word, 'prattle,' and knows only one purification and elevation, to which the prattling man, the sinner, was there submitted: judgment" (p. 71). Rereading this sentence, we must surmise that there is a difference between the knowledge of things we find in names and the knowledge of such matters as good and evil, which to Kierkegaard, Benjamin holds, amounts to prattle, that is, *Geschwätz, snak*. According to Joseph Westfall (2012), in the chapter "Walter Benjamin: Appropriating the Kierkegaardian Aesthetic," in the book *Kierkegaard's Influence on Philosophy*, Kierkegaard's *snak* is for Benjamin not something negative, but an elevation of the conception of prattle or nonsense:

> To prattle is, then, in this sense something profound. It is to speak of that which, unlike things, cannot be named. Unable to name that of which the Benjaminian-Kierkegaardian prattler wishes to speak, he or she is compelled by the external inaccessibility of the subjective to try to find new ways of speaking, ways that require allegorical thinking. Such thinking – and such language – are failures on the part of the individual to submerge himself or herself in the universality of comprehensibility (that is, for Benjamin, to be named), and thus to elevate himself or herself as subjective individual over the universal (that is, for Kierkegaard, to sin). (p. 54)

Prattle thus has a relation to the original function of language which, according to Benjamin, was characterized by the immediacy of naming. In Genesis, God created the world by naming, as in for example "Let there be light!" God, in other words, creates what he names. When it comes to human beings, Benjamin, again in "On Language as Such and on the Language of Man," states that "in the Fall, man abandoned immediacy in the communication of the concrete – that is, name – and fell into the abyss of the mediateness of all communication, of the word as means, of the empty word, into the abyss of prattle" (p. 72). With the Fall, humans were relegated to the free play of the signifier from the immediacy of presentation in which the signifier becomes the signified. In *Walter Benjamin: An Aesthetics of Redemption*, Richard Wolin (1994) states:

> As a result of the close relationship between divine language and human language, man, as it were, has been charged with the task of *completing* the process of creation. He accomplishes this by translating the imperfect, mute language of things into the language of names; that is, among creatures, man possesses a privileged status as *name-giver*. The objectivity of this process of translation is ensured by the affinity between the creative word, by virtue of which all things have come into existence, and the cognizing word of man. By bestowing names upon things man elevates them, grants them dignity, redeems them from a fate of speechless anonymity.
>
>   However, upon expulsion from paradise the pure language of man suffers degradation, resulting in the fragmentation of the original language into an impure plurality of languages [...] The original language was a *pure language of names*; it did not yet know of the (profane) separation between word and thing; that is, it had no need of "knowledge" to produce artificially an identity of subject and object. [...] In his description of this original utopian condition of knowledge, as yet unrent by the subject-object split, Benjamin makes explicit

reference to the Kabbalistic myth of the Tree of Knowledge (of good and evil). (Emphasis in the original, p. 42)

Translation before the Fall was thus an immediate practice of name-giving, in which the relation between word and thing, subject and object, signifier and signified, is uncontaminated by the foreignness, ambiguity, and plurivocity of language which followed with the Fall. Translation after the Fall, as opposed to *die Ursprache*, is forced to engage with knowledge and the ambiguity of meaning, as indeed the translation of Kirekegaard's *snak* exemplifies.

As human beings we prattle, and thus we translate; when we translate, we prattle. In Benjamin's reading of Kierkegaard's use of *snak*, *Geschwätz* arises from practice and contemplation, that is, what could be called hermeneutic negotiation, and as Westfall (2012) explains in the above quote, it is "to speak of that which, unlike things, cannot be named" (p. 54). To speak of things that cannot be named, furthermore, is what Benjamin conceives of as allegory. As he notes in *The Origin of the German Tragic Drama* (*Ursprung des deutschen Tauerspiels*) regarding Evil: "Evil as such […] exists only in allegory, is nothing other than allegory, and means something different from what it is. It means precisely the non-existence of what it presents" (Benjamin, 2003, p. 233). This is what Westfall (2012) is getting at when he writes that prattlers "require allegorical thinking" (p. 54). When it comes to translation, this means that there is no original or source text, but only the allegorical translation which lives on, survives, or *überleben*, to use Benjamin's word, by expressing that which cannot be named, namely the non-existent origin. Translation is thus allegory *par excellence*. Translation as allegory speaks about itself as language, while it, at the same time, speaks about the inexpressible, that which cannot be named, by speaking of something else, what in Benjamin amounts to the original language of God, *die Ursprache*. Accordingly, allegory is both declarative and performative, just as the word λόγος (*lógos*), which Benjamin mentions at the beginning of the essay "On Language as Such and on the Language of Man." Benjamin states:

> The distinction between a mental entity and a linguistic entity in which it communicates is the first stage in any study of linguistic theory; and this distinction seems so unquestionable that it is, rather, the frequently asserted identity between mental and linguistic being that constitutes a deep and incomprehensible paradox, the expression of which is found in the ambiguity of the word "logos." Nevertheless, this paradox has a place, as a solution, at the center of linguistic theory, but remains a paradox, and insoluble, if placed at the beginning. (p. 63)
>
> Die Unterscheidung zwischen dem geistiges Wesen und dem sprachligen, in dem es mitteilt, ist die ursprunglichste in eeiner sprachtheoretische Untersuchung, und es scheint dieser Unterschied so unzweifelhaft zu sein, daß vielmehr die oft behauptete Identität zwischen dem geistigen und sprachlichen Wesen eine tiefe und unbegreifliche Paradoxie bildet, deren Ausdruck man in dem Doppelsinn des Wortes Λόγος gefunden hat. Dennoch hat diese Paradoxie als Lösung ihre Stelle im Zentrum der Sprachtheorie, bleibt aber Paradoxie und da unlösbar, wo sie am Anfang steht. (pp. 141–142)

The double meaning of λόγος implies that it signifies both the word as such and the expression of the word, so that language always communicates that it is a medium of communication and simultaneously what is meant by a specific expression.

Λόγος, of course, also, has theological implications, as in John 1:1, where the Word of God is God, which means the Word, being God, created the world. Moreover, in Genesis 2:19, God charged Adam to name all the creatures in Eden: "And out of the ground the LORD God formed every beast of the field, and every fowl of the air; and brought *them* unto Adam to see what he would call them: and whatsoever Adam called every living creature, that *was* the name thereof" (Genesis, 2:19 King James Bible). This immediacy of naming when λόγος creates what is named is lost with the Fall, when Adam eats of the fruit from the tree of knowledge of good and evil: "But of the tree of the knowledge of good and evil, thou shalt not eat of it: for in the day that thou eatest thereof thou shalt surely die" (Genesis, 2:17 King James Bible). To gain knowledge of good and evil thus means to lose the gift of naming as a creative act; this is why Benjamin refers to the knowledge of good and evil as giving rise to prattle, that is to say, when humans after the Fall speak of good and evil they are only able to talk, meaning prattle, intermediately. There is no direct relation between language and thing; in other words, naming and thing do not coincide, which means a foreignness is instilled within language. To have λόγος no longer means being able to name in a way in which signifier and signified coincide.

Incidentally, we encounter the notorious difficulty of translating λόγος in Aristotle; specifically, in the *Nicomachean Ethics*, addressing the dual nature of the soul, Aristotle states:

> Thus we see that the irrational (ἄλογον) part, as well as the soul as a whole, is double. One division of it, the vegetative, does not share in rational principle at all; the other, the seat of the appetites and of desire in general, does in a sense participate in principle, as being amenable and obedient to it (in the sense in fact in which we speak of 'paying heed' (ἔχειν λόγον) to one's father and friends, not in the sense of the term 'rational' in mathematics). And that principle can in a manner appeal to the irrational part, is indicated by our practice of admonishing delinquents, and by our employment of rebuke and exhortation generally. (1934, 1102b25)

The heart of the difficulty lies in the parenthetical note, which impelled the translator, Harris Rackham, to provide the following note to his translation:

> This parenthetical note on the phrase "to have logos" is untranslatable, and confusing even in the Greek. According to the psychology here expounded, the intellect "has a plan or principle," in the sense of understanding principle, and being able to reason and make a plan: in other words, it is fully rational. The appetitive part of man's nature "has a plan or principle" in so far as it is capable of following or obeying a principle. It happens that this relationship of following or obeying can itself be expressed by the words "to have logos" in another sense of that phrase, viz. "to take account of, pay heed to." To be precise the writer should say that the appetitive part λόγον ἔχει τοῦ λόγου "has logos (takes account) of the logos." The phrase has yet a third sense in mathematics, where "to have logos" (ratio) means "to be rational" in the sense of commensurable. (Aristotle, 1934, *Nicomachean Ethics*, note 6).

As Rackham makes evident, we find in Aristotle the paradoxical character of λόγος (which also Benjamin points out), namely in the phrase "λόγον ἔχει τοῦ λόγου 'has logos (takes account) of the logos'," that is, λόγος is translated by λόγος, and is so both subject and object. This intralinguistic confusion of the word λόγος is, if we take our cue form Benjamin in "On Language as Such and on the Language of

Man," what characterizes human language after the Fall. As human beings we have been condemned to prattle, which means that we are caught up in a hermeneutical circle, trying to make sense out of the foreignness (the nonsense, prattle) that even our own language confronts us with. We must translate the expressions we are presented with (cultural, linguistic, social, etc.), in whatever medium, because even if these translations are inevitably allegorical, they provide us with the possibility to confront them by letting them guide us within what is foreign in them.

This investigation into the word prattle, which is part of Maitland's Benjamin quote that we started out with, has opened up some of the paths that a single passage from Benjamin's essay "On Language as Such and on the Language of Man" makes it possible to follow. In the course of the exposition I have moreover touched upon some of the main concepts which Benjamin engages with in his thinking. Even though I have not in any way exhausted the analysis of Benjamin and treated his thinking in a systematic way, which is something he undoubtedly deserves, my discussion of Maitland's quoted passage from "On Language as Such and on the Language of Man" to some degree reveals what is at stake in translation and about using translations for hermeneutical purposes. It suggests that Maitland's quoted passages form Benjamin's work are themselves in need of translation, but in a reverse fashion, so that we go back from the translation to the original in order to hermeneutically understand what is at stake in the quoted texts, and not take them as ways to simply strengthen Maitland's argument for her definition of cultural translation. The aporia of the definition as well as the quoted passages consist in that when we make use of them they turn out to mean too little, or too much, which means there is always a lack of meaning and understanding, or an excess of meaning and ways of understanding, since definitions and quotes always imply the whole by way of ellipsis, up to the point where we would have to read the text as a whole and quote the entire originals from which the quotes are taken. Even when we admit, and include a caveat in our definitions, that meaning and understanding are always partial, fragmentary, and never complete, it is still meaning and understanding that are the expected and the ultimate aim of a hermeneutic analysis. Likewise, in retracing prattle back to Kierkegaard's *snak* we are attempting to unravel the implications of what using Benjamin in translation *actually* means. In the end, however, we end up with the prattle of λόγος, λόγος saying λόγος, which lays bare the aporia at the origin of translation, breaking down the hermeneutical project that aims at understanding and exposing the origin or original. The allegory of λόγος, prattle as reason and reason as prattle, instead reveals the irreducible difference of language which precedes the naming power of the word or λόγος as and of God. What precedes λόγος is ἄλογον – the speechless and irrational, or (to refer to another translation of *snak*/*Geschwätz*) nonsense. The irrational does not make sense, it does not provide meaning, it is, simply put, *snak*. In the essay "Des tours de Babel," Derrida (2007) demonstrates, with the expression "*pas de sens*," how the aporia of translation extends to include the sacred texts of the Old Testament, that is, the Adamic *reine Sprache* or *Ursprache*, which Benjamin discusses. Of the event of the *pas de sens* – step of meaning, no meaning – in sacred texts, Derrida writes: "*Pas-de-sens*: this does not signify poverty of meaning but no meaning that would be itself, meaning, beyond any 'literality'. And right there is the sacred. The sacred surrenders itself to translation, which devotes itself to the sacred" (p. 224). This next to untranslatable sentence deserves to be quoted in French: "*Pas-de-sens, cela ne signifie pas la pauvreté mais pas de sens qui soit lui-même, sens, hors d'une « litteralité ». Et c'est là le sacré. Il se livre à la traduction qui s'adonne à lui*" (p. 235). The ambiguity of the sentence is challenging to disentangle, but it also stages the point Derrida is making. *Pas-de-sens* is both meaning and meaninglessness which is meaning beyond literality. The sacred is precisely the supplement of and at the origin,[7] which is restated in translation, while recognizing that translation always concerns itself with the sacred, the *pas-de-sens*. When it comes to Maitland, the task of translation, the translator's *Aufgabe*, to echo Benjamin, consists in this: by enacting the *pas-de-sens* of Maitland's method and definition of cultural translation the definition of cultural translation must itself be culturally translated. This is the critical, educational, and by extension pedagogical task of the translator.

In examining the word prattle in Maitland's Benjamin quote I have tried to confront Maitland's method of developing a definition of cultural translation. I have attempted to enact what a confrontation, an *Auseinandersetzung*, can involve in my reading of Maitland and, by extension, Benjamin. I have, to put it differently, tried to engage in a critique by pursuing what Maitland submits to be cultural translation, not by exposing its weaknesses, but by taking advantage of its merits and strengths. And, what is striking is how close Maitland's definition of cultural translation is to a certain understanding of critique, namely in that cultural translation as critique should include the three key concepts *interpretation*, *understanding*, and *transformation* (Maitland, 2017, p. 53). We have thus, once again, come up against the notion of the critical, of critique, which, under the name critical thinking, is to be learned and practiced by students in higher education.

---

[7] The supplement of (at) the origin is a phrase I borrow from Derrida's (1997) *Of Grammatology*, of which he states: "The question is of an originary supplement, if this absurd expression may be risked, totally unacceptable as it is within classical logic. Rather the supplement of origin: which supplements the failing origin and which is yet not derived; this supplement is, as one says of a spare part [*une pièce*], of the original make [*d'origine*] [or a document, establishing the origin]" (p. 313). Of the impossibility of saying, naming, or translating the movement of the supplement at the origin, Derrida continues by writing that "the impossibility of formulating the movement of supplementarity within the classical logos, within the logic of identity, within ontology, within the opposition of presence and absence, positive and negative, and even within dialectics, if at least one determines it, as spiritualistic or materialistic metaphysics has always done, within the horizon of presence and reappropriation. Of course the *designation* of that impossibility escapes the language of metaphysics only by a hairsbreadth. For the rest, it must borrow its resources from the logic it deconstructs. And by doing so, find its very foothold there" (p. 314).

Sensitive Readings and Obscuritanism: Critical Thinking in Higher Education

To continue to pursue translation as it relates to the critical, the cultural, and education, I would like to address the questions as to what critical thinking is and how it is supposed to be practiced by students in higher education. In the Delphi Report "Critical Thinking: A Statement of Expert Consensus for Purposes of Educational Assessment and Instruction," Peter A. Facione (1990) provides us with one of the most ambitious definitions of critical thinking (there are many), a definition being, as we have seen, the assignation of meaning in the service of understanding. The definition relates to skills and dispositions which together make up critical thinking:

> We understand critical thinking to be purposeful, self-regulatory judgment which results in interpretation, analysis, evaluation, and inference, as well as explanation of the evidential, conceptual, methodological, criteriological, or contextual considerations upon which that judgment is based. CT is essential as a tool of inquiry. As such, CT is a liberating force in education and a powerful resource in one's personal and civic life. While not synonymous with good thinking, CT is a pervasive and self-rectifying human phenomenon. The ideal critical thinker is habitually inquisitive, well-informed, trustful of reason, open-minded, flexible, fairminded in evaluation, honest in facing personal biases, prudent in making judgments, willing to reconsider, clear about issues, orderly in complex matters, diligent in seeking relevant information, reasonable in the selection of criteria, focused in inquiry, and persistent in seeking results which are as precise as the subject and the circumstances of inquiry permit. Thus, educating good critical thinkers means working toward this ideal. It combines developing CT skills with nurturing those dispositions which consistently yield useful insights and which are the basis of a rational and democratic society. (p. 2)

This dense and complex definition encompasses an array of skills and dispositions that sum up what the Delphi expert group considers to be the traits and characteristics of a critical thinker. The most salient notion in the definition is that of judgment – a critical thinker's ability to make sound judgments separates him or her from someone who practices poor judgment. In other words, the critical thinker is someone who uses judgment to decide. Decision is etymologically related to the words criticism, critic, critique, crisis which all stem from the Greek κρίνειν (krínein), the present active infinitive of κρίνω (krī́nō), which means to judge, to decide, to separate, to inquire, to investigate, to criticize, and so forth. We thus find that many of the skills and dispositions belonging to the definition of critical thinking are translated by the Greek **κρίνειν, which in itself contains the same paradox or aporia which Benjamin identifies in** λόγος and the *pas-de-sens* which Derrida finds at work in translation. To think critically, then, means, among other things, to decide (to take the step and not – *pas*) on a judgment, which implies assigning meaning (*sens*) to an expression of some sort. In the following I will attempt to unpack some of the assertions and assigned meanings that struggle to delimit critical thinking.

The Delphi Report, conducted by 46 experts from a variety of disciplines, with Facione as the main investigator, was aimed at teaching and learning critical thinking in K-12 schools, as well as colleges and universities, which makes it an admittedly general set of skills and abilities. However, Martin Davies (2015) has developed a model of critical thinking specifically for higher education within which the skills and dispositions that the Delphi Report identified are included, along with other abilities. Specifically, he adds the notions criticality and critical pedagogy which include a socio-cultural and performative dimension, that is to say, the dimension adds action, dialogue, and transformation as expected outcomes of developing critical thinking. These traits in a person who possesses the ability to think critically point to the agency, activism, and political and/or ethical action which bring about some kind of transformation. Criticality entails that the critically thinking individual do something, while critical pedagogy aims at change of some sort.

Now, the fault line within critical thinking studies, which divides the field in two, is where critical thinking as the debunking of all types of "relativism," in the name of the rationality of thinking, knowledge, facts, and truth, clashes with critical thinking as socio-cultural constructivism and critical pedagogy seen as (leftist/liberal) activism tied to what has been labeled "grievance studies," such as postcolonial studies, gender studies, intersectional feminist studies, racism studies, disability studies, queer studies, etc. Signs of this dividing line is present also in the debate between the "generalist" view and the "specifist" view of critical thinking, conducted over many years foremost by Robert Ennis and Tim Moore representing the specifist camp, and John McPeck and Martin Davies representing the generalist camp. However, the debate, I argue, runs deeper than a quarrel over whether critical thinking in higher education should be taught and learned as a generic skill or as a discipline specific skill. The dispute boils down to the adversity between analytic and so-called continental philosophy, conducted in an at times vitriolic tone. Nevertheless, and importantly, the debate between the specifist and generalist notions of critical thinking will, as we will see, lead us toward examining the tension between the universal and the singular or particular, and the positions posited by absolutism and relativism. To this end, I would like to examine two texts, one by a proponent of critical thinking as specific, namely Tim Moore (2013) and his article "Critical Thinking: Seven Definitions in Search of a Concept," and another by a generalist, Martin Davies (2013), with his article "Critical Thinking and the Disciplines Reconsidered." I will begin by considering Moore's article and then move on to examine Davies's text.

The incentive Moore gives for his investigation into critical thinking in higher education is that the concept to a large extent seems to be based on tacit knowledge, so that academics often intuitively know critical thinking when they are faced with it, but are at a loss when it comes to express what critical thinking actually is and consists in; that is, academics often have trouble defining critical thinking. Hence, Moore (2013) states:

> The evident importance of critical thinking in higher education, as well as the seeming pedagogical
>   uncertainty surrounding the concept, suggests there is a need to find out more about how the idea is actually understood and used by academics in their teaching in the disciplines. The present study is motivated by this interest. (p. 507)

Consequently, Moore sets out to survey how 17 university teachers conceive of critical thinking within their disciplines. The disciplines Moore chose to survey was history, philosophy, and literary/cultural studies. The teachers' all agreed that being critical was of importance within their respective discipline, and that thinking critically was expected by students and teachers alike. But when it came to the teachers' understanding and definitions of critical thinking, and how critical thinking was related to the students in teaching and instruction, the teachers' responses revealed considerable differences (p. 510). Moore next goes on to formulate definitions of critical thinking based on the surveyed teachers' notions of it. The seven definitions that Moore's analysis distinguished were the following: critical thinking as (i) judgement; (ii) as skepticism; (iii) as a simple originality; (iv) as careful and sensitive readings; (v) as rationality; (vi) as an active engagement with knowledge; and (vii) as self-reflexivity. In the following I will give examples of all seven definitions, since they reveal the teachers' disparity of understanding and definitional variation when it comes to critical thinking, which goes to illustrate Moore's specifist position.

The first definition, critical thinking as judgment, is in Moore's (2013) study, just as in the Delphi expert group's definition, the most salient conception of critical thinking (p. 510). Moore mentions several variants of what the teachers mean by judgment. For example, judgment entails different types of evaluative action, such as being able to make distinctions, taking a stand, being able to render verdicts, being able to determine what is good and bad (as in good and bad arguments, for example), being able to evaluate sources, being able to judge what a valid interpretation amounts to, and being able to determine what constitutes an acceptable interpretation or argument. Judgment also relates to such notions as truthfulness, reliability, persuasiveness, and usefulness, in Moore's study. The second definition is skepticism, which Moore defines as being "permanently cautious about accepting the judgments and ideas of others" (p. 512), but critical skepticism also, according to Moore, involves being skeptical of one's own preconceptions. The third definition is critical thinking as a simple originality, which amounts to "students coming to conclusions about issues, and making their own modest contribution to knowledge" (p. 514). This definition is, in other words, a modification of critical thinking as skepticism, which puts too much emphasis on negative evaluation, which means it runs the risk of becoming overly skeptical and, in consequence, uncritical. The fourth definition, critical thinking as careful and sensitive readings, relates to what could be called academic reading and the ability to gain a thorough understanding of a text. In literary studies, this is what a student practices and develops from the introductory course as a freshman and onwards, and is often associated with what is broadly termed "close reading." The fifth definition is rationality. This definition was, according to Moore, less common in the interviews, but very common in critical thinking literature generally. Rationality as critical thinking is defined, in Moore's study, as related to logic and reasoning, that is, finding scientific or scholarly grounds for one's argumentation. The sixth definition poses critical thinking as an activist engagement with knowledge, which means taking an ethical stand and seeing a university education as entailing social responsibility. In this definition the aim is to develop an ability for critical action. The seventh, and last, definition is self-reflexivity, which is defined in Moore's study as a meta-activity that requires an awareness and self-consciousness of, for example, how one comes to make judgments or how one engages in critical action.

These seven definitions together contain nearly the whole register of skills, dispositions, and criticality traits which, as we have seen, define critical thinking, and one of Moore's points is, precisely, the multivalent nature of the concept and that its definition depends on the context in which it is situated and engaged. The teachers' varied and at times conflicting conceptions, in trying to circumscribe critical thinking in terms of what it is, its importance, and how to engage with it, were present, according to Moore's analysis, not only between teachers, but also within their individual statements (p. 510). From the teachers' disparate and heterogenous conceptions of critical thinking, Moore singles out two consequences for teaching practice: (1) key terms must be explained and clarified to students, such as the word "critical" (p. 519). And as Moore states, "clarification will come not from some generic exposition of meaning" (p. 520), but instead, words such as "critical," "analysis," and "argument," must be situated within a specific disciplinary context for the students to be able to make sense of them. (2) Despite the many varieties and meanings of critical thinking, the students must be given the opportunity to find what is similar between the different conceptions of critical thinking. "This suggests," Moore states, "the need for a transdisciplinary approach, where students are encouraged to reflect on the variety of educational and intellectual processes they experience in the 'different specialist domains' of their studies, and to seek to recognize any coherences that might exist in these processes" (p. 520).

Moore's conclusion, based on the analysis of his survey study, and the discussion of possible consequences for teaching practice, states the importance of difference and variety. According to Moore, to reduce critical thinking to a set of skills and propensities that can be taught and learned in special critical thinking courses would stamp out the differences as well as coherences between notions of critical thinking and the way the disciplines form and engage with them. It is preferable, Moore asserts, to emphasize the ambiguity and uncertainty inherent in the notion of critical thinking, and to develop a critical stance that is more connected to and in tune with the disciplines themselves, which is something that will also help students understand differences and similarities between disciplines. This leads to a notion of critical thinking that is grounded in what Moore calls an "empathic view of knowledge and of its creators and purveyors" (p. 521).

Before addressing Martin Davies's article, I would like to return to Maitland's definition of cultural translation, in order to compare it with Moore's understanding of critical thinking. As we know, Maitland stresses the interpretative, hermeneutical, character of translation. This means that, for Maitland,

cultural translation starts from a quest for understanding – of some form of source material and in the sense that some cultural, political or social stimulus in the world sets in motion the interpretive work of translation led by a human actor. If the practice of human communication involves the continual interpretation of stimuli in the social sphere, cultural translation in my conceptualization here delineates a model for *all* meaningful exchanges in the world and is therefore not a subsection of interlingual communication. The 'agents' of cultural translation, moreover, are not the privileged polyglot elite but every single one of us engaged in the practice of encountering and questioning difference in every aspect of everyday life. (emphasis in the original; 2010, pp. 25–26)

It is not difficult to see this definition of cultural translation as a version of critical thinking, but it seems to go against Moore's insistence on specificity, that is, how critical thinking springs out of a particular disciplinary discourse with its own way of relating to knowledge, which in turn shapes the way we conceive of and practice critical thinking. We could say, perhaps, that critical thinking, as Moore conceives of it, is grounded in a specific (disciplinary) language which must be learned in order to practice critical thinking in a meaningful way. When we move across disciplines, translation is necessary, since we cannot simply transfer the knowledge of one (disciplinary) language into another discipline and expect to be able to sufficiently understand the language of the new discipline. This is expressed by one of Moore's literary studies informants in an earlier study (2011): "So I've come to recognize that the crucial part of critical thinking ... is being able to translate a number of different languages, it's about being able to move between different disciplinary languages" (p. 273). Maitland's definition of cultural translation, in contrast, stipulates that it is practiced by "every single one of us" in interpreting "all meaningful exchanges in the world" when we are "engaged in the practice of encountering and questioning difference in every aspect of everyday life." It seems, then, that Maitland's conception of cultural translation would be akin to generic critical thinking, in which, say, reasoning, when we know how to reason, can be applied to any context and any form of expression. We should also take note of the fact that difference in Maitland's version of cultural translation is not exclusively reserved for linguistic difference and the difference between one language and another, but seems to include ontological, ontic, and hermeneutic differences where ever they may occur, that is, cultural translation is concerned with "difference in every aspect of everyday life."

If we suggest that Maitland's notion of cultural translation is similar in scope to the view of critical thinking as generic, we must examine what this version of critical thinking entails in more detail. Martin Davies's (2013) article "Critical Thinking and the Disciplines Reconsidered" gives us such an opportunity. The article is an attempt to refute Tim Moore's specifist position as he lays it out in the article "Critical Thinking and Disciplinary Thinking: A Continuing Debate" (2011). What, then, does a generic understanding of critical thinking entail? Davies states that "the generic sense of critical thinking [...] explains, without residue, any other supervenient sense of critical thinking [...]. Moore does not accept this, and plumps for 'modes of discourse' and an unwillingness to accept one mode having priority over another. This results in the relativist view" (p. 536). And he goes on to state that

critical thinking *qua* logical relationships [...] explains critical thinking *qua* discipline-specificity [...] without residue, but does not explain it away. We can still *talk* about the 'diverse modes of thought' in the form of the language of the disciplines being different from the logical relationships of universal/generic critical thinking [...]. We can still *talk* about the importance of character, narratives, persuasion and so on. The critical *language* of disciplinary discourse has a harmless place in discussions on disciplinary topics. But, like talk on sun-setting, this talk adds nothing *substantive* to the nature of critical thinking. (p. 537)

On Davies's view, critical thinking is made up of a set of skills and propensities, such as logical relationships, which are independent of and unaffected by disciplinary discourse. There is no contamination and no "residue" left of discipline specific language. This would mean that the language of critical thinking is pure language, *reine Sprache* to invoke the phrase Benjamin uses, it is the language of logic, there is no noise and no distortion interfering with its execution, it is the precondition for any discipline specific language, we could even venture to say disciplinary prattle. As Davies writes, referring to literary studies: "We can still *talk* about the importance of character, narratives, persuasion and so on," but this would add "nothing substantive to the *nature* of critical thinking." Literary analysis is supervenient and, consequently, just talk, prattle, without the pure language of critical thinking; what is left if we strip literary analysis of its decorative talk of character, narrative, and persuasion is critical thinking as λόγος, that is to say, λόγος as reason and logic. Generic critical thinking, for Davies, is the universal grammar out of which disciplinary language is built.

Davies continues his exposition of generic critical thinking in relation to literary studies by invoking translation, specifically the translation of the first sentence of Albert Camus's *L'Étranger*. Davies's reading of the beginning of Camus's *The Stranger* represents a reading that not only argues for a generic view of critical thinking, but also for the validity of a reading of literature which relies on common sense rationality and formal logic. To support his argument for critical thinking as generic, Davies gives the example of a student of French who, as part of an exercise in translation (not in literary analysis or interpretation), is given the first sentence of Camus's *L'Etranger* to translate into English. The sentence runs as follows: "Aujourd'hui, maman est morte. Ou peut-être hier, je ne sais pas" (p. 5). Davies then suggests a translation that he holds would be a translation of a "good student": "Today, my mother died. Or maybe it was the day before, I don't know" (2013, p. 537). According to Davies, these two sentences, the French original and its English translation, convey the same linguistic meaning – nothing is altered or lost in translation. Moreover, Davies also claims that the sentence conveys an additional meaning, namely that the man uttering the sentence, the protagonist of the novel, Meursault, "is showing a disturbing insensitivity. He lacks what we might expect are the normal feelings of a person whose mother has just died" (pp. 537–538). This meaning, Davies maintains, can be arrived at by applying generic critical thinking skills that have little or nothing to do with discipline specific skills within literary studies as a discipline.

One does not have to be a scholar of literature to come to the conclusion that Meursault is abnormally insensitive, Davies seems to be saying. However, for a student of French, who has not read Camus's novel and is unfamiliar with its theme, Davies's interpretation is not self-evident or obvious. From reading only the sentence given, one could equally well interpret Meursault as grief stricken to the point of losing the sense of time and confusing days. Since it is his mother who has died

it even strengthens this possible interpretation. There are thus two conflicting interpretations at play here, and we cannot with absolute certainty decide on which interpretation is the more plausible one, given that we are unfamiliar with the plot and
theme of the novel. That the sentence conveys this uncertainty, indeed, its undecidability, for the purpose of letting the reader remain in uncertainty about what kind
of person Meursault is seems, in fact, perfectly conceivable. What is more, if the
student had prior knowledge of the novel a better translation might be something
like: "Today, mother died. Or maybe it was yesterday, I don't know" which would
signal an even more detached attitude to his mother's death than "my mother." If we
look to Stuart Gilbert's classical "British" translation of the novel from 1946, the
sentence reads: "Mother died today. Or, maybe, yesterday; I can't be sure" (p. 1). In
Gilbert's translation, the emphasis clearly lies on the uncertainty concerning the
time of Meursault's mother's passing. This is further clarified if we continue reading: "The telegram from the home says: YOUR MOTHER PASSED
AWAY. FUNERAL TOMORROW. DEEP SYMPATHY. Which leaves the matter
doubtful; it could have been yesterday" (p. 1). And a little further on, we read: "For
the present, it's almost as if Mother weren't really dead. The funeral will bring it
home to me, put an official seal on it, so to speak" (p. 1). Still, we cannot be sure in
what state Meursault is in and if he actually is, as Davies holds, emotionally detached
and insensitive to his mother's death. As Matthew Ward writes in his "Translator's
note" to the "American" translation of Camus's novel from 1988: "The 'simplicity'
of the text is merely apparent and everywhere paradoxical" (p. v). Moreover, Ward
specifically addresses the first sentence of the novel, of which he states:

> No sentence in French literature in English translation is better known than the opening
> sentence of *The Stranger*. It has become a sacred cow of sorts, and I have changed it [from
> Gilbert's translation]. In his notebooks Camus recorded the observation that "the curious
> feeling the son has for his mother constitutes *all* his sensibility." And Sartre, in his
> "Explication de *L'Etranger*," goes out of his way to point out Meursault's use of the child's
> word "Maman" when speaking of his mother. To use the more removed, adult "Mother" is,
> I believe, to change the nature of Meursault's curious feeling for her. It is to change his very
> sensibility. (p. vii)

The translation of the novel's first sentence, it seems, is not that straight forward
after all.[8] Not even the first word, "*maman*," is easily rendered in English. In Ward's
version, the first paragraph reads: "Maman died today. Or yesterday maybe, I don't
know. I got a telegram from the home: 'Mother deceased. Funeral tomorrow.
Faithfully yours.' That doesn't mean anything. Maybe it was yesterday" (p. 3). In
contrast, insisting on the meaning he propones as the one we could, and should,
deduce with the help of logical reasoning, Davies argues:

> A very young person possibly would not have enough life experience to realise that these
> two sentences are revealing about the character that speaks them. They may understand the
> linguistic meaning of these sentences, but not what they are telling us about Meursault's
> character. They might fail to appreciate the different kind of meaning that can be conveyed.

---

[8] For in depth analyses of the translation of *L'Étranger* into English, see, e.g. Sebba (1972) and
Kaplansky (2004).

> This appears to be a clear example of what Moore calls 'the diverse modes of thought' of the disciplines (in this case, Literature). (2013, p. 538)

Davies's interpretation presupposes that the student has read the novel, or at least has prior knowledge of its theme and content. In other words, to be able to say something of Meursault's character we must know the context, and, even then, the interpretation suggested by Davies would not amount to an interpretation that would have any scholarly value in the study of literature. If a student had proposed this interpretation in an essay and nothing else, the essay would most certainly receive a poor grade. Conversely, if the question is only about how to translate the sentence to assess the student's knowledge of the French language, no literary analysis is necessary. Clearly, there is more involved in literary analysis than in the reading that Davies proposes. In addition, even if Davies wants to call his interpretation an exercise in and application of critical thinking skills, his interpretation cannot be classified as a careful and sensitive reading which Moore suggests is a criterium for critical thinking in literary studies. This is also emphasized by the two different translations by Gilbert and Ward, as well as Ward's "Translator's note." Davies's analysis of the first two sentences of the novel, by way of logical reasoning, constitutes nothing less than a misreading of them and shows us that generic critical thinking used in this way is, in fact, the opposite of critical. Davies confuses the fundamental ambiguity of literature with relativism; because, to understand the nature of literature as, in essence, aporetic and undecidable is, for a student, more in line with the aim of critical thinking than Davies's ahistorical universalism. Davies concludes his example by stating that generic critical thinking

> explains what Camus is trying to tell us, but it does not explain it away. Literature can, of course, be enjoyed on its own terms (e.g. as beautiful language). Literature can also be ruined by over analysis. There is also more to Literature than arguments. But is there something critically special about the literary language in this example that is not captured by the argument map? Is there something unique about the 'mode of thinking' of Literature that is inaccessible to the argumentative/philosophical, mode? I think not. (p. 539)

I would, as opposed to Davis, answer "yes" to his question – there *is* something unique about the mode of thinking of Literature as a discipline. To recognize the ambiguity of Camus's language is one example; to pay close attention to the first word of the novel, "*maman*," and the difficulty of translating it in a way that is sensitive to the nuances of language is another example. These skills are important to learn for students in literary studies and they are also skills that can be termed critical thinking skills. Hence, there are other critical thinking skills that are necessary in order to critically analyze Camus's text than Davies's insistence on logical reasoning, which does not lend itself to this kind of text, but, precisely, explains away what is at stake in Camus's opening sentences. In the Coda to his article, Davies (2013) warns of the "comforting illusions offered by specifism and relativism" (p. 543). Moore's specifist view on critical thinking is dangerous, Davies holds: "The specifist approach to critical thinking is dangerous and wrong-headed. Moore's [...] papers neither support a rejection of the generalist thesis nor provide compelling reasons to accept a relativist attitude to the concept of critical thinking" (p. 543).

The assignation of relativism to such positions as Moore's and the warnings of these positions' presumptive danger are not uncommon in the dispute between analytical and continental philosophy, especially the poststructuralist strand of continental philosophy, including postcolonial studies. And it is to postcolonial studies and its presumptive obscuritanism that I will turn to next.

Thus, I would like to attend to an example which shares similarities with the Davies-Moore dispute. The example is not specifically addressing critical thinking, as such, but still insisting on the universality of logical reasoning and its ability to reveal the objective, hence true, meaning of a literary text. The example will also give us the opportunity to return to the issue of cultural translation. In "Hard and Soft Obscuritanism in the Humanities and Social Sciences," Jon Elster (2011) discusses what he terms "dishonorable failures" in scholarship, which he goes on to define as, in Elster's words, "obscurantist, by which I mean that one can say ahead of time that pursuits within these paradigms are unlikely to yield anything of value" (p. 159). He further provides two synonyms for obscuritanism, namely: "bullshit" and nonsense. As part of a version of what Elster calls "soft obscuritanism" and scholarly "waste," that is, scholarship which have no (social, cultural, moral, etc.) value, Elster argues that Edward Said is guilty of an intentional fallacy in his reading of Jane Austen's *Mansfield Park*. Elster's criticism centers on a passage in Said's seminal work *Culture and Imperialism* in which Said writes:

> The force of this paragraph[9] is unmistakable. [. . .] It is an early Protestant eliminating all traces of frivolous behavior. *There is nothing in Mansfield Park that would contradict us*, however, were we to assume that Sir Thomas does exactly the same things – on a larger scale – in his Antigua "plantations". Whatever was wrong there [. . .] Sir Thomas was able to fix, thereby maintaining his control over his colonial domain. *More clearly* than elsewhere in her fiction, Austen here synchronizes domestic with international authority, making it plain that the values associated with such higher things as ordination, law, and propriety must be grounded firmly in actual rule over and possession of territory. *She sees clearly* that to hold and rule Mansfield Park is to hold and rule an imperial estate in close, not to say inevitable association with it. (1994, p. 87) (Elster's emphases)

Elster states the following about the passage: "True, there is nothing in the work to contradict this interpretation. Nor is there anything that supports it. It is absurd to argue, as Said does, that a reading that is not explicitly contradicted by the text can

---

[9] The paragraph in *Mansfield Park* to which Said is referring is the following: "It was a busy morning with him. Conversation with any of them occupied but a small part of it. He had to reinstate himself in all the wonted concerns of his Mansfield life, to see his steward and his bailiff – to examine and compute – and, in the intervals of business, to walk into his stables and his gardens, and nearest plantations; but active and methodical, he had not only done all this before he resumed his seat as master of the house at dinner, he had also set the carpenter to work in pulling down what had been so lately put up in the billiard room, and given the scene painter his dismissal, long enough to justify the pleasing belief of his being then at least as far off as Northampton. The scene painter was gone, having spoiled only the floor of one room, ruined all the coachman's sponges, and made five of the under-servants idle and dissatisfied; and Sir Thomas was in hopes that another day or two would suffice to wipe away every outward memento of what had been, even to the destruction of every unbound copy of "Lovers' Vows" in the house, for he was burning all that met is eye" (Austen, 2012, p. 188).

ipso facto be imputed to the author as a 'clear' expression of her intentions" (p. 160). Elster's assumption is that the literary text is a self-contained whole, reminiscent of the formalism and scientism of New Criticism,[10] which is precisely what is questioned by Said. What is more, Elster's omissions from Said's text in the quoted passage seem to be made to strengthen his own argument, since if we read what is omitted we find that Said is consistently building an argument based on credible sources and constantly referring to his main thesis which, in the chapter on Austen, is the colonial worldview of the English empire during the eighteenth and nineteenth centuries. Elster's first omission, incidentally, cuts off Said's reference to *Robinson Crusoe* with its racist and colonial baggage. Elster's second omission deletes Said's reference in note 39 to two important scholarly works on Austen's novel, namely Warren Roberts's *Jane Austen and the French Revolution* and Avrom Fleishman's *A Reading of Mansfield Park: An Essay in Critical Synthesis*. These two references serve to situate the novel within the colonial paradigm that Said is analyzing, and in consequence support Said's claim about colonialism in the novel. What is true is that Austen scholarship have criticized Said both of underestimating and overstating the role of slavery and the importance of incomes from West Indian plantations to finance British country houses in relation to *Mansfield Park*.[11] Nevertheless, Said's method of analysis, with its focus on the significance of culture and history to readings of literature, and its opening up of perspectives that include colonialism and postcolonialism, can hardly be considered obscuritanism, nonsense, and so scholarly waste, as Elster claims.

To be able to make an informed assessment of Said's analyses, it is important, I would argue, to know what Said's explicitly stated method in *Culture and Empire* is. Said outlines his method in the Introduction:

> My method is to focus as much as possible on individual works, to read them first as great products of the creative or interpretative imagination, and then to show them as part of the relationship between culture and empire. I do not believe that authors are mechanically determined by ideology, class, or economic history, but authors are, I also believe, very much in the history of their societies, shaping and shaped by that history and their social experience in different measure. Culture and the aesthetic forms it contains derive from historical experience, which in effect is one of the main subjects of this book. (Said, 1994, p. xxii)

This method of reading develops into what Said has termed "contrapuntal reading," which means attending to the repressed, neglected, or untold (colonial and

---

[10] New Criticism, with its scientific approach to the analysis of literature and, especially poetry, was the dominant school of literary theory in the mid twentieth century, and has many similarities with generic critical thinking as a set of skills that can be applied to a text, expression, or discourse. New Critical close reading aims to reveal the true, objective, meaning of the text by way of, e.g., logical reasoning, so that form and content, structure and signification, provide the reader with the objective meaning of the text.

[11] For a comprehensive overview of Austen scholarship, including the debate over the colonialism of *Mansfield Park*, see Todd (2005).

postcolonial) histories of literary works.[12] Said, in fact, anticipates criticism such as Elster's when, in the chapter on Camus, he writes: "One ought to read the texts for the richness of what is there, we are likely to say, not for what if anything has been excluded" (p. 176). To counter this criticism, Said insists on the restorative element of his contrapuntal readings. Addressing Camus's writing, Said writes:

> This restorative interpretation is not meant vindictively. Nor do I intend after the fact to blame Camus for hiding things about Algeria in his fiction that [...] he was at pains to explain. What I want to do is to see Camus's fiction as an element in France's methodically constructed political geography of Algeria, which took many generations to complete, the better to see it as providing an arresting account of the political and interpretative contest to represent, inhabit, and possess the territory itself. (p. 176)

In the same vein, *Mansfield Park*, Said argues, "is about England *and* about Antigua, and the connection is made explicitly by Austen; it is therefore about order at home and slavery abroad, and can – indeed ought – to be read that way" (p. 259). In short, Said's reading of Austen's *Mansfield Park* does not pretend to argue for a certain authorial intention; rather, his reading takes the perspective that Austen and her text are representations of a specific age, during which there was a mindset and world-view that Said holds implies an untold history, which is still reflected in the text, regardless of Austen's intention. Austen's novels are the product of the time and society in which she lived in and which undoubtedly helped to shape her. What is at stake, in other words, is a cultural translation of what is untold or excluded in the language of the text. One can, no doubt, question Said's analysis on a number of grounds, as has also been done,[13] but to claim, as does Elster, that Said appeals to Austen's intention to confirm his reading of the text is to disregard both Said's *de facto* analysis of *Mansfield Park* and his explicitly stated aim with his reading.

---

[12] In *Culture and Empire*, Said (1994) describes contrapuntal reading in the following manner: "As we look back at the cultural archive we begin to reread it not univocally but *contrapuntally*, with a simultaneous awareness both of the metropolitan history that is narrated and of those other histories against which (and together with which) the dominant discourse acts" so that "alternative or new narratives emerge, and they become institutionalized or discursively stable entities" (p. 51). In *Humanism and Democratic Criticism*, Said (2004) defines contrapuntal reading in relation to the canonical humanities. Said states that "canon as a contrapuntal form employing numerous voices in usually strict imitation of each other, a form, in other words, expressing motion, playfulness, discovery, and, in the rhetorical sense, invention. Viewed this way, the canonical humanities, far from being a rigid tablet of fixed rules and monuments bullying us from the past [...] will always remain open to changing combinations of sense and signification; every reading and interpretation of a canonical work reanimates it in the present, furnishes an occasion for rereading, allows the modern and the new to be situated together in a broad historical field whose usefulness is that it shows us history as an agonistic process still being made, rather than finished and settled once and for all" (p. 25). Fazal Rizvi and Bob Lingard (2006), in the article "Edward Said and the Cultural Politics of Education," describes Said's contrapuntal method as "a view of cultures, histories, and literatures as inherently hybrid, forged out of overlapping and interdependent traditions of thought and practice. Any constructions of purity of categories are fictions, power/knowledge manifestations" (p. 301).

[13] To give but one example, Harold Bloom (1994), in *The Western Canon*, states the following: "[I]t has become fashionable to talk about the socioeconomic realities that Jane Austen excludes, such as the West Indian slavery that is part of the ultimate basis for the financial security most of her characters enjoy. But all achieved literary works are founded upon exclusions, and no one has demonstrated that increased consciousness of the relation between culture and empire is of the slightest benefit whatsoever in learning to read *Mansfield Park*" (p. 257).

These two instances, Davies's and Elster's criticism of the supposed relativism and obscuritanism of Moore's notion of critical thinking and Said's contrapuntal reading, respectively, is at bottom a question of definition. More precisely, it is a question of definition as setting limits and staking out boundaries for what should be considered to belong to reason. And, as such, dismissing any kind of exteriority that would contaminate logical reason and thus logical reasoning. What does not belong properly to reason is waste and obscuritanism, and so poses the danger of relativism. Hence the need for unity, clarity, transparence, objectivity, and truth, defined by that which is measured, that is, what is calculated, reasonable, exact and logical. Critical thinking has to be disciplined and defined independent of the disciplines, paradoxically making it into a discipline of its own. Moreover, its language must be universal and logical, transparent and without contamination. This is what Martin Davies (2013) asserts when he warns about the danger of Tim Moore's specifist and relativistic view of critical thinking: "Moore's relativist approach to critical thinking has real dangers. It fosters complacency – nonchalance even – in regard to teaching critical thinking. If critical thinking is to be understood as 'diverse modes of thinking' in the disciplines, no priority need be granted to generic skill development – for this is merely one 'mode of thought' among many" (pp. 541–542). But is it not equally complacent to disregard the discipline specific knowledge necessary to conduct a careful and sensitive analysis of the two first sentences of Camus's *The Stranger*? Since if logical reasoning cannot sufficiently account for the ambiguity and difficulty of translating and interpreting a literary work, then logical reasoning is reducing human expressions to formulae, art becomes an equation to be solved without remainder. Thus, the answer is yes, as we have seen in the case of Davies's analysis of Camus, the pure language of logical reasoning cannot escape being distorted and contaminated by what is foreign and unknown (be it the foreign in the form of culture, history, language, or other contexts), because the foreign and unknown constitutes that which makes it possible to translate what is rational in the specific context within which we are immersed. Of course, we cannot do without logical reasoning, argumentation, and so forth, but these skills are not enough to realize the significance, say, of the two first sentences in Camus's *The Stranger*. We can certainly translate them so that the meaning in French is understandable in English. But have we, solely by literal translation, then also come to the objective factual truth about these two sentences? No, we must come to terms with something else than logical reasoning, which means (to invoke Said) unraveling the contrapuntal other of the culture(s) out of which Camus wrote his novel, and we must perform a sensitive reading, as one of Moore's informants puts it, of the novel before coming to a decision regarding the possible meanings of the two first sentences of the novel. All of this must be included in a translation of Camus's text, even a translation viewed as intralingual, that is, an interpretation within a single language. Consequently, the act of translation, as a learning activity in higher education, if it wants to be critical, must take into account the hybridity of cultures and languages, which will inevitably blur the borders of disciplines, but will at the same time resist the reduction of language to a matter of logic and grammar.

Thinking at the Limits: Critique as Translation

We seem to be back where we started, with the problem Humboldt addresses in his letter to Schlegel, namely the aporia of translation, which stages itself between the familiar and the foreign. Critical thinking, in a similar manner, seems to be torn between the reductiveness of pure logic and rationality and the distortion of disciplinarity and culture. To be critical, to engage in critical thinking, is to question the limits of logical reasoning, authority, and logic; but, critical thinking must also address disciplinarity and culture as partitions that delimit and contain knowledge and language, and so restrain and censure the undecidability of meaning. We are close, in asserting this kind of critical thinking, to what Michel Foucault (1984) proposes to be the aspiration of critique in his essay "What is Enlightenment?" In this text, Foucault suggests a philosophical ethos which entails what he terms a *"limit-attitude"* (p. 45), within which

> criticism is no longer going to be practiced in the search for formal structures with universal value, but rather as a historical investigation into the events that have led us to constitute ourselves and to recognize ourselves as subjects of what we are doing, thinking, saying. In that sense, this criticism is not transcendental, and its goal is not that of making a metaphysics possible: it is genealogical in its design and archaeological in its method. Archaeological – and not transcendental – in the sense that it will not seek to identify the universal structures of all knowledge or of all possible moral action, but will seek to treat the instances of discourse that articulate what we think, say, and do as so many historical events. And this critique will be genealogical in the sense that it will not deduce from the form of what we are what it is impossible for us to do and to know; but it will separate out, from the contingency that has made us what we are, the possibility of no longer being, doing, or thinking what we are, do, or think. It is not seeking to make possible a metaphysics that has finally become a science; it is seeking to give new impetus, as far and wide as possible, to the undefined work of freedom. (pp. 46–47)

This form of critique is what Foucault calls a "critical ontology of ourselves" (p. 50), which involves a questioning of knowledge, power, and ethics. Foucault frames the possibility of a critical ontology of ourselves within three questions: "How are we constituted as subjects of our own knowledge? How are we constituted as subjects who exercise or submit to power relations? How are we constituted as moral subjects of our own actions?" (p. 49). These are the limits mounted by, for example, reason, state authority, and universal moral laws, divine and secular, of a yet unknown and so undiscovered freedom. Thus, Foucault's notion of critique involves a turn toward ourselves and how we construct ourselves as human subjects. It is a questioning of the limits of reason and culture, which means a questioning of a culture of reason as well as reason within culture. Foucault is careful to point out that it is not a matter of being for or against the legacy and history of the Enlightenment and its idea of rationality and reason (something Foucault calls the blackmail of the Enlightenment).[14] Instead, we should take our departure from the way and manner

---

[14] One of the most severe indictments of the Enlightenment and its ideas is no doubt levelled by Max Horkheimer and Theodore Adorno, who in the first essay ("The Concept of Enlightenment")

in which Enlightenment rationality has produced the possibilities and so the limits for what we can be, what we can do, and what we can think. As Foucault writes: "We must try to proceed with the analysis of ourselves as beings who are historically determined, to a certain extent, by the Enlightenment" (p. 43). The principles of reason which developed as a consequence of the Enlightenment are thus not, Foucault suggests, to be championed as being good or bad, but rather as parts of a formative process that has created a culture of reason – a culture which we still, to a large extent, rely on today, not least within the university and the pedagogy governing higher education.

Judith Butler (2012), in her essay "Critique, Dissent, Disciplinarity," points out that both Foucault and Derrida invoke a third way or path to rethink the limits of critique as neither pure rationalism or radical relativism. For Derrida, this path is what he calls thinking; for Foucault it is the unthought, and as Butler writes, "they may well mean something similar by these divergent terms" (p. 23). I have already touched on Foucault's archeological-genealogical method to address modernity and its relation to Enlightenment reason and rationality. But when it comes to Derrida, the question of thinking is posed in relation to philosophy and against techno-scientific and techno-economic performativity. As Derrida states:

> The name philosophy finds itself rightly associated with every "thinking" that no longer lets itself be determined, by rights, by techno-scientific or cultural programs, that troubles them sometimes, interrogates and affirms them, yes, affirms them, beyond them, without necessarily opposing or limiting them in the "critical" mode. The value of "critique" is only one of the philosophical possibilities; it has its history and its genealogy. What is called "deconstruction," for example, is not limited to one of those so-called critical operations whose virtue and incontestable necessity have inspired all those who defend philosophy, "critical" reflection before the powers that be. What interest me in this "deconstruction" is in particular the affirmative thinking that, while neither techno-scientific nor cultural, nor even philosophi-

---

of their work *Dialectic of Enlightenment: Philosophical Fragments*, conduct a scathing critique of Enlightenment reason and rationality, a critique which is already signaled in the first two sentences of the essay: "Enlightenment, understood in the widest sense as the advance of thought, has always aimed at liberating human beings from fear and installing them as masters. Yet the wholly enlightened earth is radiant with triumphant calamity" (p. 1), and which can, symptomatically, be summed up with their assertion: "Enlightenment is totalitarian" (p. 4). At the same time, there are, nevertheless, similarities between Horkheimer and Adorno's analysis and Foucault's treatment of the Enlightenment. For example, their emphasis on working through the historical limitations which the Enlightenment has constructed has tenets which we recognize in Foucault. As Horkheimer and Adorno states in the *Preface (1944 and 1947)*: "The aporia which faced us in our work thus proved to be the first matter we had to investigate: the self-destruction of enlightenment. We have no doubt – and herein lies our *petitio principia* – that freedom in society is inseparable from enlightenment thinking" (p. xvi). Thus: "What is at stake is not conservation of the past but the fulfillment of past hopes" (p. xvii). The influence of the Frankfurt School on Foucault's thinking has also been noted by Maurizio Passerin d'Entrèves (2000), who in "Critique and Enlightenment: Michel Foucault on 'Was ist Aufklärung?'," notes that the question of reason and power "had also been at the centre of the Frankfurt School's critique of instrumental reason, and Foucault acknowledged the deep affinity that existed between his genealogical inquiries and the work of the Frankfurt School. Both had been concerned with the question that Kant addressed for the first time in 1784 ('What is Enlightenment?') and both could be seen as continuing the interrogation of reason initiated by Kant" (p. 189).

cal through and through, maintains an essential affinity with the philosophical, which it works – in every sense of the word – in discourse as well as in its institutional, pedagogical, political, etc., structures. This "thinking" can find itself at work in all the disciplines, in the sciences and in philosophy, in history, literature, the arts, a certain manner of writing, of practicing or studying languages, without the obsession of techno-economic performativity. If there is any, this thinking is incalculable and marks every limit of technocratism. (p. 162)

We could add translation as another "discipline" in which Derrida's notion of thinking can find itself at work. Whatever the discipline, then, this notion of thinking is necessary, and as Derrida points out, the critical is only one mode, albeit a necessary mode, of thinking. This thinking, furthermore, installs itself in and as the decision before rationality or logical reasoning, before the cultural and before translation can take place. It is that sensitive reading that must accompany every rational judgment, it is thinking that opens a place for λόγος, since for us to have λόγος we must first begin to learn how to think. To learn critical thinking, and become a critical thinker, *thinking* that must take precedence, it must precede the critical in all shapes and forms, in Derrida's sense. Thinking is thus the history as well as the future of the critical. Just as with Heidegger's *Auseinandersetzung*, Derrida's thinking is, as he insists, affirmative, it does not tear down and demolish, but works with and within what one is attempting to think through.

Now, to return to cultural translation and specifically to a situation similar to the one Humboldt addresses, namely how Heidegger (1993), in "The origin of the Work of Art," invokes the Romans' translation of Greek words into Latin as part of the move to determine the Western interpretation of the Being of beings:

> The process begins with the appropriation [*Übernahme*] of Greek words by Roman-Latin thought. *Hypokeimenon* becomes *subiectum*; *hypostasis* becomes *substantia*; *symbebêkos* becomes *accidens*. However, this translation of Greek names into Latin is in no way the innocent process it is considered to this day. Beneath the seemingly literal and thus faithful translation there is concealed, rather, a *trans*lation [*Übersetzen*] of Greek experience into a different way of thinking. Roman thought takes over [*übernimmt*] the Greek words without a corresponding, equally original experience of what they say, without the Greek word. The rootlessness of Western thought begins with this translation. (p. 149).

It is thus by a translation which does not consider the original Greek experience of Being as presence, and simply places the literal meaning over and above the Greek word and so covers over its original meaning, that Western philosophy loses touch with its origin. The Greek words are appropriated without considering the culture out of which they came, a culture and experience which is subsequently forgotten in the development of Western philosophy. This, in turn, forms the thinking which Western philosophy is capable of, and which ends, Heidegger claims, with the dissolution of philosophy into separate disciplines. The end of philosophy in technocybernetic disciplinarity highlights the need for thinking as something other than the impatience that comes with the torrent of information which characterizes the ground for knowledge, and the decisions based on this knowledge, in the technological and digital age. There is no time for aporetic thinking, that is, a thinking which abides in indecision and uncertainty. Thinking as critical thinking thus ends up in a debate over definitions, relativism, rationality, and disciplinarity. This is a difficulty that higher education stands to grapple with and must face if it is to survive the challenges of, for example, distance education and the digital turn that is starting to pervade education on all levels. In a text closely related to his essay "The End of Philosophy and the Task of Thinking," entitled "On the Question Concerning the Determination of the Matter for Thinking" Heidegger (2010) formulates this challenge in the following manner:

> The difficulty lies in a lack of education [*Unerzogenheit*] in thinking that is conditioned by the matter [*Sache*] of thinking and is, therefore, not fortuitous, and which already Aristotle suggested in his own way (Metaphysics IV, 4, 1006 a 6ff.). The sentence reads: ἔστι γὰρ ἀπαιδευσία τὸ μὴ γιγνώσκειν τίνων δεῖ ζητεῖν ἀπόδειξιν καὶ τίνων οὐ δεῖ. "For it is a lack of education (in thinking) not to have an eye for that regarding which it is necessary to seek a proof and that regarding which this is not necessary." This lack of education in today's thinking is great. It is even greater with respect to the task of asking, first of all, the question concerning the determination of the matter for thinking and of unfolding it sufficiently. Therefore, the words of Aristotle demand careful reflection. Since, so far, it remains undecided in what way that which does not require a proof for becoming the thought-worthy matter for thinking is experienceable and sayable. (p. 222)

The task of thinking, I argue with Heidegger, is an urgent task also for education, and this is a matter, furthermore, which constitutes the precondition of both critical thinking, as it is conceived of in higher education, and cultural translation as defined by, for example, Sarah Maitland. One way of approaching thinking and the task of thinking is, I suggest, through translation as an aporetic activity, a performance which holds and remains in the unresolved and irresolvable, but at the same time affirmative, *pas* or no-step, with which Derrida engages. It is a questioning of limits, of definitions, and so of the limits of reason, imposed by culture, politics, disciplines, and what Derrida calls technocratism, and what Heidegger in the just-quoted essay terms "the sciences and their cybernetictechnical organization" (p. 222), which decide what is possible to think under the conditions they authorize.

References

Aristotle. (1934). *Nicomachean ethics* (H. Rackham, Trans). In Aristotle, *Aristotle in 23 volumes*. (Vol. 19, 1102b25) (H. Rackham, Ed.). Harvard University Press. Retrieved from http://www.perseus.tufts.edu/hopper/text?doc=Perseus:text:1999.01.0054.

Austen, J. (2012). *Mansfield park*. Penguin.

Benjamin, W. (1991). Über Sprache überhaupt und über die Sprache des Menschen. In W. Benjamin, *Gesammelte Schriften II* (R. Tiedemann & H. Schweppenhäuser, Eds.) (pp. 140–157). Suhrkamp.

Benjamin, W. (1999). *The arcades project* (H. Eiland & K. McLaughlin, Trans.). Harvard University Press.

Benjamin, W. (2003). *The origin of the German tragic drama* (J. Osborne, Trans.). Verso.

Bloom, H. (1994). *The western canon: The books and school of the ages*. Harcourt Brace.

Butler, J. (2012). Critique, dissent, disciplinary. In K. de Boer & R. Sonderegger (Eds.), *Conceptions of critique in modern and contemporary philosophy* (pp. 10–29).

Camus, A. (1954/1946). *The stranger* (S. Gilbert, Trans.). Originally published in Britain as *the outsider*). Vintage.

Conway, C. (2012). A conceptual and empirical approach to cultural translation. *Translation Studies, 5*(3), 264–279.

Cunningham, V. (1994). Sticky transfers. In H. Grabes (Ed.), *REAL: Yearbook of research in English and American literature, Vol. 10., Aesthetics and contemporary discourse* (pp. 325–354). Gunter Narr Verlag.

d'Entrèves, M. P. (2000). Critique and enlightenment: Michel Foucault on 'Was ist Aufklärung?'. In N. Geras & R. Wokler (Eds.), *The enlightenment and modernity* (pp. 184–203). Macmillan.

Davies, M. (2013). Critical thinking and the disciplines reconsidered. *Higher Education Research & Development, 32*(4), 529–544.

Davies, M. (2015). A model of critical thinking in higher education. In M. B. Paulsen (Ed.), *Higher education: Handbook of theory and research* (Vol. 30, pp. 41–92). Springer.

Derrida, J. (1997). *Of grammatology* (G. Spivak, Trans.). The Johns Hopkins University Press.

Derrida, J. (2007). Des tours de Babel (J. F. Graham, Trans.). In J. Derrida (Ed.), *Psyche: Inventions of the other, Vol 1* (P. Kamuf & E. Rottenberg, Eds.) (pp. 191–225). Stanford University Press.

Dickinson, C., & Symons, S. (Eds.). (2016). *Walter Benjamin and theology*. Fordham University Press.

Elster, J. (2011). Hard and soft obscuritanism in the humanities and social sciences. *Diogenes, 58*(1–2), 159–170.

Facione, P. (1990). *Critical thinking: A statement of expert consensus for purposes of educational assessment and instruction* (pp. 1–20). The California Academic Press.

Figueira, D. M. (1994). *The exotic: A decadent quest*. State University of New York Press.

Foucault, M. (1984). *What is enlightenment? The Foucault reader* (Paul Rabinow, Ed. & Catherine Porter, Trans.) (pp. 32–50). Pantheon Books.

Gibbs, R. (1998). Lines, circles, points: Messianic epistemology in Cohen, Rosenzweig and Benjamin. In P. Schäfer & M. Cohen (Eds.), *Toward the millennium: Messianic expectations from the Bible to Waco* (pp. 363–382). Brill.

Heidegger, M. (1993). The origin of the work of art (A. Hofstadter, Trans.). In M. Heidegger, *Basic writings* (D. F. Krell, Ed.) (pp. 143–212). HarperCollins.

Heidegger, M. (2010). On the question concerning the determination of the matter for thinking (R. Capobianco & M. Göbel, Trans.). *Epoché, 14*(2), 213–223.

Kaplansky, J. (2004). Outside *the stranger*? English retranslations of Camus' *L'Étranger*. *Palimpsestes: Revue de traduction, 15*, 187–198.

Maitland. S. (2017). *What is cultural translation?*. Bloomsbury.

Moore, T. (2011). Critical thinking and disciplinary thinking: A continuing debate. *Higher Education Research and Development, 30*(3), 261–274.

Moore, T. (2013). Critical thinking: Seven definitions in search of a concept. *Studies in Higher Education, 38*(4), 506–522.

Naishtat, F. (2019). Benjamin's profane use of theology: The invisible Organon. *Religions, 10*(93), 1–16.

Pierce, G. (2018). *Introducing translational studies*. ED-Tech Press.

Plate, S. B. (2005). *Walter Benjamin, religion, and aesthetics: Rethinking religion through the arts*. Routledge.

Pym, A. (2010). *Exploring translation theories*. Routledge.

Rizvi, F., & Lingard, B. (2006). Edward Said and the cultural politics of education. *Discourse: Studies in the Cultural Politics of Education, 27*(3), 293–308.

Said, E. (1994). *Culture and imperialism*. Vintage.

Said, E. (2004). *Humanism and Democratic Criticism*. Columbia University Press.

Sebba, H. (1972). Stuart Gilbert's Mersault: A strange "stranger". *Contemporary Literature, 13*(3), 334–340.

Todd, J. (Ed.). (2005). *Jane Austen in context*. Cambridge University Press.
von Humboldt, W. (2017). Briefe. *Band 3, Juli 1795-Juni 1797* (P. Mattson, Ed.). Walter de Gruyter.
Westfall, J. (2012). Walter Benjamin: Appropriating the Kierkegaardian aesthetic. In J. Stewart (Ed.), *Kierkegaard's influence on philosophy: Tome I German and Scandinavian philosophy* (pp. 49–65). Routledge.
Wolin, R. (1994). *Walter Benjamin: An aesthetic of redemption*. University of California Press.

Chapter 5
The Nature of Learning and the Aporia of "Words"

Psychagogia, Pure Finding, and the Matter for Thinking

To pick up where we left off in the previous chapter, in "On the Question Concerning the Determination of the Matter for Thinking" Heidegger (2010) mentions a lack of education [*Unerzogenheit*] which is especially critical when it comes to thinking. And he refers us to Aristotle to emphasize his point:

> The difficulty lies in a lack of education [*Unerzogenheit*] in thinking that is conditioned by the matter [*Sache*] of thinking and is, therefore, not fortuitous, and which already Aristotle suggested in his own way (Metaphysics IV, 4, 1006 a 6ff.). The sentence reads: ἔστι γὰρ ἀπαιδευσία τὸ μὴ γιγνώσκειν τίνων δεῖ ζητεῖν ἀπόδειξιν καὶ τίνων οὐ δεῖ. "For it is a lack of education (in thinking) not to have an eye for that regarding which it is necessary to seek a proof and that regarding which this is not necessary." This lack of education in today's thinking is great. (p. 222)

As we can see, Heidegger relates education, and the lack thereof, to thinking; more specifically, he states that it is the matter [*die Sache*] for thinking that still remains to be ascertained. For Heidegger, then, the matter for thinking is, as he states, still undecided: "[T]he words of Aristotle demand careful reflection [*sorgsame Besinnung*]. Since, so far, it remains undecided in what way that which does not require proof for becoming the thought-worthy matter for thinking is experience-able and sayable" (p. 222). Since we do not, yet, know how, perhaps even if, the matter for thinking can be experienced or expressed, the first step, Heidegger suggests, is to reflect on, that is, think through, the words of Aristotle. In other words, we need some form of education in what Aristotle is saying to be able to come to a decision as to the question if and how that which require no proof for becoming the matter for thinking is experienceable and sayable. Now, the specific passage Heidegger refers to in Aristotle is where Aristotle is discussing the principle of non-contradiction or, as it is also called, the law of contradiction, which states that a thing cannot be and not be at the same time. This is, says Aristotle (2016), "the most stable starting point of all,"

> that the same thing cannot at the same time belong and also not belong to the same thing and in the same respect (and let us assume that we have also added as many other qualifica-tions as might be needed to respond to logico-linguistic difficulties). This, then, is the most

© Springer Nature Switzerland AG 2022
E. Schwieler, *Aporias of Translation*, Contemporary Philosophies and Theories in Education 18, https://doi.org/10.1007/978-3-030-97895-2_5

stable of all starting points, since it has the aforementioned distinguishing feature. For it is
impossible to take the same thing to be and not to be, as some people think Heraclitus says.
(p. 53, *Metaphysics*, Book 4, 1006a 18-24)

This law, then, is what requires no proof, according to Aristotle, because it is that on
which every inquiry should be grounded. If one questions the law of contradiction,
Aristotle goes on to say, it would indicate a lack of education in the person demanding proof. The law of contradiction is the unshakable foundation on which the
λόγος, including logic, rests. We can assume that Heidegger did not choose this
specific passage from Aristotle haphazardly. On the contrary, it stages the fundamental challenge of thinking, the question which searches for the matter for thinking, which for Heidegger amounts to the question of the thinking of Being. Aristotle's
first principle of non-contradiction thus serves as a point of contestation, which
leads Heidegger to attend to the law of contradiction as relating to Aristotle's assertion of a first philosophy, namely the philosophy of the Being of beings.[1] More
precisely, it is in his confrontation with Nietzsche that Heidegger situates his reading of the first principle of Aristotle's first philosophy, which is to say the law of
contradiction, and in what way the beginning of metaphysics, as rendered in
Aristotle's first philosophy, relates to the consummation of metaphysics in
Nietzsche's will to power. Moreover, Heidegger (1991b) asserts that Nietzsche's
reading of Aristotle and the law of contradiction is misinformed:

> Nietzsche knows that the law of contradiction is a law concerning the Being of beings. Yet
> Nietzsche does not know that this interpretation of the law of contradiction was expressed
> by precisely that thinker who for the first time posited and conceived the law entirely as a
> law of Being. If Nietzsche's not-knowing were only a historiological oversight, we would
> pay no further attention to it. But it means something else. It means that Nietzsche fails to
> recognize the historical ground of his own interpretation of beings and does not judge the
> scope of his own positions. Thus he cannot make out his *own standpoint*, so that he also
> cannot get at the opposition he wants. For an opponent must first of all be grasped and
> attacked on the basis of his own very position. (*Nietzsche Vol. III-IV*, p. 112)

Here Heidegger reiterates his aim to engage in an *Auseinandersetzung*, a confrontation, with Nietzsche (as outlined in Chap. 3), which means that Heidegger is not
seeking to tear down without any concern for the merits of Nietzsche's thinking, but
precisely build on its significance for thinking. As Heidegger points out, Nietzsche
"fails" in his analysis of the law of contradiction, because he does not consider the
"historical ground" of his reading and so misses the emphasis on Being in Aristotle's
position, a position which is crucial to Heidegger's thinking. What Heidegger wants
to argue is that if the law of contradiction is, in fact, grounded in the notion of the
primacy of Being, then it is Being that gives rise to the law of contradiction, but that
Being itself is not governed by this law. However, the law of contradiction has come
to cover over the primacy of Being and foregrounded the logic, and so by extension

---

[1] As Heidegger (1991b) writes: "Ever since the Aristotelian elucidation of the law of contradiction
the one question has haunted us as to whether this law is a logical principle, a highest rule of thinking, or whether it is a metaphysical law, that is, a law that decides something about beings as such –
about Being" (p. 104).

the scientism, of the law of contradiction. Heidegger even states that "[i]f Being itself had to be what it is by grace of lack of contradiction in human thought, then it would be denied in its own proper essence" (p. 202). That is, if we take Being as ruled by the law of contradiction, we fail to attend to what Being "is" in its essence. We would rely on logic to solve the equation of Being, or to put it differently, we would translate Being literally, logically, and in accordance with determined meanings, that is, by confusing Being with being.

Now, formal logic and scientism, Heidegger argues, displace a more fundamental thinking, a thinking that prepares the way for thinking the matter of thinking itself. This thinking, Heidegger (1993b) suggests by way of a question, is a search which aims at "pure discovery" (*reines finden*). In his 1929 inaugural lecture at the University of Freiburg, "What is Metaphysics?" where we find the expression "pure discovery," Heidegger (1993b) asks: "Is there ultimately such a thing as a search without that anticipation [*vorwegnahme*], a search to which pure discovery belongs?" (p. 98). This would amount to a search in which we as human beings search without having anticipated (*vorweggenommen*) that which we set out to search for. I will come back to the word *vorwegnnahme*, since it comprises some of the guiding words which belong to Heidegger's philosophical vocabulary. The German word will also be of importance for how the anticipated and unanticipated are related to how we may conceive of the notions teaching and learning in Heidegger's work. (Incidentally, *reines finden*, pure discovery, is addressed by Derrida (2007) in "Psyche: Invention of the Other," more precisely in his discussion of the aporia of invention and how it relates to creation and discovery.)

Where do we turn, if neither science, nor philosophy, nor education sufficiently prepare us for the unanticipated? The Greeks looked to poetry for that which cannot, yet, be explained or understood. As Werner Jaeger (1946) writes in his seminal work *Paideia: The Ideals of Greek Culture*, discussing Homer as educator:

> Art has a limitless power to convert the human soul – a power which the Greeks called *psychagogia*. For art alone possesses the two essentials of educational influence – universal significance and immediate appeal. By uniting these two methods of influencing the mind, it surpasses both philosophical thought and actual life. Life has immediate appeal, but the events of life lack universal significance: they have too many accidental accompaniments to create a truly deep and lasting impression on the soul. Philosophy and abstract thought do attain universal significance: they deal with the essence of things; yet they affect none but the man who can use his own experience to inspire them with the vividness and intensity of personal life. Thus, poetry has the advantage over both the universal teachings of abstract reason and the accidental events of individual experience. It is more philosophical than life (if we may use Aristotle's famous epigram in a wider sense), but it is also, because of its concentrated spiritual actuality, more lifelike than philosophy. (pp. 36–37)

We find the notion of ψυχαγωγία (*psychagogia*) in Plato's *Phaedrus*, where it is a rhetorical concept, meaning "guidance of the soul." As Elizabeth Asmis states (1986) in her essay "'Psychagogia' in Plato's 'Phaedrus'": "Socrates serves as an example of a true rhetorician and true 'psychagogue'. Against Aristophanes' portrait of Socrates as conjuror of souls, Plato sets a portrait of Socrates as a 'psychagogue' who guides souls to the truth by seeking it himself" (p. 157). As Socrates declares, rhetoric is, specifically, a ψυχαγωγία through words: "Is not rhetoric in its entire nature an art which leads the soul by means of words?" [ἆρ' οὖν οὐ τὸ μὲν ὅλον ἡ ῥητορικὴ ἂν εἴη τέχνη ψυχαγωγία τις διὰ λόγων] (Plato, 1914, *Phaedrus*, 261a, pp. 516, 518). It is, in other words, art as τέχνη (*tékhnē*) we are dealing with, which means that what Jaeger is referring to is the art of poetry and its power to guide the soul to knowledge through the word. And, according to Jaeger, the power of the word and the ψυχαγωγία of poetry has the advantage over both philosophy and life to educate by combining "universal significance and immediate appeal" (p. 36). By intertwining reason and experience, poetry works to educate, that is, to address the urgency of living and the limits of reason. More precisely, the ψυχαγωγία of poetry responds to the question of beings and what it means to be. This is the guiding of the soul that Socrates unravels in the *Phaedrus* – an education of beings.

However, for Heidegger, such an education would be remiss of asking the grounding question, which is the question of the truth of Being. It is this question that must be responded to without knowing it, without having anticipated its call. It is precisely this kind of thinking which, Heidegger maintains, we are uneducated in; we neglect to attend to the fundamental matter (*die Sache selbst*) of thinking. The education of beings through a poetry that addresses the question of the meaning of beings concerns itself with what the poetry represents, and this goes for both its form and its content, that is, what is necessarily anticipated, which means there is no pure finding (*reines finden*) in such an education, but simply a retelling of what is known. If we follow Heidegger, an education which would aim to discover pure finding would concern itself with Being as such, before any prohibition against contradiction and aporia. Such education is possible only if we let go of representational interpretations of the meaning of beings, and attend to the word in a different manner. As it was for the Greeks, poetry is for Heidegger what can educate us in thinking the matter for thinking, namely Being. It is when we let go of the anticipation of what a poem might mean that the notion of pure finding can find us as readers. And, in such finding, we learn how to listen to the poem differently, and so attend to the words of the poem as the poem's saying and naming. But what, if we follow Heidegger way of thinking, does such a saying and naming of the unanticipated entail?

Heidegger's "Words"

Heidegger's (1982b) essay "Words," published in the collection *On the Way to Language*, and in German in *Unterwegs zur Sprache* (GA: 12) as *"Das Wort,"* was first given as a lecture at the Burgtheater in Vienna on May 11, 1958, with the title *"Dichten und Denken. Zu Stefan Georges Gedicht* Das Wort." Now, the first detail to take notice of is the English translation of *"Das Wort"* into "Words." The German title has *das Wort* in the singular, while the English translation renders it as words in the plural. Moreover, the title of Stefan George's poem under discussion in Heidegger's essay uses the singular, "Das Wort." So why, then, has the translators,

Joan Stambaugh of the essay and Peter Hertz of the poem,[2] preferred to use the
plural? The most likely explanation is that since *das Wort* in German can signify the
word in general, which makes it reasonable to translate it into the English plural:
words. However, it could be argued that translating "das Wort" with "the word" is
an equally feasible alternative, since it works grammatically as a collective noun in
the same way as in German to signify words in general. Another angle to this is that
the Word in English can mean that which is communicated, as in the Word of God,
Λόγος. Whatever the reason for deciding to translate "*das Wort*" with "words," we
are obliged to look closer at Heidegger's reading to George's poem and what we can
learn from the reading in terms of poetry and education (education taken as an activity consisting of teaching and learning) and their interrelationship with the unanticipated and the matter for thinking.

Heidegger begins the essay by invoking two lines of Hölderlin's elegy "Bread
and Wine" ["*Brod und Wein*"]: "Why are they silent, too, the theaters ancient and
hallowed? / Why not now does the dance celebrate, consecrate joy?"[3] These two
lines represent the absence of the old gods, and the words uttered by the Greek
poets. But what is even more critical is the absence of how these words were
expressed. However, it is of significance that Heidegger has chosen to refer to two
questions in Hölderlin's poem, since, as we will see, the ability to question is a basic
skill in philosophy and also related to how we teach and learn. We need only to think
of Socrates to be reminded of the importance of questions in order to learn and gain
knowledge. As for Heidegger, he often reminds us that the question of the truth of
Being is, precisely, a questioning.[4] Now, the significance of these two lines for
Heidegger is that "[t]he word is withheld from the former place of the gods' appearance, the word as it once was word" (p. 139). Both Hölderlin and Heidegger emphasize the loss of a previous state of abundance and presence, which the poets were
able to express in and through the word. Heidegger goes on the say that the loss of
the word as it once was has turned it into an enigma [*Rätsel*] and the poetic word has
withdrawn in silence. We can begin to reflect on the enigma of the word, Heidegger
suggests, by reading Stefan George's poem "The Word." The crucial line in the
poem for reflecting on the enigma and silence of the word is the last line of the

---

[2] It should be noted that Stefan George's poem is translated by Peter Hertz as "The Word" in
Heidegger's essay "The Nature of Language" in *On the Way to Language*. I will refer to Heidegger's
essay "The Nature of Language" and George's poem "The Word" included in that essay in the
course of this chapter.

[3] Hölderlin's elegy "*Brod und Wein*" is perhaps his most famous poem, but also the best introduction both into Hölderlin's poetics and philosophy. It was written in 1801 when Hölderlin's schizo-
phrenia had already started to affect him. The elegy can be seen as an attempt to reconcile classical
Greek culture with Christianity; however, the elegy is first and foremost a didactic poem
(*Lehrgedicht*) that communicates Hölderlin's worldview, or as it says in the *Hölderlin Handbuch*
(2011): "*vor allem als weltanschauliches Lehrgedicht aufgefaßt*" (p. 327).

[4] For example, as Heidegger (1991a) states in part 2, volume 4 of his Nietzsche lectures, "Nihilism
and the History of Being": "Any discussion of 'Being itself' always remains interrogative"
(p. 201). See also Chap. 1 of Heidegger's *Introduction to Metaphysics* (2014) for a discussion of
the nature of questioning, a text which I will touch on in what follows.

poem: "Where word breaks off no thing may be" [*Kein ding sei wo das Wort gebricht*].[5] The line presents substantial difficulties for a translator, but a tentative, alternative, and admittedly unpoetic, translation of the line might be: "No thing is given being where the word lacks." The crux is first and foremost George's use of "*sei*" which cannot be translated simply as "is." Instead some kind of paraphrase is necessary, such as "may be" or as my own suggestion has it "given being." Obviously, both these translations break off (*gebricht*), to invoke what the poem states, the original German. The challenge of translation, which entails the exposure to that which is lost or gone missing in a translation, the silence of the word, which in translation turns out to be an enigma, is what the poem stages by the use of a variant of the word for being. The last line of the poem, I tentatively suggest, defines what the poem presents as a whole, which is the act of translation – the poet's struggle to translate experience into words and the reader's labor to translate the words into an experience of the words. Heidegger's restatement of the line points in a similar direction: "It is only the word at our disposal which endows the thing with Being" (p. 141). This means that the word as broken off, the word that has withdrawn, is no longer present in our thinking. And, as Heidegger suggests, the difficulty facing the reader attempting to make sense of the poem, and especially this last line, gives rise to unrest in our thinking. Or, rather, it causes unrest when we think again and think back (*Nachdenken*). The last line of the poem "forces us to the unrest of thought" [*drängt uns in die Unruhe des Nachdenkens*] (p. 141). Thus, the poem stages the work of the translation of words, which is a statement that adds to Heidegger's proposition as to what "is the poetic intent of the whole poem: Words [*das Wort*]" (p. 141).

Next, after concluding that the "poetic intent" of the poem is the word, Heidegger goes on to discuss the penultimate line and the final stanza as a whole: "So I renounced and sadly see: [*So lernt ich traurig den verzicht*]" (p. 142). Again, an alternative translation of the line might be: "So I learned, sadly, to renounce:" which has the advantage of spelling out the word "learn," which is important for my discussion of education (which includes considering learning, teaching, being educated and lacking education, etc.). The word "learn" is also important to highlight, since Heidegger a little later on in the essay discusses its meaning and relevance in the poem. As for the penultimate line of the poem, Heidegger finds the keyword of the line in the word "renounced" (*verzicht*). Heidegger's reading of the word *verzicht* is a good example of his method of paratactic translation, which Miles Groth describes in his study *Translating Heidegger* (2017): "Heidegger's translation practice, which is determined by his philosophy of translation, is characterized by a procedure that works paratactically, word by word, rather than syntactically, by way of an analysis of propositions" (p 165). Heidegger's translation of *verzicht* displays, in an exemplary manner, the way he practices his philosophy of translation and reading of poetry. The passage on the word *verzicht* reads as follows:

[5]The German text is from Stefan George, (2004), *Gesamtausgabe der Werke*. Vol. 9. Berlin: Directmedia, p. 134 (1.023).

Renouncing is not stating [*Aussagen*], but perhaps after all a Saying [*Sagen*]. Renouncing belongs to the verb to forgive [*verzeihen*]. Accusing [*zeihen*], charging [*zichten*] is the same word as showing [*zeigen*], in Greek *deiknumi*, Latin *dicere*. To accuse, to show means: to allow to be seen, to bring to appearance. This, however, showing and allowing to be seen, is the meaning of the old German word *sagan*, to say. To accuse, to charge someone means: to tell him something straight to his face. Accordingly, Saying dominates in forgiving, in renouncing [*Im Verzeihen, Verzichen waltet demnach ein Sagen*]. How so? Renouncing means: to give up the claim to something, to deny oneself something. Because renouncing is a manner of Saying, it can be introduced in writing by a colon. Yet what follows the colon does not need to be a statement. The colon following the word "renounce" does not disclose something in the sense of a statement or an assertion. Rather, the colon discloses renunciation as Saying of that with which it is involved. With what is it involved? Presumably with that which renunciation renounces. (p. 142)

Heidegger begins by saying that renouncing is not a statement but, perhaps, a Saying, and Saying is "to allow to be seen, to bring to appearance [*Vorschein*]," that is, Saying is revealing.[6] Heidegger then connects renouncing to forgiving, accusing, charging, and showing, which he then translates, by way of the old German word *sagan*, to say, into Saying. Renouncing is thus, Heidegger claims, "a manner of Saying." This tracing of words, their interrelated meanings and connections, is typical of Heidegger's paratactic method of translation. However, not only words carry signification, but also the punctuation in the poem. Thus, Heidegger turns his attention to the significance of the colon in the poem. When it comes to the last stanza, the colon opens up [*öffnet*] renunciation "as Saying of that with which it is involved [*worauf es sich einläßt*]." Alternatively, the colon opens up for renunciation as "Saying of what it lets in," or as "Saying of what it is getting itself into". The point to take note of is how Heidegger draws on words that suggest opening up and letting in. The phrase "*worauf es sich einläßt*" brings with it the sense of taking a risk, that one knows the risks or dangers of that with which one is getting involved in, as in "*wissen, worauf man sich einlässt*," meaning to understand the risks. Now, when we

---

[6] If renouncing is not a statement (*Aussage*), but a saying (*Sagen*) which reveals and shows, then what is a statement, according to Heidegger? In "What is a Thing?" (a text to which I will return in connection to the concept of learning), he states, in the course of discussing Kant's major work *Critique of Pure Reason*, and more specifically λόγος as *ratio*, reason, *Vernunft*: "The assertion [*Aussage*] is a kind of λέγειν – addressing something as something. This implies something taken as something. Considering and expressing something as something in Latin is called *reor*, *ratio*. Therefore, *ratio* becomes the translation of λόγος. The simple asserting simultaneously gives the basic form in which we mean and think something about things. The basic form of thinking, and thus of thought, is the guideline (*Leitfaden*) for the determination of the thingness of the thing. [...] To ask about the being of what is, what and how what is, is at all, counts as philosophy's principal task. To ask in this way is first, first-ranking, and proper philosophy, πρώτη φιλοσοφία, *prima philosophia*. [...] 'Guideline' (*Leitfaden*) here means that the modes of assertion (*Ausgesagtheit*) direct the view in the determining of presence (*Anwesenheit*), i.e., of the being of what is" (Heidegger, 1967, p. 64). As we can infer from this passage, *Aussagen* (assertion, statement) is a word Heidegger connects to the language of metaphysics, here represented by Aristotle's first philosophy, that is, the question of "the being of what is, what and how what is, is at all," as Heidegger pus it here. Thus, *Sagen* belongs to something else than philosophy, or first philosophy, or metaphysics, Heidegger claims. In what follows, I will address the significance of *Sagen* as Heidegger develops it in "Das Wort."

know that renunciation is a Saying that says what it is getting itself involved in, that is, it says what it is letting in while understanding there might be a risk involved in doing so, Heidegger asks what, precisely, it is getting itself involved in? "Presumably," Heidegger responds, "with that which renunciation renounces [*Verzicht verzichtet*]" (p. 142).

The Saying of renunciation is the poet's Saying and a renunciation, since, according to Heidegger, it means "to deny [*versagen*] *oneself* something" (emphasis added, p. 143). "Accordingly," Heidegger continues, "the final verse must, after all, tell of what the poet denies [*versagt*] himself" (p. 143). Thus, the poet denies (himself) by saying, while what he says is denied, since both Saying and denying are implied in *versagen*: *ver-sagen*, which combines the negative *ver-* with *sagen*.[7] Heidegger replies to the proposition that the poet denies himself by stating: "Yes and no" (p. 143). So, how is the poet both denying himself and not denying himself at the same time? This is the question which Heidegger commits himself to address in the remaining part of the essay. Moreover, it is at this moment in the essay that Heidegger addresses learning by pointing to the last line and its invocation of learning renunciation: "*So lernt ich traurig den verzicht.*" The last line says that the poet, by denying himself, and in Saying, has learned what renunciation means, which leads Heidegger to provide a very condensed theory of learning:

> The poet has learned renunciation. To learn means: to become knowing. In Latin, knowing is *qui vidit*,[8] one who has seen, has caught sight of something, and who never again loses

[7] See, "*versagen*" in the *Grimm Wörterbuch*, for the etymological link between *versagen* and *sagen*.

[8] It is somewhat unclear how Heidegger relates knowing to *qui vidit*. The connection of seeing with knowledge goes back, at least, to Plato and Aristotle, and is later expressly invoked in Meister Eckhart's work. However, one possible source, specifically for Heidegger's Latin quote, might be Augustine's (2019) *Confessions*, Book X: "There is yet another kind of temptation, one that is far more dangerous. For besides the lust of the flesh, which concerns the enjoyment of all the senses and of pleasures – ruinous to those whom it enslaves, who take themselves far away from you – there is in the soul a certain empty and inquisitive passion, not for enjoyment in the flesh, but for experience through the flesh, through the same bodily senses, a passion that disguises itself under the name of understanding and knowledge. Now because this passion is a desire to know, and the eyes are foremost among the senses as sources of knowledge, the language of Scripture calls it 'the lust of the eyes'. Strictly speaking, seeing is the function of the eyes, but we use the verb 'to see' of the other senses as well when we make use of them to know something. We do not say 'hear how it glows red' or 'smell how bright it is' or 'taste how shiny it is' or 'feel how it gleams' – but we do speak of seeing all these things. For we say not only 'See how bright it is' (something only the eyes can perceive) but also 'See how it sounds', 'See what it smells like', 'See how it tastes', 'See how hard it is'. And so, as I have said, the endeavor to gain knowledge through any of the senses is called 'the lust of the eyes', because the other senses claim for themselves by analogy the function of seeing, which belongs to the eyes first of all, whenever they seek any kind of knowledge" (p. 192). ["Huc accedit alia forma temptationis multiplicius periculosa. praeter enim concupiscentiam earnis, quae inest in delectatione omnium sensuum et voluptatum, cui servientes depereunt qui longe se faciunt a te, inest animae per eosdem sensus corporis quaedam non se oblectandi in carne, sed experiendi per carnem vana et curiosa cupiditas nomine cognitionis et scientiae palliata. quae quoniam in appetitu noscendi est, oculi autem sunt ad noscendum in sensibus principes, concupiscentia oculorum eloquio divino adpellata est. ad oculos enim videre proprie pertinet : utimur autem hoc verbo etiam in ceteris sensibus, cum eos ad cognoscendum intendimus. neque enim

sight of what he has caught sight of. To learn means: to attain to such seeing. To this belongs our reaching it; namely on the way [*unterwegs*], on a journey [*Fahrt*]. To put oneself on a journey, to experience [*Er-fahren*], means to learn. (p. 143)

To have seen, here, should be related, in Heidegger's reading, to the etymology of *verzicht* as showing and allowing to be seen, and not to the word "see" that concludes the penultimate line of the poem in its English translation, since "seeing" as such, is not literally stated in the poem. Nevertheless, Heidegger connects knowledge and learning to sight and vision throughout his work. For example, in "The Origin of the Work of Art," Heidegger (1993a) states: "The word *technê* denotes rather a mode of knowing. To know means to have seen [*Wissen heißt: gesehen haben*], in the widest sense of seeing, which means to apprehend what is present, as such" (p. 184). To know is to have seen, and to learn is to reach such knowledge through having seen. Learning is a journey, says Heidegger, one learns on the way [*unterwegs*]. To gain experience from the journey one sets oneself upon is to learn: "*Sich in das Er-fahren schicken heißt: lernen*" (GA 12, p. 211). Thus, seeing, journeying, and experiencing amount to learning and how we gain knowledge.[9]

However, when it comes to learning, Heidegger addresses it in slightly different ways throughout his work. In *What is a Thing?* he traces teaching and learning as stemming from the Greek expression τὰ μαθήματα (*ta mathêmata*), meaning, in Heidegger's translation, "what can be learned and thus, at the same time, what can be taught" (p. 69). After discussing what kind of learning the Greek sense of the word mathematics presupposes, *viz.* that it is a teaching and learning of what is already known, Heidegger states: "The mathematical, in the original sense of learning what one already knows, is the fundamental presupposition of 'academic' work" (p. 76). Thus, in order to be able to learn, in a supposedly academic way, to use and handle a thing, we must first know what the thing is, we have to be familiar with the thing to be learned, which is called μαθήματα (*mathémata*). Heidegger's example of μαθήματα is by way of a weapon:

> This [what a weapon is] must be known in advance, and must be learned, and be teachable. [...] We do not first learn what a weapon is when we become familiar with this rifle or with a certain model of rifle. We already know that in advance and must know it; otherwise we could not perceive that rifle as such at all. Because we know in advance what a weapon is, and only in this way, does what we see [*Gesehene*] laid out before us become visible [*sichtbar*] as what it is. (p. 72)

---

dicimus : audi quid rutilet, aut : olefac quam niteat, aut : gusta quam splendeat, aut: palpa quam fulgeat : videri enim dicuntur haec omnia, dicimus autem non solum : vide quid lucct, quod soli oculi sentire possunt, seel etiam : vide quid sonet, vide quid oleat, vide quid sapiat, vide quam durum sit. ideoque generalis experientia sensuum concupiscentia, sicut dictum est, oculorum vocatur, quia videndi officium, in quo primatum oculi tenent, etiam ceteri sensus sibi de similitudine usurpant, cum aliquid cognitionis explorant" (2016, pp. 160, 162).

[9] The etymological relation between the words to see and to know can be traced back to the proto-indo-european base *weid, meaning both to know and to see, cf. *videre* (Lat.) and *Wissen* (Ger.).

Heidegger here invokes seeing and being visible as conditions of knowing, learning, and teaching, which we recognize from the essays referenced so far, namely "Words" and "The Origin of the Work of Art." What is known, what has been seen, as μαθήματα, is accordingly the task of what Heidegger calls academic work. This kind of knowledge is, in other words, anticipated and governed by the law of contradiction: it is the knowledge of science and metaphysics. Knowledge of this kind constitutes what is to be learned, for example in a course of study in a particular discipline, governed by disciplinary rules, conventions, and traditions. But, as Heidegger maintains: "[M]athematics itself is only a particular formation [*Ausformung*] of the mathematical" (p. 68), that is, mathematics, as a discipline, is not identical with and does not define the mathematical. This leads Heidegger to, as we have seen, appeal to the etymology of the word mathematics as meaning teaching and learning.[10]

Now, when it comes to learning and its relation to teaching, Heidegger identifies the essence of learning (*Wesen des Lernens*) with what he calls "*zur Kenntnis Nehmen*" (1985b, GA 41, p. 73), which is translated in English as "take cognizance of" (p. 73). Learning, on the one hand, and as Heidegger conceives of it here, is an "extremely peculiar" (*höchst merkwürdiges*) taking, a taking, moreover, of what the learner already is in possession of. "Teaching," on the other hand, Heidegger says, "is a giving [*ein Geben*], an offering [*Darbieten*]"

> but what is offered in teaching is not learnable, for the student is merely instructed to take for himself what he already has. If the student only takes over something which is offered he does not learn. He only comes to learn when he experiences what he takes as something he himself already has. True learning only occurs where the taking of what one already has is a self-giving [*Sichsebtsgeben*] and is experienced as such. Teaching, therefore, does not mean anything else than to let the others learn, i.e., to bring one another to learning. Learning is more difficult than teaching; for only he who can truly learn – and only as long as he can do it – can truly teach. The genuine teacher differs from the pupil only in that he can learn better, and that he more genuinely wants to learn. In all teaching, the teacher learns the most. (p. 73)

This way of learning applies to how we come to learn and know about things as they present themselves to us in their thingness [*Dingheit*]. Heidegger identifies how learning works in how the Greeks understood the notion μάθησις, the mathematical. The notion of the mathematical, Heidegger points out, is ambiguous (*Doppeldeutig*), since it designates what can be learned, how we learn, and the process of learning. It denotes our experience of things, our pre-knowledge of them, and also the foundational stance (*Grundstellung*) for our disposition toward things, that is, how we understand them as already given to us. "Therefore," Heidegger states, "the

---

[10] It also prompts Heidegger to disparage the disciplinary organization of the university: "Mathematics is as little a natural science as philosophy is one of the humanities. Philosophy in its essence belongs as little in the philosophical faculty as mathematics belongs to natural science. To house philosophy and mathematics in this way today seems to be a blemish or a mistake in the catalogue of the universities. But perhaps it is something quite different, [...] namely a sign that there no longer is a fundamental and clarified unity of the sciences and that this unity is no longer either a necessity or a question" (p. 69).

mathematical is the fundamental presupposition [*Grundvoraussetzung*] of the knowledge of things" (p. 75).

To sum up Heidegger's exposition of learning in *What is a Thing?*: In order to learn about things, we must recognize that we can only learn about things that are already familiar to us; we must attend to how things are given, more specifically, how things are given to us, which is what Heidegger calls self-giving. This means that when we teach we let the learners take what is given, which is something that the learners can only give themselves. We learn, moreover, by experience (*erfahren*) and seeing (*sehen*) what is there, things we are already familiar with. Thus, the basic concepts of learning and knowing that Heidegger mentions in "Words" are also part of his exposition of learning in *What is a Thing?*

To highlight another instance where Heidegger refers to learning, I would like to turn, shortly, to his *Introduction to Metaphysics*, in which we again find the notion of learning but from a slightly different perspective, namely learning and its relation to questioning. First, however, Heidegger juxtaposes knowledge (*Wissen*) and information (*Kenntnisse*):

> Merely to have information, however wide-ranging it may be, is not to know. Even if this information is focused on what is practically most important through courses of study and examination requirements, it is not knowledge. Even if this information, cut back to the most compelling needs, is "close to life," its possession is not knowledge. One who carries such information around with him and has added a few practical tricks to it will still be at a loss and will still bungle in the face of real reality, which is always different from what the philistine understands by closeness to life and closeness to reality. Why? Because he has no knowledge, since to know means *to be able to learn* [*Wissen heißt*: lernen können]. (2014, p. 24)

It must be noted that *Kenntnisse* in German implies more than information; Kenntnisse is a form of knowledge, such as knowledge of facts, or being able to do something without knowing the functioning or theory behind what one is doing, for example. *Wissen*, in contrast, is all encompassing knowledge, which includes experience, practical knowledge, theoretical knowledge, self-reflection, etc. However, what Heidegger is after is something else than outlining a taxonomy of knowledge or developing an epistemology. We get a hint at what Heidegger means by reading the beginning sentences of the paragraph from which the above quoted passage is taken. The sentences read: "But to know means to be able to stand in the truth. Truth is the openness of beings. To know is accordingly to be able to stand in the openness of beings, to stand up to it. [*Wissen aber heißt: in der Wahrheit stehen können. Wahrheit is die Offenbarkeit des Seienen. Wissen ist demnach: in der Offenbarkeit des Seienden stehen können, sie bestehen*]" (p. 24; GA 40, p. 23). To know is to be able to learn, which means to "stand in the truth," which in turn means "to stand in the openness of beings," meaning to persist, subsist, survive [*bestehen*] in the openness where beings unfold.[11] Furthermore, the prerequisite for being able to learn is being able to question. To be able to question, Heidegger says, is having "the resoluteness to be able to stand in the openness of beings" (p. 24). The question that Heidegger is asking in *Introduction to Metaphysics* is the one that Leibniz famously asked, namely, in Heidegger's wording: "Why are there beings at all instead of nothing?" (p. 1). When we have the ability to ask this question in an essential way we are also able to learn. This is one of the aims of *Introduction to Metaphysics*.

The notion of learning put forward in *Introduction to Metaphysics* is noticeably different from the one Heidegger submits in *What is a Thing?* But they are similar in the way they emphasize the learner's ability learn and, importantly, the learner's ability to learn how to learn. Together, these two notions of learning in Heidegger's thinking provide us with an intimation of how to contextualize the way learning is dealt with in the essay "Words." In that essay, as we have seen, learning is to become knowing, and to know is to see. We reach this knowledge by experience (*Er-fahrung*), by setting out on a journey (*Fahrt*). Given the notions of learning proposed by Heidegger so far, we could say that what we learn is what we take (*nehmen*) as given (*gegeben*) by experience on the way (*unterwegs*) on our journey. This movement of learning reminds us of Heidegger's question (posed almost as an aside) concerning the possibility of a pure finding that I referred to above, a finding that is not antici-pated [*vorweggenommen*]. Let's look closer at the paragraph in "What is metaphys-ics?" where Heidegger (1993b) mentions the word *vorwegnahme*:

> Where shall we seek [*suchen*] the nothing? Where will we find [*finden*] the nothing? In order to find something must we not already know in general that it is there? Indeed! At first and for the most part man can seek only when he has anticipated [*vorweggenommen*] the being at hand [*Vorhandensein*] of what he is looking for. Now the nothing is what we are seeking. Is there ultimately such a thing as a search without that anticipation [*vorweg-nahme*], a search to which pure discovery belongs? (p. 98)

---

[11] The open in which Dasein stands in the openness of beings is the lighting/clearing [*Lichtung*], as in a cleared space in the forest which lets light shine through. As Gert-Jan van der Heide (2010) explains it: "Heidegger describes lighting as the open place occurring in the midst of being as a whole. This open place 'grants and guarantees to us humans a passage to these beings'. As such, beings can only appear to us if they stand within this lighting. Truth takes place as this lighting in a 'battle' with concealment as *Verstellen* and as *einfaches Versagen*, both as displacement and as simple refusal. Therefore, he can claim that the essence of truth is untruth, that is to say that truth only occurs in a struggle with appearances that displace the whole of the lighting in which we are. And truth is also a struggle with the concealment that simply refuses us any appearance at all and that stands at the origin of the open place in which beings appear in the first place" (p. 44). I refer to van der Heide's explication of lighting and the open since it connects it to an important aspect of my own reading in this chapter, namely the word *Versagen*. For an excellent analysis of the notion *Lichtung* and its development in Heidegger's thinking from *Being and Time* to the late writ-ings of the 1960s, see Richard Capobianco's (2010) book *Engaging Heidegger*, especially Chaps. 5 and 6. As Capobianco states, "the story reads from 'the lighting' to 'the clearing'" (p. 99.), implying the shift in Heidegger's thinking from conceiving of *Lichtung* as light (*lumen naturale*) to thinking *Lichtung* in terms of unconcealment (ἀλήθεια), comparable to a forest clearing.

We recognize in this passage Heidegger's discussion of learning in *What is a Thing?* where her insists on how we must already be familiar with what we learn to be able to learn it. In effect, Heidegger here asks if there is such a thing that can be learned without any knowledge of it in advance, a way to take what is given before choosing to take the way that is known, so to speak. This would be a search without having a staked-out way, a finding that does not know what it finds, discovers, or reveals. It seems that what Heidegger is implying is that it is the nothing that cannot be found or discovered with the help of science in the manner of scientific exploration. In consequence, we cannot learn the nothing, we cannot learn about it, what it consists of and its functioning, its characteristics, because it "is" not, it is not a being. But at the same time, Heidegger argues, it is the nothing that makes beings possible in the first place, it is the nothing that lets us learn. But if we cannot learn about the nothing from science, then from what can we learn it? Heidegger's answer is that we can learn about the nothing in philosophy and poetry. In *Introduction to Metaphysics* he is equally explicit about the inadequacy of science in this respect as he is confident about the ability of philosophy and poetry to talk about the nothing:

> In truth, it is only an illusion of rigor and scientificy when one appeals to the principle of contradiction, and to logic in general, in order to prove that all thought and talk about Nothing is contradictory and therefore senseless. "Logic" is then taken as the tribunal, secure for all eternity, and it goes without saying that no rational human being will call into doubt its authority as the first and last court of appeal. Whoever speaks against logic is suspected, implicitly or explicitly, of arbitrariness. [...] One cannot, in fact, talk about and deal with Nothing as if it were a thing, such as the rain out there, or a mountain, or any object at all; Nothing remains in principle inaccessible to all science. Whoever wants to talk of Nothing must necessarily become unscientific. But this is a great misfortune only if one believes that scientific thinking alone is the authentic, rigorous thinking, that it alone can and must be made the measure even of philosophical thinking. The reverse is the case. All scientific thinking is just a derivative and rigidified form of philosophical thinking. Philosophy never arises from or through science. Philosophy can never belong to the same order as the sciences. It belongs to a higher order, and not just "logically," as it were, or in a table of the system of sciences. Philosophy stands in a completely different domain and rank of spiritual Dasein [*Die Philosophie steht in einem ganz anderen Bereich und Rang geistigen Daseins*]. Only poetry is of the same order as philosophical thinking, although thinking and poetry are not identical. [...] But aside from the philosopher, the poet can also talk about Nothing [...] in comparison to all mere science, an essential superiority of the spirit holds sway in poetry [*eine wesenhafte Überlegenheit des Geistes gegenüber aller bloßen Wissenschaft waltet*]. (pp. 28–29)

The poet and the thinker, Heidegger says, are the ones who can teach us about the nothing, since they are of a higher order of spiritual Dasein, and not constrained and limited by the principle of contradiction and formal logic. But, even though the thinker and the poet can address the nothing, it is still impossible to talk about the nothing as a thing, which leads us to wonder how it stands with learning what the nothing is, learning from out of the nothing, and learning by taking the nothing in consideration, since Heidegger's exposition of learning takes its cue from what is already known and about, precisely, the thing. Even in Stefan George's poem "*Das Wort*" the emphasis lies on what cannot be expressed, that which the poet has to learn to renounce.

There seems, then, that there is a prior knowledge, or rather precondition of knowledge, which is related to poetic saying and philosophical thinking. However, poetry can only say what is unsayable by way of a detour. What is unsayable remains unsayable and has to be renounced and so can only be learned in the act of renouncing it. This is where the word breaks off in Stefan George's poem. What the poet mourns is the loss of the unanticipated finding which belongs to Being and which is expressed only in contradiction and aporia. Even the poet and the thinker have to renounce when faced with the nothing, which can only be found, and by extension learned, by letting it be. There is no act of (scientific) discovery or logical reasoning that can explain the nothing of the poem. The nothing is only made manifest by that which it is not, namely something, for example a poem. Every poem, every act of thinking, must, in consequence, be translated into a thing which can be seen, known, and so learned. But prior to knowing and learning there is that pure finding, the unanticipated finding, the nothing, which cannot be discovered and known, but is intimated in the saying of a poem or the saying of a thinker.

The Learning of Being: The Being of Learning

Let us return to Heidegger's reading of the poem "*Das Wort*," a poem which according to Heidegger concerns itself with the word and its possibility, the poet and the poet's saying. Moreover, we were introduced to learning as a way of seeing, more precisely, learning by experiencing what one sees when undertaking a journey. However, what, more specifically, does the poet learn by renouncing? We get an answer in Heidegger's (1982a) treatment of George's poem in the lectures published in *On the Way to Language* with the title "*Das Wesen der Sprache*," translated as "The Nature of Language." The three lectures making up "The Nature of Language," Heidegger informs us, "are intended to bring us face to face with a possibility of undergoing an experience with language [*mit der Sprache eine Erfahrung zu machen*]" (p. 57). What we must attempt to clarify is what Heidegger means by "undergo an experience [*eine Erfahrung machen*]." As we have already indicated, Heidegger in the essay "Words" tells us that to experience something is related to travel, to being underway, which he highlights by writing experience as "*Er-fahrung*," emphasizing the word "*fahren*" meaning to travel, move, navigate. As for the word "undergo," which translates "*machen*," Heidegger points out that we should understand it to mean something other than a subject or agent doing something, but rather implies, as Heidegger states, "that we endure it, suffer it, receive it as it strikes us and submit to it. It is this something itself that comes about, comes to pass, happens" (p. 57). To know the essence, nature, or Being of language, we must, in other words, learn it, since what Heidegger here submits as the criteria for undergoing an experience are also, as we have seen, what he takes learning to mean. And it is this learning experience that he sets forth to investigate in the three lectures making up "*Das Wesen der Sprache*." What is more, this learning experience, which is the aim of the lectures, is closely connected to, or rather, belongs to the same neighborhood as thinking, poetry, and language. Thus, Heidegger defines what it means to undergo an experience with language in the following way: "To undergo an experience with language, then, means to let ourselves be properly concerned by the claim of language by entering into and submitting to it [*Mit der Sprache eine Erfahrung machen heißt dann: uns vom Anspruch der Sprache eigens angehen lassen, indem wir auf ihn eingehen, uns ihn fügen*]" (1982a, p. 57; 1985a, GA: 12, p. 149). In this definitional sentence Heidegger is playing on the words "*Sprache*" and "*gehen*." Language, *Sprache*, makes an *Anspruch*, that is, a claim, a demand on us, a claim that we must let concern, *angehen*, us when we enter into or arrive, *eingehen*, in language, which we do by submitting to, and join together, *fügen*, with language. If we manage to engage with language in this way, we have the possibility, Heidegger says, of undergoing an experience with language. Such a possibility is opened up to us by Stefan George's poem "*Das Wort*," since to think poetry and thinking essentially, meaning to learn, and so understand, their respective and shared nature or being, *Wesen*, which given to us as a possibility in the saying, *sagen*, that is, in the showing of poetry and thinking.

What Heidegger aspires to achieve with his lectures (in "The Nature of Language" as well as in "Words") is, as he suggests in the third lecture, to hint at a possible transformation of our way of thinking so that we can see what the word shows us, or rather gives us to see. That from which we are to take a hint is, according to Heidegger, what he calls the "guide word" (*Leitwort*) that shows the way to the possibility of undergoing an experience with language: "The being of language: the language of being [*Das Wesen der Sprache: Die Sprache des Wesens*]" (1982a, p. 94; 1985a, GA: 12, p. 189). Again, Heidegger calls attention to the significance of the colon, as he does in his reading of the poem "*Das Wort*." Heidegger states:

> Two phrases held apart by a colon, each the inversion of the other. If the whole is to be a guide-word, then this colon must indicate that what precedes it opens into what follows it. Within the whole there plays a disclosure and a beckoning that point to something which we, coming from the first turn of phrase, do not suspect in the second; for that second phrase is more than just a rearrangement of the words in the first. If so, then what the words "being" and "language" on either side of the colon say is not only not identical, but even the form of the phrase is different in each case. (p. 94).

As was the case with the colon in the last stanza of Stefan George's poem, that which follows the colon is not a mere statement (*Aussage*), but also an opening up to a Saying. Moreover, we should not read the two phrases of the guide-word as a simple inversion of the pharses, but rather as translations – the second phrase translating the first, while the first translates the second. The guide-word includes both the original and the translation, and each phrase is at the same time an original as well as a translation; they are, as Heidegger suggests, neighbors dwelling within the same neighborhood (*Nachbarschaft*). Moreover, just as with the act of translation the phrases of the guide-word give us a hint, beckons us, toward a way to read each of the phrases, and also, since poetry and thinking are ways of saying, how to read the whole of the guide-word taken as a Saying:

> If we were to succeed for once in reaching the place to which the guide-word beckons [*winkt*] us, we would arrive where we have a possibility of undergoing an experience with

language, the language known to us. Thus, much depends on our keeping to the direction of that indication [*Wink*] which the clarified guide-word gives us – this guide-word which we can now paraphrase as follows: what concerns us as language receives its definition from Saying as that which moves all things. A hint beckons [*Ein Wink winkt*] away from the one, toward the other. The guide-word beckons [*winkt*] us away from current notions about language, to the experience of language as Saying. (pp. 95–96)

To learn how we can start to think the guide-word, we must, accordingly, set out to translate it. But even though we follow the hint that it gives us, it is not certain that we arrive at a conclusion about the nature, essence, being (*Wesen*) of language. Why? Because what we find cannot be anticipated when it comes to the Saying of language, which implies an other way of perceiving language than the scientific, rational model of accounting for what language is. This is the lesson learned by the poet in "*Das Wort.*" The poet's experience shows him, and us, that we must learn how to renounce, since "Where the word breaks off no thing may be." But, we must still as readers learn how to read, or as Heidegger would have it, hear the poem as a Saying. The poem as Saying opens up a possibility for us to experience language. If we follow the way of the hint (*Wink*) that the guide-word opens up, it means we have to translate the poem through the guide-word, "away from the one, toward the other." However, what is indicated by translation here does not, first and foremost, give rise to a thing, a being, but to Saying. Since, to repeat the last line of the poem once more: "Where the word breaks off no thing maybe," and the word, Heidegger insists, "which itself is supposed not to be a thing, not anything that 'is', escapes us. It seems as though what is happening here is just like what happens with the prize in the poem" (p. 86). The prize, in the poem, "does not reach being a thing, it does not come to be a treasure, that is, a poetically secured possession of the land" (p. 69). Nevertheless, it gives the poet an experience with language, even though the prize withdraws as soon as it is within reach. The poet's experience with language, as Heidegger puts it, "shows what is there and yet 'is' not. The word, too, belongs to what is there – perhaps not merely 'too' but first of all, and even in such a way that the word, the nature [*Wesen*] of the word, conceals [*verbirgt*] within itself that which gives being" (pp. 87–88). Likewise, if we attempt a translation of the poem through the guide-word, it will not reveal or disclose what its Being is, or what gives being, since it remains hidden and out of reach of any statement, or definition of it. It belongs to the silent "is" that is not a thing or being, and so cannot be determined by knowledge of or familiarity with it as a thing/being.

In consequence, we cannot rely on the same approach to learning that the Saying of the poem shows, as was the approach indicated by Heidegger when it comes to learning about a thing or being, since Saying is not concerned with the knowledge of beings but, to put it bluntly, to experience Being through an experience with the Being of language, that is, what gives being, meaning, things, and so forth. Learning what shows itself in Saying must remain a possibility and cannot be verified or exposed, but follow the hint the leads to the ways that language opens up. It means to learn by intimating, to experience that which cannot be known by measuring, calculating and accounting for in order to give evidence of what is there, that is, prove the existence of things-beings – and so catalogue and categorize their qualities, attributes, and characteristics. It means learning how to wait for the unanticipated, which amounts to the pure finding (*reines finden*), which Heidegger mentions. Learning, in this way, means being able to remain in what Heidegger calls "the mysterious wonder that makes us wonder [*das geheimnisvoll Erstaunende, was staunen läßt*]" (1982a, p. 88; 1985a, GA: 12, p. 183).

Learning, as waiting for the unanticipated, comes about through translation, when we understand translation as the "possibility of undergoing and experience with language." This possibility must necessarily endure the aporia of translation, that is, the withdrawal of that which shows itself in translation as Saying. This experience is staged by Stefan George in the poem "*Das Wort*" as the possibility of Saying that which must be renounced, which is the full meaning and explanation of the relation between word and thing. In the final paragraphs of the third lecture of "The Nature of Language" Heidegger suggests a "supposition" (*vermutenden sagen*) in response to his reading of the last line of "*Das Wort*": "An 'is' arises where the word breaks up [*Ein »ist« ergibt sich, wo das Wort zerbricht*]" (1982a, p. 108; 1985a, GA: 12, p. 204). The springing word here is "*ergibt*" which should be related to the giving or gift of Being which is the "is," which gives without revealing itself, and only shows itself as the residue of Being in the "is" when the word breaks up. In Heidegger's words: "To break up here means that the sounding word returns into soundlessness, back to whence it was granted: into the ringing of stillness which, as Saying, moves (*be-wëgt*)[12] the regions of the world's fourfold into their nearness (*Nähe*)." And he ends the lecture with the words: "This breaking up of the word is the true step back on the way of thinking" (p. 108). The poetic words that guide us on the way to experience the Being of language, meaning the guide-word translated through the words of the poem, which leads to its Saying (*Sage*), are as word-things broken up, beyond their literal and figural meaning, to give us an intimation of what the poet cannot express. That for which there are no words, and so what cannot be expressed, is Being, as such, since "it" "is" not a being, a thing. But still, the experience transforms us, which is what happens, as a happening, an event (*Ereignis*),[13] when what Heidegger calls the fourfold (sky, earth, gods, and mortals) gather into

---

[12] Heidegger's use of *be-wëgen* and *be-wëgt* is drawing on its use in the Swabian dialect, where it means "to give way," "prepare a way," and "clear a way." See 1985a, GA: 12, p. 186, and the translator's note of the omitted passage of Heidegger's text, 1982a, p. 92.

[13] On the notion of *Ereignis* and its relation to language, Heidegger (1982c) in "The Way to Language," a lecture given in 1959, states: "In order to pursue in thought the being of language and to say of it what is its own, a transformation [*Wandel*] of language is needed which we can neither compel nor invent. This transformation does not result from the procurement of newly formed words and phrases. It touches on our relation [*Verhältnis*] to language, which is determined by our destiny [*Geschick*]: whether and in what way the nature of language, as the arch-tidings of Appropriation [*Ur-Kunde des Ereignisses*], will retain us in Appropriation [*Ereignis*]. For that appropriating, holding, self-retaining [*eignend-haltend-ansichhaltend*] is the relation of all relations. Thus *our* saying – always an answering – remains forever relational. Relation is thought of here always in terms of the appropriation, and no longer conceived in the form of mere reference. Our relation to language defines [*bestimmt*] itself in terms of the mode in which we, who are needed in the usage of language, belong [*gehören*] to the Appropriation" (pp. 135–136).

nearness. Accordingly, and as Heidegger notes, we cannot reach such an experience with the Being of language by asking questions, which will not move (*be-wëgen*) us out of the realm of attempting to determine the meaning of beings. Instead, we must listen to that which is given, Heidegger says, since "the authentic attitude of thinking is not a putting of questions – rather, it is listening to the grant, the promise of what is to be put in question" (p. 71). And, such listening to the gift of language prepares a way for learning the possibility of undergoing an experience with language by thinking through the guide-word: "No matter how we put our questions to language about its nature [*Wesen*], first of all it is needful that language vouchsafe itself to us. If it does, the nature of language becomes the grant of its essential being [*Wesens*], that is, the being of language becomes the language of being" (p. 72). Before we ask questions, we must learn how to listen to what gives rise to our questioning, which is what Heidegger attempts to do in his lectures on the nature of language and the poem "*Das Wort*." To find a way, "differing from all other ways [*anders den jeder andere Weg*]," toward hearing the Saying of thinking and poetry, we need an escort that reaches ahead (*vorausreichenden Geleites*) of us (1982a, p. 93; 1985a, GA: 12, p. 188). The escort (*Geleit*), says Heidegger, is part of the guide-word (*Leitwort*) which leads and guides us on the way toward learning the possibility of undergoing an experience with language. Heidegger's guide-word, the Being of language: the language of Being, is also a fitting escort to the aporia of translation, which in the same way (although it, too, is other than all other ways) is a listening to that which withdraws, making way for the unanticipated, when the word breaks off, where no thing may be.

Concluding Thoughts: Translating Heidegger and Another Way of Learning

Along these lines, what can be hinted at, by way of the preceding discussion, and in the final analysis, is a transformation of learning and our way of thinking, a way which pays heed to the aporia of translation which precede Aristotle's law of contradiction, and so the scientism of rationality and formal logic which developed out of it. In the final paragraph of the chapter, entitled "Overcoming Metaphysics," in *The End of Philosophy*, Heidegger (1974) in a condensed manner broaches many of the key words we have encountered. He begins the paragraph by stating: "No transformation comes without an anticipatory escort." And then goes on to pose the question: "But how does an escort draw near unless Appropriation opens out which, calling, needing, envisions human being, that is, sees and in this seeing brings mortals to the path of thinking, poetizing building" (p. 110). The paragraph deserves being repeated in Heidegger's German: "*Kein Wandel kommt ohne vorausweisendes Geleit. Wie aber naht ein Geleit, wenn nicht das Ereignis sich lichtet, das rufend, brauchend das Menschenwesen er-äugnet, d.h. er-blickt und im Erblicken Sterbliche auf den Weg des denkenden, dichtenden Bauens bringt?*" (GA: 7, p. 98). The extreme difficulty of translating this passage sums up many of the issues I have attempted to approach in my reading of Heidegger in this chapter. In fact, the simultaneous reading of Heidegger in English and German stages what is at stake when trying to undergo an experience with the Being, essence, nature, that is to say, *Wesen* of language. The difficulties, or rather, aporias, arise not only in the translation between German and English, but also in the intricate style of language Heidegger uses in German. Consider, for example the word *Wesen*, which has several different, not to say, conflicting, meanings, and which we have to keep in mind simultaneously when we read. Or the many possible meanings gathered in the word λόγος that Heidegger often invokes in his work. The same can also be said of many other keywords in Heidegger, such as the play on *Weg-bewegung*, *hören-gehören*, to give just two examples. Thus, it is not simply a question of literally translating Heidegger's language into another language, but of constantly being aware of what is intimated, left out, silent, and ambiguous, as well as the words' etymological registers. In the reading I propose, there is the example of the word "*verzicht*" in Stefan George's poem "*Das Wort*" which, as Heidegger underscores, takes on several different possible meanings. These aporias of translation are an essential part of Heidegger's thinking and affect the way we understand it. The most notable and important consequence is that the open-endedness of language opens up possibilities for us to learn how to think with, but also differently than Heidegger. This does not, in any way, mean that we can interpret Heidegger's language and thinking however we want. On the contrary, the open-endedness of his language and thinking imposes on us an even greater responsibility to closely read the tradition on which Heidegger insists that we as human beings are immersed in and dependent on. This too is why we cannot simply proclaim an end to metaphysics and state that we are now speaking outside of that tradition. This would, for Heidegger, be impossible, since we are in constant confrontation (*Auseinandersetzung*) with the metaphysical tradition; in other words, there is no neutral or objective point of view or place from which we would be completely cut off from the history of being. For example, this is the aim, as Heidegger points out, of the lectures making up the three volumes devoted to Nietzsche. Nietzsche, of whom Heidegger says that he constitutes the crowning achievement of metaphysics and so its consummation.

What Heidegger wants to prepare for, by what he calls the step back (*schritt zurück*), is a thinking that would not disregard and dismiss the progress and benefits of science and rationality, as grounded in, for example, the law of contradiction, but to break down their presuppositions and what they fail or forget to think through. This includes what he calls philosophy, by which he means metaphysics and academic philosophy, which leads him to ask about the matter for thinking at the end of philosophy. Such asking, as we have seen, demands a thorough reading of the tradition one is asking about; we cannot simply position ourselves free of context or history to speak of the matter for thinking. Moreover, it obliges us to learn how to think in another, wholly other, way (*anders den jeder andere Weg*), which means not shying away from thinking within contradiction, the nothing, the unsaid, and the foreign, since, as Heidegger maintains, it is by attending to the unfamiliar that we are given the possibility of understanding what the familiar entails in an essential way. Poetry, or rather what Heidegger considers great poetry, constitutes such a way, a way or path that can guide us toward learning, and thus seeing and hearing the Saying which the matter for thinking gives us to think.

To conclude this chapter, I would like to refer to the passage in Heidegger's "On the Question Concerning the Determination of the Matter for Thinking," which I quoted at the outset, and more specifically to the sentence that Heidegger quotes from Aristotle's *Metaphysics* (Metaphysics IV, 4, 1006 a 6ff.), which it has been the aim of the chapter to, in a somewhat roundabout way to relate to: ἔστι γὰρ ἀπαιδευσία τὸ μὴ γιγνώσκειν τίνων δεῖ ζητεῖν ἀπόδειξιν καὶ τίνων οὐ δεῖ. "For it is a lack of education (in thinking) not to have an eye for that regarding which it is necessary to seek a proof and that regarding which this is not necessary." What I have suggested in the chapter amounts, hopefully, to one possible way to confront this lack of education in thinking by attending to Heidegger's notions of learning and to hint at a possible other, or alternative way, of thinking about what it means to learn, that is, to have an eye for, seeing, coming to know that of which we do not need to seek proof.

References

Aristotle. (2016). *Metaphysics* (C. D. C. Reeves, Trans.). Hackett Publishing.
Asmis, E. (1986). Psychagogia in Plato's "Phaedrus". *Illinois Classical Studies, 11*(1/2), 153–172.
Augustine. (2016). *Confessions, Volume II, Books 9-13* (C J.-B. Hammond, Trans.). Harvard University Press.
Augustine. (2019). *Confessions* (T. Williams, Trans.). Hackett Publishing.
Capobianco, R. (2010). *Engaging Heidegger*. University of Toronto Press.
Derrida, J. (2007). Psyche: Invention of the other (P. Kamuf, Trans.). In J. Derrida, *Psyche: Inventions of the other, Vol. 1* (P. Kamuf & E. Rottenberg, Eds.) (pp. 1–89). Stanford University Press.
George, S. (2004). *Gesamtausgabe der Werke* (Vol. 9). Directmedia.
Groth, M. (2004). *Translating Heidegger*. University of Toronto Press.
Heidegger, M. (1967). *What is a thing?* (W. B. Barton, Jr. & V. Deutsch, Trans.). Gateway Editions.
Heidegger, M. (1974). *The end of philosophy* (J. Stambaugh, Trans.). Harper & Row.
Heidegger, M. (1982a). The nature of language (P. D. Hertz, Trans.). In M. Heidegger (Ed.), *On the way to language* (pp. 57–108). Harper & Row.
Heidegger, M. (1982b). Words (J. Stambaugh, Trans.). In M. Heidegger, *On the way to language* (P. D. Hertz, Trans.) (pp. 139–156). Harper & Row.
Heidegger, M. (1982c). The way to language (P. D. Hertz, Trans.). In M. Heidegger, *On the way to language* (pp. 111–136). Harper & Row.
Heidegger, M. (1985a). Das Wesen der Sprache. In M. Heidegger, *Underwegs zur Sprache* (GA 12) (pp. 147–204). Vittorio Klostermann.
Heidegger, M. (1985b). *Die Frage nach dem Ding* (GA 41). Vittorio Klostermann.
Heidegger, M. (1991a). *Nietzsche, Vol. I-II* (D. F. Krell, Trans.). HarperCollins.
Heidegger, M. (1991b). *Nietzsche, Vol. III-IV* (J. Stambaugh, D. F. Krell, & F. A. Capuzzi, Trans.). HarperCollins.
Heidegger, M. (1993a). The origin of the work of art (A. Hofstadter, Trans.). In M. Heidegger, *Basic writings* (D. F. Krell, Ed.) (pp. 143–212). HarperCollins.

Heidegger, M. (1993b). What is metaphysics? (A. Hofstadter, Trans.). In M. Heidegger, *Basic writings* (D. F. Krell, Ed.) (pp. 93–110). HarperCollins.

Heidegger, M. (2010). On the question concerning the determination of the matter for thinking (R. Capobianco & M. Göbel, Trans.). *Epoché, 14*(2), 213–223.

Heidegger, M. (2014). *Introduction to metaphysics* (G. Fried & R. Polt, Trans.). Yale University Press.

Jaeger, W. (1946). *Paideia: The ideals of Greek culture, Vol. I* (G. Highet, Trans.). Basil Blackwell.

Kreuzer, J. (Ed.). (2011). *Hölderlin Handbuch: Leben, Werk, Wirkung.* J. B. Metzler Verlag.

Plato. (1914). Phaedrus (H. N. Fowler, Trans.). In J. Henderson (Ed.), *Plato: Euthyphro, Apology, Crito, Phadeo, Phaedrus.* Harvard University Press.

van der Heide, G.-J. (2010). *The truth (and untruth) of language: Heidegger, Ricœur, and Derrida on disclosure and displacement.* Duquesne University Press.

Chapter 6
The Aporias of Translation in Poetry and Aesthetic Education: Reading John Ashbery

Introduction

Since this chapter is, to a large extent, concerned with the poetry of John Ashbery, a short introduction seems in order. John Ashbery was born in Rochester, New York, in 1927. His second collection of poems, *Some Trees*, published in 1956, was selected by the poet W. H. Auden for the Yale Younger Poets Series, which set the stage for his success as a poet. He came to publish over 30 collections of poetry, including, just to mention some of his perhaps most well-known collections, *The Tennis Court Oath* (1962), *The Double Dream of Spring* (1970), *Three Poems* (1972), *Self-portrait in a Convex Mirror* (1975), *Houseboat Days* (1977), *As We Know* (1979), *A Wave* (1984), *Flow Chart* (1991), *Hotel Lautréamont* (1992), and *Where Shall I Wander* (2005). Ashbery has been loosely connected with the, so called, New York School, an avant-garde school of poetry, music, and art, inspired by French surrealist poetry and characterized by cosmopolitan themes and stream of consciousness or automatic writing. The New York School included poets such as Frank O'Hara, Kenneth Koch, and James Schuyler. With time, Ashbery disassociated himself from the New York School as he developed his personal highly influential style of poetry. The subject matter that much of his poetry is concerned with is the act of writing poetry, its creation and the experience of experiencing as poetry. His style is characterized by a fluid, dissociative poetry often with a strain of humor and parody. He has been labelled a poet's poet and as obscure, as well as, importantly, questioning what we take for granted as rational and true. Poetic meaning in Ashbery's poetry is hard to pin down, since one of its main themes is to question what we, in fact, mean by poetic meaning. His poetry often shies away from the obvious meaning we might anticipate by sudden metaphorical twists and linguistic play.

In the course of the chapter I will not refer to many of Ashbery's poems, but rather focus on two of them, "One Hundred Multiple-Choice Questions" and *Three Poems*, which I believe speak to my overall aim, namely to problematize the notion

© Springer Nature Switzerland AG 2022
E. Schwieler, *Aporias of Translation*, Contemporary Philosophies and Theories in Education 18, https://doi.org/10.1007/978-3-030-97895-2_6

of aesthetic education. I will not give a definitive answer to how I believe aesthetic education can be developed, or provide a program for how one could structure and systematize it in a more efficient and improved way. Rather, my reflections on Ashbery's poetry and aesthetic education are meant to indicate a counter-project, in George Bataille's sense of this term, which will hopefully offer us an opening up for how we can continue to think through what in poetry and aesthetic education remain unthought.

Multiple Choice Questions as Poetry

Among his uncollected poems, published in the first volume of *Collected Poems 1956-1987* (2008), we find John Ashbery's poem "One Hundred Multiple-Choice Questions." The poem exposes, with ironic clarity, the difference between a genuine poetic experience, or rather the possible experience and insight that is opened up by poetry, and the rational force behind certain educational assessment practices. More specifically, Ashbery's poem points to the defectiveness of assessing someone's knowledge of the existential and ontological dimensions of poetry by using multiple choice questions, that is, knowledge beyond factual and lower order knowledge and skills. In the poem, Ashbery creates a tension between our urge to answer the MCQ questions and the necessity to look beyond factual correctness when reading and relating to the poem. A poem in the form of an MCQ test is thus a paradox, or a contradiction in terms, since what the poem stages is an impossible test. The questions are portrayed as having factual answers, while they on closer inspection are too complex to answer by simply choosing the letter or letters corresponding to what are supposedly the right answers. Added to this is Ashbery's ironic or humorous tone, which in a sense makes fun of the rigidity and reductive nature of MCQ tests. To give but one example of a multiple choice question and its answer choices in the poem, which relates to the theme of thinking that runs through the present study, I will quote the first question of the poem: "1. Thinking can help to solve problems because A) problems exist only in the mind B) problems must be taken seriously C) mind triumph over matter D) not to think would be to avoid the problem E) no problem can be completely solved anyway F) it is our duty to think our way out of problems" (p. 938). We could, of course, relate the answer alternatives to different kinds of knowledge and make assumptions about learning contexts in which the five answers would correspond to a specific stance toward thinking and problem solving. We could, for example, conceive of a context in which the moral obligation to think in order to solve a problem would not be completely up the wall. Similarly, there could certainly be instances where the mind-matter dichotomy in relation to thinking and problem-solving would be a feasible topic to test students on. However, this would be somewhat beyond the point of the poem, since the impossible, nonsense, and at times absurd character of the questions and answers will signal to the reader the MCQ items rather being a parodic wink to those who would be quite familiar with the form and jargon of multiple choice tests.

More importantly, perhaps, is that the MCQ's determinate form (with a question, the stem, and answer alternatives, consisting of the key(s), which is the right answer or answers, and distractors, which could be false answers or less plausible answers) functions as a verse form providing the poet with predetermined rules for composing the poem. In this sense, Ashbery is using the MCQ test as a form of poetry comparable to, for example, the sonnet, the heroic couplet, or the haiku. Ashbery's MCQ poem is, from this perspective, an experimentation with form. The form, however, is part of the content of the poetry since its language follows the idiom of the form. The paradox is that the form and language of the poem follow a strictly factual and rational discursive strain, in which poetry as commonly conceived has no place. The poem is, in other words, a clash between rational and poetic ways of thinking and representation. But what, then, is the relation between the rational and the poetic, and their respective form and content, which Ashbery stages in his poem?

Blanchot and the Significance of Poetry

The tension between the rational and the poetic is something that Maurice Blanchot (2001) broaches in his essay "Is Mallarmé's Poetry Obscure?" While attempting to answer the question his title poses, Blanchot's main focus in the essay develops into a reflection on the sense or meaning of poetry; but, as he makes clear, a poem's sense cannot be separated from neither its form, nor its language. When it comes to sense in poetry, Blanchot writes: "Those who claim that every poem has a sense and who await its revelation have a perfectly correct attitude; their mistake begins as soon as they understand the word *sense* as they would try to understand it in reference to a text concerned with exposition of rational thought" (p. 108). What is at stake is thus two different modes of discourse, rational thought and poetic thought. Poetry certainly conveys meaning and sense; it is when we begin translating poetry in an interpretation using the language of rationality that the poetic sense withdraws. However, this constitutes the necessary aporia of poetry – to make sense of poetry we are obliged to explicate it in some way, but as soon as we do, its meaning withdraws. We translate the language of poetry into the language of rationality to lay bare what the poem objectively states. But, according to Blanchot, this move is precisely what covers up and diverges from the sense of the poem. This too is what Ashbery's MCQ poem attempts to highlight, namely that the rational desire to answer the questions correctly conceals the poetic sense of the poem, or in Blanchot's words, "[t]he first reflex when faced with some lines of verse that discursive reasoning would like to elucidate is to give them another form" (p. 108). But how, then, do poetic and nonpoetic language and their relation to meaning differ? Blanchot states:

> The first characteristic of poetic meaning is that it is linked, without possible change, to the language that manifests it. In nonpoetic language we know that we have understood the idea whose presence discourse brings us when we can express it in various forms, making ourselves master of it to the point of freeing it from all determined language. On the contrary, if poetry is to be understood, it demands a total acquiescence to the unique form it proposes.

> The sense of the poem is inseparable from all the words, from all the movements, from all the accents of the poem. It exists only in this ensemble, and it disappears as soon as one seeks to separate it from the form it has taken. What the poem signifies coincides exactly with what it is. (p. 108)

This would mean that poetry is essentially untranslatable, since if the poem "coincides exactly with what it is" its rendering in another language and in other words would make it into what it is not. This is even more the case if the poem is transformed into the prose of a language of interpretation. At the same time, translation and interpretation are necessary for us to be able to approach the poem and experience the sense of it. The reader of poetry is thus faced with an insurmountable aporia, which cannot be overcome by any rational knowledge of the poetic or specific poems. Consequently, we stray from the sense of a poem if we attempt to answer the questions it raises in the fashion of nonpoetic language, such as surrendering to the desire to choose ready-made answers to Ashbery's multiple choice questions. What Ashbery's poem is corresponds to its unique form and to understand it we must, in Blanchot's words, lend "total acquiescence to the unique form it possesses." Every critique, analysis, and translation of the poem makes it other than what it is, which means that its essential sense and meaning withdraws. Blanchot stresses the uniqueness of poetry and poetic sense:

> Poetic meaning is not a matter of some generalization for which many means of expression are possible and that can be applied to a number of cases. It works only once, and it makes the system of images, symbols, and consonances that is inextricably associated with it untransferable. It belongs to the category of the Unique. It is not only that which depends essentially on language but also that which calls language back to its essence and prevents it from being confused with its intentions. (p. 109)

That a poem is "untransfereable" in effect means that it is also untranslatable, in the sense that a poem "belongs to the category of the Unique" – an experience that happens only once. Translation, in contrast, is in essence a repetition, but a repetition in the sense an allegory repeats the mythical disguised in the language of culture. Translation takes the form of allegory, just as Ashbery's poem takes the MCQ as its form. The MCQ form, then, is a form of poetry in Ashbery's case, and not a form for assessing knowledge, which means that the poem under the guise of rationality works poetically. But this uniqueness and the aporia it gives rise to is also a possibility, in that it constitutes a call to respond to the impasse between uniqueness and generality. The aporia of poetic saying urges us to respond to it and recognize in it the perfomative of a promise. To understand poetry means performing it in a way that responds to the uniqueness of its expression. If we were to analyze a poem in terms of what it has to say about education and assessment in formal educational settings, and perhaps claim that, for example, Ashbery's MCQ poem constitutes a critique and problematization of traditional assessment practices and the discrepancy between methods of assessment and the nature of poetry, would this analysis reflect what the poem essentially is, its essential sense? No, according to Blanchot; this kind of analysis would be an example of how assessment practices fail to account for the nature of poetry and poetic knowledge, but it would not say anything about the poem as such and its essence. It would be a paraphrase of the poem in a language alien to it, a rationalization of a determined exterior meaning imposed on the poem which does not correspond to what it is. It would be a restatement of the poem which, in Blanchot's words, would constitute an "exposition of rational thought" (p. 108). To analyze a poem by breaking it up and categorizing it according to its constituent parts, or relating it to social history, the poet's biography, or the ideal reader's most likely reading of it, will certainly result in an understanding of the poem, its conditions and social significance. But, will it yield what the poem in essence is? Will we learn about what Blanchot calls the poem's uniqueness? Blanchot would answer that we do not. So, then what is the essential sense of poetry, of a unique poem as such? Blanchot:

> Poetry thus suggests a sense whose structure is unique to it. Whereas rational signification implies an idea that can be detached from words, which even denies all importance to words and which, apart from them, assures intelligibility and understanding between beings, poetic signification is that which cannot be separated from words, that which makes each word important and that reveals itself in the fact or the illusion that language has an essential reality, a fundamental mission: to establish things by and in the word. (pp. 109–110)

We are here reminded of Walter Benjamin's notion of language and his invocation of the paradox of λόγος,[1] that is, the word's simultaneous performative and constative nature, to use J. L. Austin's vocabulary.[2] While rational discourse transforms poetry into a different form under the aegis of making it more understandable, treating poetry as being sprung out of rationality and logical reason, poetic sense as such, on the contrary and as Blanchot conceives of it, performs itself into existence while it at the same time describes this process. As such, it cannot be severed from its form and its words, but exists only because of them and through them. It is in this way, in its aporia of translation, that poetry stages and performs what it means, which, Blanchot suggests, tells us something about existence – human as well as poetic existence:

> And one understands a poem not when one grasps its thoughts nor even when one formulates its complex relationships but when one is led by it to the mode of existence that it signifies, provoked to a certain tension, exaltation, or destruction, led to a world whose logical content is only one element. One could say that poetic meaning has to do with existence itself, that it is the understanding of the situation of man, that it calls what he is into question. (p. 110)

Of the sense of poetry and poetic meaning, what Ashbery's MCQ poem teaches us, and so what we can learn from it, is not, first and foremost, about the experimentation of poetic form, or the inadequacy of MCQ assessment methods to capture and measure a person's knowledge of some aspect of poetry, but, rather, it reveals "existence itself" so that we more deeply, hopefully, can come to understand "the

---

[1] See Chap. 4 of the present study.

[2] In *How to Do Things with Words*, based on his William James Lectures given in 1955 at Harvard University, Austin developed his Speech Act Theory, which differentiates between performative and constative utterances. A performative utterance performs an act rather than describes it (for example "I do" when uttered in a marriage ceremony); a constative utterance, in contrast, describes the world (for example "The sky is blue"). See Austin (1962).

situation of man." And the poem does this by the performative nature of its words and their inseparable relation to its form; it calls our existence into question, and our responsibility is to answer this call in its uniqueness. Only then can we take a step closer to learn the (non)sense – *pas-de-sens* – of the poem.

Catachresis: Poetry, Aesthetic Education, and the Double Bind

This way of approaching poetry, and by extension the experience and learning of poetry, is other than the assignment of meaning to situations external to poetry, as well as art generally, which we find in critical theory and also in, what is called, aesthetic education. In these discourses we find how poetry and art are used to explain or exemplify a social or pedagogical situation, condition, or position. As Alison Ross notes in *The Aesthetic Paths of Philosophy: Presentation in Kant, Heidegger, Lacoue-Labarthe, and Nancy*:

> In critical theory, 'art' is often used to bestow meaning, in the emphatic sense of this term, on social life, perspectives, and practices. In general, the significance of art relates to the role art is given as a vehicle of insight into prevailing social relations. The 'referential ideality' of artworks here meets a pressing need of social criticism that would not otherwise be had. (Note 2, p. 216).

In critical theory, as in aesthetic education, art functions as, in Ross's words, a "vehicle of insight," which is to say that art transfers and translates an ideal of social reality. Art is made to function as a trope that highlights and reveals the state of affairs in society; art is considered a metaphor which elucidates and exposes social, cultural, and also educational conditions. Art as a "vehicle of insight" presupposes that the work of art is given a specific meaning. We have, then, the prescription of meaning that Blanchot pointed to in rational, scientific discourse, and the urge to "bestow meaning" that Ross highlights in critical theory. This bestowing of meaning is also, as noted, present in aesthetic education. To give an example of this common practice within education we can refer to a noteworthy text by Adrienne Pickett on Hannah Arendt's response to the photographs depicting the Little Rock Crisis in 1957, "Images, Dialogue, and Aesthetic Education: Arendt's Response to the Little Rock Crisis":

> To cultivate a disposition of wide-awakeness, openness to difference, and an enlivened social imagination in aesthetic education, we begin by perceiving works of art, engaging them experientially and in dialogue with others whose experiences with art differ from ours. When we participate in this kind of aesthetic education, the hope is that our experiences with art will change the way we see and live in the world and relate to the people in it, as we aspire to improve the human condition overall. (p. 196)

Pickett argues that art, in aesthetic education, has the potential to develop students into enlightened and empathic human beings, who strive to "improve the human condition overall." But for this to happen art must first be "bestow[ed] with meaning," which is to say that it must be interpreted in a way that corresponds to the aims and goals of education, which might be to, for example, develop democratic citizens. There is, then, given what Blanchot and Ross maintain, a confusion of what art "is" and what art can be translated to mean. Certainly, art can be used as a vehicle to convey a predetermined ethical stance or ideological preference. Thus, Pickett's notion of art as an educational tool goes by way of a preconceived idea of what the work of art means, its "referential ideality," which Ross mentions, and it relies on the art work to, by way of metaphorical transfer, translate a certain ethical or ideological principle.

This stance is further problematized by Gayatri Spivak (2012) in her dense and demanding introduction to her collection of essays titled *An Aesthetic Education in the Era of Globalization*. In the introduction she deals with aesthetic education from the perspective of the double bind, which she defines as "learning to live with contradictory instructions" (p. 3), and indeed designates translation as a double bind. Her introduction, Spivak continues, "traces a Kant-Schiller-Marx-de Man trajectory, where the European proper names are metonyms of epochal changes" (p. 39). I will not go into detail about this trajectory, but focus on what Spivak means by double bind and its relation to another notion she frequently makes use of, namely "ab-use," and their relation to aesthetic education. Some of the double binds that Spivak mentions are those between class and race, self and other, mind and body, action and thinking, the sensual and the rational, and between practical and pure reason. These are double binds that problematize the binary opposites which, by way of the Enlightenment, structure the idea of the aesthetical, ethical, as well as the rational. Now, for Spivak, it is not a question of overcoming, solving or resolving, the double binds, but to learn to accept and endure them, and more importantly to expose their creative performative power. To accept and endure a double bind is not to resign and concede to its impossibility; rather, it is a move to consider that for which there is no, and cannot be any, evidence or proof. It is learning the truth from the untrue, that is, untrue if we assume that, for example, a work of art is not a constative statement about truth or of a determined truth, but always a probing of what is not yet truth or what might, under certain conditions, be true.[3] In other words, the

---

[3] This idea of poetic truth goes back at least to Aristotle's (1997) *Poetics*, for example when he states: "It is clear too from what has been said that the poet's business is to tell not what is happening but the sort of things that might [be expected to] happen – things that, according to likelihood and necessity, can [happen]. For the distinction between the historian and the poet is not whether they give their accounts in verse or prose (for it would be possible for Herodotus's work to be put into verses and it would be no less a kind of history in verse than [it is] without verses). [No,] the [real] difference is this: that the one [i.e. the historian] tells what happened, the other [i.e., the poet] [tells] the sort of things that can happen. That's why in fact poetry is a more speculative and more 'serious' business than history: for poetry deals more with universals, history with particulars" (1451a 37-40-1451b1-8, p. 81). As Butcher (1920) states in his classic interpretation of Aristorle's *Poetics*: "The world of poetry, it is said, presents not facts but fiction: such things have never happened, such beings have never lived. 'Untrue' (οὐκ ἀληθῆ) 'impossible' (αδύνατα), said the detractors of poetry in Aristotle's day: 'these creations are not real, not true to life.' 'Not real,' replies Aristotle, 'but a higher reality' (ἀλλὰ βέλτιον), 'what ought to be (ὡς δεῖ), not what is.' Poetry, he means to say, is not concerned with fact, but with what transcends fact; it represents things which are not, and never can be in actual experience; it gives us the 'ought to be'; the form

double bind is an epistemology of art, an education in aesthetics – an aesthetic education – in which the rational and ethical are never denied, but continuously questioned by the force of aporia or double bind. It is in this context that Spivak comes to employ the notion "ab-use," which with its prefix "ab" signals, as she notes, "below," "motion away," "agency, point of origin," "supporting," and "the duties of slaves" (pp. 3–4). To ab-use, as Spivak uses the word, is to turn something against itself, to confront something by both acknowledging its strongest points while using these points to move away and create something other – what I have, in previous chapters, called *Auseinandersetzung*, or deconstruction. What is more, an aspect of ab-use, not mentioned by Spivak, is its relation to the Latin rhetorical trope *abusio* and its translation of the Greek κατάχρησις (*katakhresis*), used in rhetoric for the misuse of a word or trope. The relationship between catachresis and metaphor is, however, more complex than taking catachresis as merely being the misuse, and metaphor as the proper use, of a word or trope. As Patricia Parker (1990) shows, in her essay "Metaphor and Catachresis," the relationship between metaphor and catachresis is portrayed, throughout the history of rhetoric, as one between need and necessity (catachresis) on the one hand, and one of abundance and freedom (metaphor) on the other hand. The partition of the two terms also takes on the character of an opposition between the barbaric and foreign and the refined and familiar, the unconscious and the conscious. It is a question, Parker notes, of an economy of tropes, remembering the etymology of the word economy as stemming from οἶκος (*oikos*), the family home or dwelling, that is, a familiar and friendly abode, as opposed to the strange, other, and unknown (barbaric). These characterizations of catachresis and metaphor stem from the basic definition of the two terms which she traces back to Quintilian. Thus, taking her departure in Quintilian's definitions of metaphor and catachresis in his *Institutio oratoria*, Parker unravels the history of the concepts and the recurring blurring of the boundaries between the two, especially how metaphor cannot avoid taking on the characteristics of what is supposed to differentiate it from catachresis. Accordingly, Quintilian (1959) defines catachresis as "the practice of adapting the nearest available term to describe something for which no actual term exists" (p. 320). Hence, as Parker explains:

> The lack of an original proper term – the lexical gap or lacuna – is in this passage the clear basis for Quintilian's distinction between catachresis, or *abusio*, and metaphor, or *translatio*: catachresis is a transfer of terms from one place to another employed when no proper word exists, while metaphor is a transfer or substitution employed when a proper term does already exist and is displaced by a term transferred from another place to a place not its own. (p. 60)

Catachresis is thus a trope that functions as a supplement at the origin – there is no word which it translates, but rather it provides an approximation for that which cannot be expressed, since there is no original word or term for it. It signifies the

---

that answers to the true idea. The characters of Sophocles, the ideal forms of Zeuxis, are unreal only in the sense that they surpass reality. They are not untrue to the principles of nature or to her ideal tendencies" (pp. 167–168). As we will see, this "ought to be" comes back in Kant as "as if [*als ob*]."

nonsense or *pas-de-sens*, which Derrida mentions in his reading of Benjamin's essay "The Task of the Translator."[4] Catachresis is the tomb of meaning, out of which meaning nevertheless is born; and it signifies only by way of approximation, as a translation that originates as translation, as if it were the origin of language.

Now, having addressed Blanchot's insistence on the uniqueness of poetic meaning, by way of aesthetic education and Spivak's double bind, to the lacuna of catachresis, I would like to move on to consider Johan Ashbery's *Three Poems*, and then conclude with a reconsideration of aesthetic education. Hence, as an introductory observation, Ashbery's purpose in *Three Poems*, is to pose two possible answers to the lacuna of catachresis which the poem works to fill: to put it all down or leave everything out. This is what Ashbery stages in his poetry as the aporia of the "experience of experience"[5] and, as we will become clear, it is also what is at stake in his prose poem *Three Poems*. Just as aesthetic education is caught in a double bind, or founding catachresis, so is the notion of a prose poem, particularly in the version which Ahbery gives it in *Three Poems*. Consequently, what Ashbery's poem sets out to explore is the limits of poetry and poetic experience, precisely by acknowledging, although tacitly, the aporia of the double bind connecting poetry and experience, aesthetics and education. We could call it an ab-use, an erring attempt to understand experience and its translation into poetry, in which sense and meaning are secondary to the searching movement of the words filling the pages that make up the poem. The aporia of translation is, furthermore, if not a necessity, then at least a possibility for how we might attempt a reading of *Three Poems* as a self-exploratory text.

Ashbery's *Three Poems* and Aesthetic Education

John Ashbery's method of writing in *Three Poems* has been termed "translative" by Stephen Fredman (1990) in his study of the prose poem, titled *Poet's Prose: The Crisis in American Verse*. With "translative" Fredman refers to the difference

---

[4] In the essay "White Mythology," Derrida conducts a reading of metaphor and catachresis which centers on the foundational catachresis of philosophical and scientific language. His reading of metaphor and catachresis takes its departure in Pierre Fontanier's *Figures of Discourse* with the aim to deconstruct the presupposed meaning that philosophical language has to assume, "the already-there of a meaning" (p. 257), which philosophy then attempts to reveal, uncover, bring to light, as truth – a meaning which, Derrida shows, relies on catachresis. Philosophical language turns out to be, in Derrida's words "a system of catachreses" (p. 257) rather than a revelation of meaning as truth. As I will argue in what follows, the same tropological, or "translative," aporia is to be found in in Ashbery's *Three Poems* and its relation to aesthetic education.

[5] In an interview with Alfred Poulin (1981), Ashbery expressly mentions this phrase to describe his poetry: "I mean it doesn't particularly matter about the experience; the movement of experiencing is what I'm trying to get down. [...] Most of my poems are about the experience of experience. As I said before, the particular occasion is of lesser interest to me than the way a happening or experience filters through to me. I believe this is the way in which it happens with most people. I'm trying to set down a generalized transcript of what's really going on in our minds all day long" (p. 245).

between the intention of the poet and the intention of the translator that Walter Benjamin identifies in "The Task of the Translator": "The intention of the poet is spontaneous, primary, graphic; that of the translator is derivative, ultimate, ideational" (*Illuminations*, pp. 76–77). Ashbery, in *Three Poems*, Fredman contends, employs a method which is more similar to the translator's than the poet's, hence the designation "translative" to denote Ashbery's writing style in these prose poems: "John Ashbery, as a poet, leans heavily toward the translative half of Benjamin's distinction, especially in the prose of *Three Poems*" (p. 106), that is, they should be characterized as, in Benjamin's words, "derivative, ultimate, ideational." The characterization of Ashbery's *Three Poems* as translational thus presents us with an aporetic double bind in Spivak's sense. Friedman formulates this aporia in a manner we should recognize by now. Speaking of Ashbery's aim with *Three Poems*, Friedman states: "This attempt to present unmediated experience ultimately comes up against the bounds of the medium used for presentation. Language, for instance, will always convey to us an experience structured by its own characteristic means: No work of writing can evade its status as writing and reach us as mere reality" (p. 103). Writing, it is implied, always changes the experience it wants to express, so that the poet always represents what he or she wants to present, and is constrained by, in Friedman's words, "the impossible goal of total mimesis" (p. 103). Ashbery's poem is, in consequence, related to translation in an essential way; and, once again, we are faced with the aporia of translation, just as we were when considering the death of education in Bernhard, the paradox of Λόγος in Benjamin, the double bind in Spivak, and renouncing in Heidegger. To be more precise, poetry is *translatio* as κατάχρησις, that which is the beginning of language, where the aporia of κατάχρησις is *abusio*, the false or untrue word for what cannot be said, or rather that for which there is no word.

This is also the manner in which poetry turns toward the didactical, that is, it attempts to fill the space where there is a lack of knowledge; accordingly, education as poetry begins in catachresis. It is with this situation that Ashbery's *Three Poems* begins: It begins by staging the catachresis of self-exploration as the educational journey of poetry and experience: "I thought that if I could put it all down, that would be one way. And the next thought came to me that to leave all out would be another, and truer, way" (p. 247). The poem starts with two impossible extremes: absolute knowledge as excess or nothingness, and it does so as a response to the aporia of origin, that is to say, the discrepancy, or rather difference, which situates itself as the catachrestic origin of the poem, which is manifested in the tension between language and experience. *Three Poems* sets out to explore, and so to negotiate, the challenge that consists in the possibility of poetry and experience, respectively, namely what can be expressed and what can be learned. Its beginning is a reflection on poetry as such, a poetry on poetry; in other words, a poetics. What is of special interest, if we want to investigate both its metaphysical and educational implications, is the "I" and the "it" of the quoted passage. For the "I" to be able to put "it" down, the "I" and the "it" must stand in a special relationship, i.e. as mutually implied, when it comes to their enunciating force. The "it" must be able to express the "I," while the "I" must know what the "it" is able to express. This is what the first sentence of the poem circles around in order to express the "I" and the "it" in a new way, which is also signaled in the title of the first of the three poems: "The new spirit." Ashbery's project, in *Three Poems*, is a project that ends up working against itself, toward its own disintegration. In other words, it ends up in paradox or, better, aporia, an unresolved attempt to know, to understand and gain knowledge about "it" that is the project, the poetry, and the self which is the "I."

This situation, as the point of departure of *Three Poems*, relates to what Stephen Fredman (1990) terms "not-understanding" in Ashbery's poetry (pp 108–109). And, based on Fredman's notion of not-understanding I would like to suggest a complementing conceptualization of what is at stake in Ashbery's poem, namely Bataille's notion "nonknowledge." This concept introduces ideas of experience and education, which are notions that relates in important ways to my reading of Ashbery's *Three Poems*. Although Fredman's idea of not-understanding points to some interesting correspondences with what can be said to be the motivating force in Ashebery's poem, I believe that Bataille's idea of nonknowledge can be seen to add to Fredman's idea of not-understanding, first of all because Ashbery's poem is not, at least not primarily, concerned with understanding as such, but rather with knowledge, what we can know and so experience and express. Thus, as we will see, Bataille's development of what he calls "inner experience" and nonknowledge, together with the grounding paradox which Bataille identifies as governing his thinking, namely the critique of what he calls "the project," which he conceives of as a mode of subjectivity,[6] come closer to Ashbery's *Three Poems* than Fredman's not-understanding does, although his analysis of Ashbery by centering on not-understanding, pure language, translation, experience, and reality provide critical insights into Ashbery's *Three Poems*. Hence, before taking on Bataille and Ashbery, an elucidation of Fredman's notion not-understanding is necessary.

Fredman suggests that not-understanding is a mental state that we can strive to realize when reading or writing:

> Not-understanding is a positive experience available to translators, writers, readers, or anyone involved in a complex hermeneutic experience. Not-understanding of this sort is a

---

[6] I will come back to the "project" in Bataille when exploring the notion of non-knowledge. However, an indication of what Bataille means by "project" is in order. Ben Brewer (2013) provides a lucid explanation of the notion in his essay "Unsaying Non-Knowledge: Georges Bataille and the Mysticism of Writing": "Project, broadly speaking, is a mode of being-in-the-world in which we experience the world and the things that populate it as distinct from ourselves and as defined by their use. The division of the subject and the object introduced by project degrades the object by making it valuable only to some higher end, and degrades the subject. In entering the world of project, the subject 'puts off existence' indefinitely (*Inner Experience* 46). The present becomes valuable only insofar as it is relatable to a future to come. Thus, to live in project, for Bataille, is 'not to die but to be dead' (46). In response to this, Bataille attempts a performative writing capable of *enacting*, rather than describing, a unification of subject and object. He does this by bringing the reader to maddening experiences of aporia that call into question the apparatus of discursive reason and that provide an opening for the unification of subject and object. In this way, Bataille radically undermines the classic conception of what it means to do ethics or to act ethically and undertakes a writing that would not just describe, but would perform, enact, and breathe" (pp. 116–117).

pleasurable, relaxed, and receptive state (what Ashbery calls the delicious sensation of drowning) in which a feeling of strangeness or mystery hints that certain ineffable thoughts or connections may be possible. It is a prelude to a new understanding. This state occurs in relation to language, whether spoken, written, or about to be composed; around the language hovers a kind of aura that we invest with unexpressed feelings, desires, or insights, hoping that they may find form in this language. It is always possible for this to take place if we allow ourselves to dwell in not-understanding. (p. 108)

What Fredman indicates is that not-understanding is a state before which poetic or hermeneutic meaning is articulated, an experience that can be made with language which gives rise to a sense of the inexpressible, it is an emotive sensation beyond or rather prefiguring the discursive structuring of language into meaning. And, importantly, Fredman holds, this state of being, comparable (perhaps) to a meditative state, is a way to engage with pure language; that is, the poet, translator, reader, or person engaged in a hermeneutical activity, who achieves a state of not-understanding, is able to translate the ineffable into a new understanding – the new spirit. As Fredman asserts: "The state of not-understanding is available any time we trust in a meaning beyond our present understanding, and it manifests as an aura around language" (p. 108). However, while Fredman maintains that we are still within the dimension of meaning, I would suggest, with Blanchot (as discussed above) and Bataille (discussed in what follows), that even a "meaning beyond our present understanding" still belongs to the rational order of the sentence, the teleological promise of discursive unity, full understanding, and absolute knowledge. There is a will to understand at work in Fredman's reading of Ashbery which, I suggest, is undermined by Ashbery's *Three Poems*. Not only is this will to understand present in Fredman's own reading, but he also asserts this will to understand in Ashbery, so that the poem's meaning falls into place while the meaning extracted from it is precisely the deconstruction of meaning. In other words, on Fredman's view, the poem does not enact a deconstruction of meaning, but rather describes it.

Thus, Fredman finds in Ashbery's text a recuperation of meaning and understanding in which pure language manifests itself as an object disclosed to a subject: "When one relaxes one's quest for the unachievable goal of absolute understanding [...], the pure language that hides in not-understanding becomes available again" (p. 125). Even though one could argue that Fredman does recognize the unattainability of absolute understanding, the promise of pure language is still the motivating force that he finds in Ashbery's poem. His qualification of pure language as a possibility for understanding reads as a poetics of mimesis with didactic or educational nuances: "If art were to move [too] close to life, it would lose its redemptive power, its ability to promote understanding, to frame questions for evaluation" (pp. 125–126). To put it differently, Fredman finds in Ashbery's poem a fundamental discrepancy between poetry and reality, since if art and life or reality were to coincide we would not be able to differentiate neither the ethical, nor the aesthetic, from our lived experience; there would be no ethics and no aesthetics, and we could not, as Kant insists, rely on the "as if" (*als ob*)[7] to make judgments about ethical or aesthetic matters. We could not, Feldman seems to argue, relate the aesthetic to the real, or the ethical to the rational, if aesthetics and ethics coincide with the empirical. Ashbery's poem, in consequence, ends up as a *Bildungs* narrative, in the manner of Hegel's *Phenomenology of Spirit*, in which the educational journey is infinite, but still has a final outcome as the ultimate goal.

Admittedly, Ashbery's *Three Poems* could be read as such an educational journey, an exploration of the limits of knowledge and understanding, of the intricate relationship between reality and experience, life and poetry, with the poem describing the journey without enacting it, but still ending in triumph, its goal achieved, the subject comes to dominate its object, the reader mastering the text, the learner passing the exam in his or her program of aesthetic education. *Three Poems* would be a didactic poem teaching us how to come to terms with its content, no matter how

---

[7] As Eva Scharper (1964–1965) explains in her essay "The Kantian 'As-If' and Its Relevance for Aesthetics": "In Section 45 [of the *Critique of Aesthetic Judgement*] Kant states: 'Nature was beautiful when it appeared as art; and art can only be called beautiful when we are conscious of its being art whilst it yet appears to us as if it were nature'. Here Kant's aesthetic key term, 'beautiful', indicates the fundamental requirement for an aesthetic object: that it must appear. Natural objects must appear *as if* wrought by art, art objects *as if* produced by nature; yet in both cases we know that this is only an appearance" (p. 229). When it comes to ethics, the "as if" relates to Kant's categorical imperative of duty. As Kant (2011) states in the *Groundwork of the Metaphysics of Morals*: "[A]ct only according to that maxim through which you can at the same time will that it become a universal law" (p. 71), a statement, however, which he says can be rephrased: "Since the universality of the law according to which effects happen constitutes that which is actually called nature in the most general sense (according to its form), i.e. the existence of things insofar as it is determined according to universal laws, the universal imperative of duty [*Pflicht*] could also be expressed as follows: *so act as if the maxim of your action were to become by your will a* UNIVERSAL LAW OF NATURE [handle so, als ob die Maxime deine Handlung durch deinen Willen zum ALLGEMEINEN NATURGESETZE werden sollte" (pp. 71; 70). As a final, but important, comment about the notion of "as if," it should be noted that it is prominent in Jacques Derrida's later work, perhaps most succinctly in the essay "The University Without Condition" (2002a), where Derrida addresses the "as if" in relation to Kant, the university, and the future of the Humanities. Derrida suggests that any discourse that aspires to truth, whether in the sciences or the humanities, introduces knowingly or unknowingly the modality of an "as if" into the logic of its presentation. Derrida (2002b) calls this, in "Typewriter Ribbons: Limited Ink 2," a "supplement of fiction" (p. 82). This supplement of the "as if" makes the propositions of discourse, truth, reason, logic, etc., happen and take place, it is an event. However, as Derrida (2002a) states in "The University Without Condition": "As long as I can produce and determine an event by a performative act guaranteed, like any performative, by conventions, legitimate fictions, and a certain 'as if', then, to be sure, I will not say that nothing happens or comes about, but I will say that what takes place, arrives, happens, or happens *to me* remains still controllable and programmable within a horizon of anticipation or precomprehension, within a *horizon*, period. [...] Which is to say that this event takes place only where it does not allow itself to be domesticated by any 'as if', or at least by any 'as if' that can already be read, decoded, or articulated as such. So that this small word, the 'as' of the 'as if' as well as the 'as' of the 'as such' – whose authority founds and justifies every ontology as well as every phenomenology, every philosophy as science or knowledge – this small word, 'as', might well be the name of the true problem, not to say the target, of deconstruction" (pp. 233–234). The relevance of Derrida's deconstruction of the "as if" to my reading of both Ashbery and Bataille will be addressed in what follows.

difficult its form, regardless of its traps and pitfalls. This is, undeniably, a convincing reading of the poem. But, I would like to ask, could it not be read otherwise? To counter Fredman's reading, we could begin by considering the presentation of the pome's major theme, which is basically made up of the question: All or nothing? The catachresis at the origin, which, as we know, means that what is "left out" or even absent from the outset is always, sooner or later, filled with prattle, or as Ashbery (2008) has it, when you leave things out "something soon comes to stand in their place" (p. 247). And he goes on to pursue the dream of the new spirit as "the last chance to escape the ball / of contradictions" (p.247). In doing so he invokes the law of reason to tackle the confusion of silence: "It is the law to think now. To think becomes the law. [...] We must drink the confusion, sample that other, concerted, dark effort that pushes not to the light, but toward a draft of dank clammy air" (p. 247). Thus, Ashbery's first move seems to be to attempt to fill the pages with the light of reason in order to break "through into the meaning of the tomb" (pp. 247–248). The absence of meaning is, in other words, the grave of reason, knowledge, and understanding. However, this call to action in the name of reason remains a call, a slogan, without a clear idea of how to accomplish it and heed its call: "But the act is still proposed, before us / it needs pronouncing. To formulate oneself around this hollow, empty sphere" (p. 248). To fill the "hollow, empty sphere" the poet must formulate and pronounce, that is to say, express and communicate experiences, old and new, in a systematic way – the new spirit needs a system. However, and to rush ahead into the second poem, "The System," with its foreshadowing first line: "The system was breaking down" (p. 280). And finally, to jump to the third poem, "The Recital," where the attempt to discover, uncover, create, or more precisely, *enact* the new spirit ends in bathos. Thus, in the very last sentence of *Three Poems*, Ashbery likens his effort to a play or reading by stating: "The performance had ended, the audience streamed out; the applause still echoed in the empty hall. But the idea of the spectacle as something to be acted out and absorbed still hung in the air long after the last spectator had gone home to sleep" (p. 326). In this last sentence we have a telling example of the "as if" that supposedly works to make judgment possible and differentiate between reality and fiction, experience and poetry. Ashbery stages the poem *as if* it were presented at a recital, as the title of the third poem signals, or as Ashbery has it in the last sentence, performance or spectacle, which ends on a note that leaves the audience with a sense of the recital being unfinished, that the experience of the poem still needed to be enacted to be understood. The poem, already an "as if" in itself, stages another "as if" to express its conclusion, the conclusion being that the new spirit has not been actualized or enacted, that its system broke down, since the system in itself was that which had to be overcome. Consequently, instead of the translative "as if" that would supposedly bring us in touch with pure language through not-understanding, which Fredman suggests is the success of *Three Poems*, we must conclude with Ashbery that this is exactly what makes the systematicity of the poem break down, ending in an "as if" *en abyme*.

How, then, can we approach the important themes that Fredman nevertheless and rightly identifies in the poem, which also include themes I am concerned with in this study, namely its searching, exploring educational trajectory; its scrutiny of understanding and knowledge; and its attempt to pose the challenge of all-inclusiveness against emptiness; in short, its attempt at a poetic enactment of the experience of experience? I would suggest that instead of following in Hegel's footsteps in *The Phenomenology of Spirit*, the educational journey staged in *Three Poems* is more akin to Bataille's project, as a project against itself, a counter-project to which I will now turn. As noted, the opening of *Three Poems* broaches two important themes that guide the poem throughout: 1) To endeavor a poetic work which is encyclopedic and all-inclusive or strives toward the nihility of absolute ellipsis; and 2) the place, function and poetic consequence of the "I" and the "it," the subject and the object. These two themes together with the prominent topics of knowledge and understanding, experience and reality of and in poetry, work to enact the poetry as an event. However, as I want to suggest, this project, which Ashbery calls the new spirit, just like Bataille's project, is a counter-project that turns against itself. And it does so by turning toward nonknowledge. Accordingly, the journey of exploration, with its aim of discovering, in the mode of "pure finding" (*reines finden*) that Heidegger mentions, the pure language (*reine Sprache*) we find discussed in Benjamin, this journey can only succeed by failing. In fact, it is a lost cause from the outset. The endeavor to "put it all down" competing with the struggle to "leave all out" in the end signify the same thing, the silence of death. Or as Bataille (2001) has it in his lecture notes titled "The Teaching of Death": "The search for the most perfect silence, the search that actually takes place, the search for what approaches the maximum silence" (p. 123) is the search for the silence of death. The silence of death, in Bataille's lecture, more precisely, denotes what he calls "the death of thought," which in turn is the essence of nonknowledge. "Death can teach us nothing," Bataille says, because we cannot have an experience of death. However, the death of thought gives rise to what Bataille calls "the sovereign moment," a concept which is most fully developed in Bataille's work *The Accursed Share*. The instant of the sovereign moment is the nonknowledge that disrupts a project as work or utility. Bataille likens the sovereign moment to the death of thought which we experience in, for example, ecstasy, intoxication, laughter, and, importantly, poetry. "The sovereign individual," Bataille (1991) states in *Inner Experience*, "consumes and doesn't labor, whereas at the antipodes of sovereignty the slave and the man without means labor and reduce their consumption to the necessities, to the products without which they could neither subsist nor labor (p. 198). Thus, "we may call sovereign the enjoyment of possibilities that utility doesn't justify (utility being that whose end is productive activity). Life beyond utility is the domain of sovereignty" (p. 198). It is in this light we must understand what Bataille means by "project," that is, as part of what Bataille calls work or labor. Moreover, Bataille differentiates between project-oriented writing and necessary writing. As Stuart Kendall writes in his introduction to *The Unfinished System of Nonknowledge*:

In his preface to *Inner Experience*,[8] Bataille distinguishes between project-oriented writing and necessary writing: "The only part of this book written out of necessity – in accordance with my life – are the second, *Torture*, and the last [the poetry]. I wrote the others with the laudable concern of writing a book" (xxxi; translation modified). He returns to this same distinction again and again, always admitting the inevitability of project-oriented thought, of system building, yet always valorizing another necessity. "Project is the prison from which I wish to escape (project, discursive experience): I formed the project to escape the project! (59). The project, then, "the laudable concern of writing a book," is set in motion against itself. The book, written against itself, sets out to describe an experience (torture), an experience that eludes all attempts at its designation. Like the tragic hero, the project is doomed from the beginning. This demonstration of the failure of all designation is the central movement and paradox of Bataille's oeuvre. (xxiv–xxv)

Keeping in mind the concept of the sovereign, and Kendall's account of Bataille's notion of project-oriented and necessary writing, we begin to discern the similarities between Ashbery's proposition of a project for a poetic system resulting in the new spirit and Bataille's project as a project against itself.

In Bataille, there is no "pure language" and no "not-understanding," but rather the disruption of communication and meaning, system and convention, translation and method. Correspondingly, in Ashbery's *Three Poems*, there is, in the end, no pure language to be found, not even by adhering to translative not-understanding, since the "as if," the fictionalization of discourse, breaks down in Ashbery's poem; in fact, just as with Bataille's project, Ashbery's poetics in *Three Poems* is from the beginning destined to fail. To fail, in this context, is not something altogether negative, but rather a necessity, since the counter-project Bataille engages in works to interrupt the movement toward completion, which means that the success of his project, paradoxically enough, is its fall into crisis. His project is thus governed by the double bind that Spivak mentions, or the aporia, which is one of the main themes of the present study. What we encounter in *Three Poems*, then, is a necessary project of translation – the experience of experience – which is a translation that inevitably fails, as all translations in one way or another arguably do, since they must come to terms with the silence, pause, absence, or catachresis of the original. *Three Poems* is the staging of the "I" and the "it," which dissolves in, what Bataille calls, moments of sovereignty, which are instants that cannot be predicted or accounted for, since they occur as the death of thought. The subject's definition, description, analysis, explanation, and subsequent determination of the object is the unavoidable outcome of Ashbery's poem, while it at the same time sets out to interrupt and disrupt such movements. The nonknowledge in which the subject and the object merge is the sovereign moments of aporia that the poem not only describes and performs, but also that which happens in the poem and because of the poem despite itself. There is no system or method, no path, leading to the "meaning of the tomb," since those sovereign moments of nonknowledge keep silent, they don't arrive (as Derrida would say) to the "I," the subject, since they cannot be posed, "put down," as objects neither of poetry, nor teaching, nor learning. They remain as inaccessible as death.

---

[8] Kendall quotes from the following translation: Bataille, G. (1988). *Inner Experience* (L. A. Boldt, Trans.). Albany: State University of New York Press.

The teaching of death, as Bataille notes, is impossible, and so is, if we follow Bataille, the sovereign moment of education, since any type study, whether as a noun or a verb, must be considered a "productive activity" in Bataille's sense, and so functions as work or labor. To come closer to understanding what this moment, happening, or event consists in I would like to return to the modality of the "as if." I will expand the already quoted passage from Derrida's (2002a) "The University Without Condition":

> That which happens, takes place, comes about in general, that which is called event, what is it? Can one ask with regard to it: "What is it?" It must not only surprise the constative and propositional mode of the language of knowledge (S is P), but also no longer let itself be commanded by the performative speech act of a subject. As long as I can produce and determine an event by a performative act guaranteed, like any performative, by conventions, legitimate fictions, and a certain "as if," then, to be sure, I will not say that nothing happens or comes about, but I will say that what takes place, arrives, happens, or happens to me remains still controllable and programmable within a horizon of anticipation or precomprehension, within a *horizon*, period. It is of the order of the masterable possible, it is the unfolding of what is already possible. It is of the order of power, of the "I can," "I may," or "I am empowered to . . ." No surprise, thus no event in the strong sense.
>
> Which is as much as to say that, to this extent at least, it does not happen, it does not come about, or, as I would say in French: *cela n'arrive pas*, it does not arrive. If there is any, if there is such a thing, the pure singular eventness of *what* arrives or of *who* arrives and arrives *to me* (which is what I call the *arrivant*), it would suppose an *irruption* that punctures the horizon, *interrupting* any performative organization, any convention, or any context that can be dominated by a conventionality. Which is to say that this event takes place only where it does not allow itself to be domesticated by any "as if," or at least by any "as if" that can already be read, decoded, or articulated *as such*. (pp. 233–234.)

In terms of Ashbery's *Three Poem*, that "it," which does not reveal itself is in the poem described in a constative manner, precisely as that which eludes knowledge, that which does not present itself to us neither as a constative, nor a performative expression. We find this in a passage where the poet describes how he senses the pressure of silence weigh down on him, waiting for him to "say the word," and how his beloved is also waiting for him to say it, but he finds himself unable to express what this word is that also waits for him to say it, and he starts "talking about extraneous matters." But then:

> Suddenly you realize that you have been talking for a long time without listening to yourself; you must have said *it* a long way back without knowing it, for everything in the room has fallen back into its familiar place, only this time organized according to the invisible guidelines that radiate out from both of you like the laws governing a kingdom. [...] And the word that everything hinged on is buried back there; by a mutual consent neither of you examined it when it was pronounced and rushed to its final resting place. It is doing the organizing, the guidelines radiate from its control; therefore it is good not to know what it is since its results can be known so intimately, appreciated for what they are; it is best then that the buried word remain buried for we were intended to appreciate only its fruits and not the secret principle activating them – to know this would be to know too much" (p. 310).

Perhaps this is as close we get to an explanation of the event, or in Bataille's language, a sovereign moment. However, this moment or event is unteachable, it belongs to the (ir)responsibility of teaching (which I will address in the next chapter), a teaching that teaches nothing. The sovereign moment comes or arrives when the "performative organization" of teaching is interrupted, a moment that we perhaps do not even notice before it is past, and we only took notice of it because its silence affected us, that is, its not being there. This unknown and silent event sets us, teachers and students, in a certain way, on a certain path, giving us a method, a system, to begin translating what can never be presented as such, that is, as an "unfolding of what is already possible," to use Derrida's words.

Conclusion: Reconsidering Aesthetic Education

To conclude, I wish to briefly address John Stuart Mill's (1981) idea of an Art of Life, as it is developed in his *A System of Logic*, since Mill's philosophy of aesthetics can shed some light on the foundation of aesthetic education as a teleological pursuit, that is, its purpose of developing character.[9] As Colin Heydt (2006) states in *Rethinking Mill's Ethics: Character and Aesthetic Education*:

> Mill divides education into three varieties: intellectual, moral and aesthetic. Intellectual education covers cognitive development. Moral education, which occasionally overlaps with the aesthetic, promotes feelings of duty, i.e. the development of conscience. Aesthetic education is 'the education of the feelings, and the cultivation of the beautiful', which amounts to the development of dispositions of feeling and of imagination. 'Aesthetic' here is employed ambiguously. It connotes both the means whereby one gets an aesthetic education, i.e. 'poetry and art', and the major goals of that education, namely the culture of specific feelings and of an aesthetic sensibility whose foundation is a developed imagination. Aesthetic education, however, is also broader than what might be suggested by the connection to art. [...] [T]he cultivation of feeling and imagination relies just as much on institutional structures and habitual activities as it does on our experience of art. (p. 6)

Again, we notice in Heydt's account of Mill's proposed system of education that the concept of the aesthetic is used to refer to, besides the art object itself, something exterior to the aesthetic object. Poetry, for example, seemingly has the power by its form and content to cultivate and develop a sensitivity to other things than poetry. Having developed a propensity for appreciating the beauty of poetry consequently means that one has the ability to transfer this propensity into other contexts, such as social and cultural situations which demand, for example, a moral judgment. To become aesthetically educated thus implies work and a sense of duty. Work or utility is also related to Mill's definition of art which states that art correlates to practice generally. This means that not only the fine arts, but also that, for example, the work of carpenters and medical doctors, belong to art. What differentiates art from science is, according to Mill, the following: "Propositions of science assert a matter of fact: an existence, a coexistence, a succession, or a resemblance. The propositions [of art] do not assert that anything is, but enjoin or

---

[9] Mill's calls the formation of character ethology and states that it is "he science that corresponds of education" (p. 869).

recommend that something should be" (p. 949). Mill then goes on to propose a "body of doctrine" that he calls the "Art of Life," and which he divides into three "departments": "Morality, Prudence or Policy, and Aesthetics; the Right, the Expedient, and the Beautiful or Noble, in human conduct and works" (p. 949). These three departments have a common goal, and this goal, says Mill, is happiness: "[T]he promotion of happiness is the ultimate principle of Teleology" (p. 951). Hence, the teleology of aesthetic education in Mill, as Heydt also points out in the quoted passage above, amounts to develop and cultivate a sensitivity based on the imagination for what is beautiful and noble, which in turn depends not solely on art or practice, but also on "institutional structures and habitual activities" (p. 6), as Heydt suggests of Mill.

What is quite evident from this brief sketch of the Art of Life in Mill is that his aesthetic education is the exact opposite of the way Bataille's approaches the same topics. It is also evident that Mill, more than Bataille, must be seen as the predecessor of much of the kind of aesthetic education that I have addressed in this study. Except, it should be noted, for Spivak, whose notion of aesthetic education takes its cue from her notion of the double bind. Nevertheless, the emphasis on work and utility is present in much of how aesthetic education posits the object of study as the source of change and transformation into an idea of the good and the beautiful. This is a different focus than Bataille's interest in the states of mind that come about through ecstasy, intoxication, laughter, tears, and pain. These are sovereign moments for which there are no words, nor a teleological purpose of usefulness. The "buried word," "the tomb of meaning," and "the death of thought," are, consequently, what aesthetic education do not consider when we bestow the aesthetic object with meaning and teleology, be it ethical, cultural, social, or aesthetic. By engaging in a "supplement of fiction," to use Derrida's term, the purpose of aesthetic education has often been, and still is, to develop, for example, empathy, moral sensitivity, a sensitivity to the beautiful, and social awareness. It is a movement of the "as if" which in Mill is present in his insistence on art as something that proposed a "should be." This since if we posit something as it "should be," then, clearly, we enter the world of fiction.

To return, in closing, to Ashbery and his "One Hundred Multiple-Choice Questions," a poem that we could read, as I suggested at the outset of the chapter, as an ironic statement on the unpoetic character of assessment practices in education, or a humorous experimentation with poetic form. However, I would like to argue that this poem that on the surface seems to be a digression from what is usually considered "serious" poetry hides that event, or sovereign moment, that word, which in *Three Poems* is never expressed, but in its silence makes us wonder and question if there is not something else, another way, or a different path to take. To revisit the very last sentence of *Three Poems*, "the idea of the spectacle as something to be acted out and absorbed still hung in the air long after the last spectator had gone home to sleep" (p. 326), which is a sentiment that also haunts the reader of "One Hundred Multiple-Choice Questions," and much of Ashbery's poetry in general, because of its character of sidestepping poetic meaning, in favor of a flow of words that give rise to an aesthetic experience of sovereign moments.

The question that emerges from these reflections on poetry and aesthetic education is if there is not another aesthetic education, one in which the main concern is to contemplate that which is unsaid and has no meaning, but still carries a significance beyond work or labor, any utility or cultivation, any systematicity or convention, any educational program, beyond, as Derrida (2002a) has it, the "unfolding of what is already possible" (p. 234). One could, for example, explore an idea within aesthetic education that I have left in silence in this chapter, namely the notion of *Spieltrieb* that is, play drive or impulse, which Schiller introduces in Letter 14 of his *The Aesthetic Education of Man*. The notion of play, in turn, would lead to a consideration of, for example, Kant's idea of play, how play figures in Gadamer's hermeneutic phenomenology, and also how play is conceived of in Derrida's thinking. However, I will leave this thought suspended, while recognizing its potential significance.

References

Aristotle. (1997). *Poetics* (G. Whalley, Trans.). McGill-Queens University Press.

Ashbery, J. (2008). *Collected poems 1956-1987*. The Library of America.

Austin, J. L. (1962). *How to do things with words*. Clarendon Press.

Bataille, G. (1988). *Inner experience* (L. A. Boldt, Trans.). State University of New York Press.

Bataille, G. (1991). *The accursed share: An essay on general economy, vol. II (history of eroticism) and III (Sovereignty)* (R. Hurley, Trans.). Zone Books.

Bataille, G. (2001). The Teaching of death. In *The unfinished system of nonknowledge* (M. Kendall & S. Kendall, Trans.) (pp. 119–128). University of Minnesota Press.

Blanchot, M. (2001). "Is Mallarmé's Poetry Obscure?" In *Faux Pas*. (C. Mandell, Trans.). Stanford University Press.

Brewer, B. (2013). Unsaying non-knowledge: Georges Bataille and the mysticism of writing. *Res Cogitans, 4*(1), 116–130.

Butcher, S. H. (1920). *Aristotle's theory of poetry and fine art, with a critical text and translation of the poetics*. Macmillan.

Derrida, J. (2002a). The university without condition. In *Without Alibi* (P. Kamuf, Trans.) (pp. 202–237). Stanford University Press.

Derrida, J. (2002b). Typewriter Ribbons: Limited Ink 2. In *Without Alibi* (P. Kamuf, Trans.) (pp. 71–160). Stanford University Press.

Fredman, S. (1990). *Poet's prose: The crisis in American verse*. Cambridge University Press.

Heytd, C. (2006). *Rethinking Mill's ethics: Character and Aesthetic education*. Continuum.

Kant, I. (2011). *Groundwork of the metaphysics of morals. A German-English edition*. (M. Gregor, Trans. & J. Timmerman, Rev.). Cambridge University Press.

Mill, J. S. (1981). A system of logic: Ratiocinative and inductive, book IV-VI. In *Collected works of John Stuart Mill* (Vol. 8). Toronto University Press.

Parker, P. (1990). Metaphor and catachresis. In *The ends of Rhetoric: History, theory, practice* (J. Bender & D. E. Wellbery, Eds.) (pp. 60–74). Stanford University Press.

Poulin, A., Jr. (1981). The experience of experience: A conversation with John Ashbery. *Michigan Quarterly Review, 20*(3), 242–255.

Quintilian. (1959). *The* Institutio oratoria *of Quintilian* (H. E. Butler, Trans.). Vol. III. Harvard University Press.

Schaper, E. (1964–1965). The Kantian 'as-if' and its relevance for aesthetics. *Proceedings of the Aristotelian Society, 65*, 219–234.

Spivak, G. C. (2012). *An aesthetic education in the era of globalization.* Harvard University Press.

Chapter 7
The Aporia of Teaching: Translating the Other

Introduction

In *The Gift of Death*, Jacques Derrida (1996) argues, concerning the concept of responsibility:

> What is thus found at work in everyday discourse, in the exercise of justice, and first and foremost in the axiomatics of private, public, or international law, in the conduct of internal politics, diplomacy, and war, is a lexicon concerning responsibility that can be said to hover vaguely about a concept that is nowhere to be found, even if we can't go so far as to say that it doesn't correspond to any concept at all. It amounts to a disavowal whose resources, as one knows, are inexhaustible. One simply keeps on denying the aporia and antimony [sic], tirelessly, and one treats as nihilist, relativist, even poststructuralist, and worse still deconstructionist, all those who remain concerned in the face of such a display of good conscience. (p. 85)

This passage touches on more, I contend, than the discourses of law and the everyday, it touches on the self's relation to the other; in other words, it concerns what, within education, is often termed diversity and the related notion of Social Justice Education. Hence, Derrida's argument is important because it relates to an issue that is of importance for how we conceive of diversity and Social Justice Education in teaching and learning in higher education, and it concerns the importance of being critically and theoretically thorough. As Derrida puts in the passage above, it involves "those who remain concerned." And what I would like to explore here is precisely the aporia, or impasse, of responsibility and how it affects the discourse of the other, and also how it comes to be expressed in teaching and learning in higher education.

To set the stage for my reflections on education, the other, and responsibility I would like to begin by addressing Sharon Todd's (2003) study of the other and ethics in education, since it broaches similar themes as the ones I will pursue, and more importantly she does this from a similar philosophical and theoretical perspective to the one I take in what follows. Todd's study is noteworthy also for the reason that it is a study which, in an original way, thinks through the implications of ethics and

E. Schwieler, *Aporias of Translation*, Contemporary Philosophies and Theories in Education 18, https://doi.org/10.1007/978-3-030-97895-2_7

the other in education. As her guiding question in the study makes clear, she sets out
to explore: "'What constitutes ethical possibilities in relation to learning from others?'" (p. 3.) The title of her study, *Learning form the Other: Levinas, Psychoanalysis
and Ethical Possibilities in Education*, indicates that her notions of the other and
ethics are mainly based on Levinas's thinking and Freud's psychoanalysis. When it
comes to education, Todd is concerned with Social Justice Education, by which she
means "a wide range of pedagogies that seek to ameliorate social harm wrought
through inequitable practices and structures" (p. 1). In this kind of education, Todd
notes, ethics and the notion of the other are prominent features used to address, for
example, marginalized, racialized, poor, and oppressed people. (It is also to this
kind of discourse that the notion of diversity within higher education belong). Social
Justice Education thus works on two levels, on one level it addresses social justice
within education itself, that is, in schools and institutions of higher education; on a
second level it is part of the curriculum and constitutes a subject taught in schools
and in higher education. Social Justice Education, then, is an attempt to promote
equality and equity in education through applying a set of pedagogies. The aim of
these pedagogies is to confront otherness as being an effect of often oppressive
social and educational structures. As Todd puts it: "Within the terms of social justice
education, the 'Other' is seen to be the consequence of social, economic, or political
disaffiliation, and thus to be 'Other' signals that which is undesirable by virtue of its
formation within oppressive circumstances. It is an attribute obtained through material, ideological, and discursive practices, and it is therefore viewed as a construction of time and place" (p. 2). However, as Todd rightly points out, the other is also
a philosophical concept that entails an entirely different way of conceiving of the
other and otherness. Consequently, I will turn to address the concept of the other
and how it has been represented in philosophy as well as theories within the social
sciences and humanities.[1]

The Concept of the Other

As noted, Social Justice Education and diversity, both in practice and theory, in
higher education, often take their departure from the concept of the other, and as
such diversity, specifically, is a means to address otherness in a student population.
Now, the theoretical discourses, within Social Justice Education, which relate to
diversity, such as critical pedagogy, cultural studies, postcolonialism, gender studies, new historicism, and queer studies, to name a few, conceive of the concept of
the other in different ways. The other in these discourses can, for example, signify a
racial or ethnic other, or being other on the basis of social class, religion, sexual
orientation, gender, age, physical or mental disability.

---

[1] I will come back to Todd's study later in the chapter.

There is, however, also a philosophical mode of analysis of the concept of the other, which goes beyond traits and characteristics such as race, class or sexual orientation. Two philosophers who have engaged in this type of analysis are Emmanuel Levinas and Jacques Derrida. The development of the theories relating to the other in the disciplines mentioned above stem to a large part from their analyses of the other, which is why I will focus on the thinking of these philosophers in order to explore a possible approach to the praxis of responsibility in teaching.

First, however, I want to situate the concept of diversity. Diversity means, according to the OED, in its etymological sense, "[t]he condition or quality of being diverse, different, or varied; difference, unlikeness."[2] This definition begs the questions: Different from what?

Different according to whom, and under what circumstances and conditions? What does it mean to be different? At a seminar on diversity[3] I once attended, one of the keynote speakers answered the question of how we should come to terms with diversity in education by saying that we should "Celebrate difference". This statement, however optimistic and encouraging it might sound, is problematic. If we are to "celebrate difference" we run the risk of reducing difference to identity and to "the same," to use the language of Emmanuel Levinas. The statement makes difference into what I am as a human being, it makes "being apart," and "separated from," into who I am. In other words, it functions as an onto-theology of difference. This stance, I would like to argue, can lead to exclusion instead of inclusion; it can lead to being excluded from what creates a genuine interest in and of difference. Interest here meaning to be in between, to exist as and with the interest in and of difference (cf. the Latin etymology, *interesse*),[4] which, Levinas maintains, implies that one can suggest a possible ethics of difference as a precondition for what Martin Heidegger calls the ontological difference (i.e., being(s)-in-the-world as different from Being-as-such). This problematic of difference is also recognized by the literary theorist Terry Eagleton, who, in his short essay with the title "Five types of identity and difference," notes the following:

> A genuine concept of equality [...] deconstructs the notions of identity and non-identity, sameness and difference, the individual and universal, in contrast to those more rigidly binary theorists of postmodernism who would line up difference on one side of the onto-logical fence and abstract universality on the other. (p. 50)

In the same essay he provides a solution to the problem of difference when he writes: "The goal is no longer either difference or identity, but an attempt to reconstruct, on the basis of the fullest possible liberation of difference, new forms of human solidarity" (p. 52). However, Eagleton's, in my view, justified critique of difference is informed by his explicit political stance, and his use of deconstruction

---

[2] See OED, Diversity.

[3] Curriculum innovation for diversity, York St John University College, UK, September 12, 2006.

[4] See OED, interess, "ME. and AF. interesse, a. med. L. interesse compensation for loss, compensatory payment, n. use of L. interesse to be between, to differ, make a difference, to concern, be of importance."

is similar to how cultural studies critics use it, as I will try to show in what follows. But first I want to mention another instance of a justified critique that falls short mainly because it lacks reference back to the origins of the theories with which it engages.

In "The Study of Diversity: The 'Knowledge of Difference' and the Limits of Science," Benjamin Baez (2004) asserts: "A critical study of diversity should uncover which practices and discourses create and use racial differences and why. Such differences are mediated by discursive practices, which implicate systems of knowledge [...]. The study of diversity should not just focus on individuals and their differences but also on discursive practices and their uses of difference" (p. 290).[5] Baez points to the importance of recognizing the potential subversiveness of the concept of difference, but also its potentially reductive effects. However, while developing this notion of difference, his essay builds on philosophical perspectives that are not fully explicated. That is, Baez's arguments are implicitly grounded in philosophical reflections of the concept of the other, while his explicit theoretical point of departure can be found in cultural studies, postmodern and poststructural theories, and consequently, by extension, what is known as critical pedagogy. This, I argue, is symptomatic of the discourses of cultural studies and critical pedagogy. These discourses hover between practical and theoretical rigor and do not pay either of them well enough attention. As the philosopher Alain Badiou (2002) writes, in *Ethics: An Essay on the Understanding of Evil*, regarding the uses of the concepts of ethics and the other:

> The conception of ethics as the "ethics of the other" or the "ethics of difference" has its origin in the theses of Emmanuel Lévinas rather than those in Kant.
> Lévinas has devoted his work [...] to the deposing of philosophy in favour of ethics. It is to him we owe, long before the current fashion, a kind of ethical radicalism. (p. 18)

Badiou, in fact, discards the entire discourse of the other and of cultural differences, that is, what, in higher education, is commonly known as diversity, on the grounds that, as he writes, "genuine thought should affirm the following principle: since differences are what there is, and since every truth is the coming-to-be of that which is not yet, so differences are then precisely what truths depose, or render insignificant. No light is shed on any concrete situation by the notion of the 'recognition of the other'" (p. 27). This means that Badiou's idea of truth also renders insignificant for thought the ethics of Levinas and Derrida.

However, this is a debate, between Badiou and his English translator Peter Hallward on one side, and Simon Critchley on the other. And in his recently published work *Infinitely Demanding: Ethics of Commitment, Politics of Resistance*, Critchley (2007) argues against Badiou:

> I have some reservations about Badiou's work. They concern his rather dogmatic attempt to exclude religion as one of the conditions for an event (there are only four conditions for the event: mathematics, politics, art and love), his questionable use of Lacanian psychoanalysis in explaining the relation between subject and event, and a certain heroism of the decision

---

[5] It should be noted that Baez's argumentation holds for any type of diversity, not just race.

that I detect in Badiou, particularly in his political pronouncements. Most significantly, I have reservations about Badiou's talk of truth. (pp. 47–48)

To counter Badiou's disregard for Levinas' ethics of the other, Critchley's move is to install the other, once again, into the argument, as the other in me, as conscience. And conscience, moreover, leads up to Critchely's notion of ethics: "Conscience is not the work of God within us, but the work of ourselves upon ourselves. This work on the self can be excessively demanding work. On my account, conscience is the location of the ethical demand, a demand that is impossibly demanding, a demand to be infinitely responsible, a demand that divides us, that sunders us" (p. 87). I would argue that to be infinitely responsible by a demand that divides us is similar to and, again, demands the same kind of vigilant praxis that Derrida asks for in his appeal to those who remain concerned. I will not go deeper into this debate here, but rather focus on Levinas's and Derrida's thoughts on the topic at hand. To be able to do that I want, first, to relate to two of the theoretical discourses that use the concept of the other in order to establish how the concept of diversity in higher education is founded on them. What follows are two examples:

Example number one. One of the major theoretical perspectives that focuses on diversity in education is the perspective known as critical pedagogy. Critical pedagogy takes its name from what is called critical theory, also known as the Frankfurt School. Moreover, critical theory as well as critical pedagogy is developed in a similar way as interdisciplinary subjects such as cultural studies and postcolonial studies, and could in this way be said to build on a wide range of theories within the humanities and social sciences. They are, to put it differently, eclectic disciplines. The theorist that has perhaps most influenced the development of critical pedagogy is Paolo Freire (1996), with his seminal work *Pedagogy of the Oppressed*. One reservation that one can have against Freire's pedagogy is that the Marxist vocabulary limits and restricts its theoretical and political force. Furthermore, Freire is undoubtedly conscious of the danger of stagnation in political leadership and of the necessity to renegotiate the grounds for one's pedagogical as well as political action. If this is not done the danger of oppression and the restriction of liberty and freedom is imminent (pp. 76–77). But, despite Freire's caveats, his application of Marxist terminology on educational matters renders it pedagogically, politically, and ethically problematic. The politization of education can, in Freire, be said to lead to an ideological blindness with the consequence that its pedagogy remains concerned only politically and not, I would argue, ethically. This kind of tension between politics and education is something which Tyson E. Lewis (2012) addresses in his book *The Aesthetics of Education: Theatre, Curiosity, and Politics in the Work of Jacques Rancière and Paulo Freire*. Lewis affirms the political bearing of Freire's thinking, but at the same time wants to, as he writes, translate Freire's work, so that his study is not reduced to "summaries of what Freire said about art or aesthetics but will be an *active* translation of his work in order to probe the latent potentiality of his thought for further educational experimentation" (p. 13). This translation is what he calls a repositioning of Freire "in relation to major political thinkers such as

Peter McLaren's (2000) rehabilitation of Freire's Marxist Humanism or Raymond Morrow and Carlos Alberto Torres's (2002) interpretation of Freirian dialogue as a form of Habermasian communicative action. While perhaps methodologically similar, my book stands resolutely opposed to these other texts which, in their own ways, demonstrate how critique itself always displaces the political (and perhaps the educational) onto another scene" (pp. 13–14).[6] In line with Lewis's argumentation, when it comes to the development of Freire's pedagogy into critical pedagogy, I would say that it, as a critical and theoretical perspective, comes to suffer from the same difficulties as cultural studies and postcolonial theory. That is, when politicizing these disciplines, the theoretical and critical rigor is sometimes lost or made secondary to meet their political or ideological ends. This teleological "higher cause," in consequence, jeopardizes a sustained and thorough critique, which would mean that it does not effectively confront the critic's perspective's possible bias, be it political or ideological. It is when these different theories, as critique, slides into a more or less fixed methodology which is applied to, seemingly, any object of analysis that they become questionable. Hence, I would like to argue that Social Justice Education and diversity, in themselves diverse subjects or disciplines, must be included within the theories and discourses that run the risk of the same philosophical reductionism.

Example number two. Cultural Studies as a discipline builds on and makes use of a wide range of theories: postmodern, poststructural, feminist, Marxist, deconstructive, historical, and sociological. It has an explicit political agenda in that, by the study of cultural texts, the aim is to enact social and/or cultural change. Cultural Studies, furthermore, acknowledges its situatedness, that is, its subjective character. Instead of feigning objectivity, cultural studies critics explicitly draw on their subjective position in order to critique the positivist emphasis on

---

[6]Drawing on Rancière's thinking Lewis defines his use of translation in the following way: "Translation enables new metaphors to appear through the collisions of atoms that have suddenly fallen off course and tumbled into one another. If translation is a philosophical method, then theatrical performance is its social and political equivalent. Or, perhaps we can think of the two operations working in unison: translation creates the script for political performance to emerge and announce a wrong" (p. 51). Lewis's application of translation as an aesthetical and philosophical method nevertheless overlooks the radical otherness that all translation brings with it, and which can only be expressed as an aporetic alterity, a catachresis that produces a metaphor for the silence in which the wholly other rests, for example as the metaphor of the collisions of atoms Lewis uses to describe the work of translation, or education as the staging, acting, and performing of teaching and learning (p. 52). These metaphors that appear and become manifest are, in turn, the concepts which generate the methods of philosophy. Drawing on Rancière, Lewis suggests what he calls a dramaturgy of universal teaching which is a dramaturgy that is also part of the formation of politics. As Lewis writes, "education, like politics, is linked directly with the theatrics of improvisation" (p. 52). There is, then, an aesthetics of performance involved in shaping both education and politics through the act of improvisation. In teaching as well as in political action, there is an element of imitation in that the agents (teachers, politicians) act as someone else than themselves. In other words, these agents are involved in acts of translation, Lewis claims, just like actors on the stage translate the characters of a play into a performance (p. 51). We could say that this is translation as the staging of the self as other. However, this other is an other, and not that wholly other that, as we will see, figures in Levinas and Derrida.

objectivity and the exclusivity of truth. Cultural Studies is concerned with analyzing the marginalized or oppressed other in culture, be it a racial, social, or sexual other. Thus, the analysis of knowledge and power underlying a given cultural or social discourse constitutes the cultural studies critic's main interest. As two Cultural Studies critics, Robert Davis and Ronald Schleifer (1992), note in their book *Criticism and Culture*:

> The critique of the subject is key to cultural studies and formulates a critique of 'culture' itself. In this critique, critics read the discourses and texts of contemporary culture to expose crucial oppositions and contradictions that govern the exercise of power, to expose what Homi K. Bhabha calls at one extreme "the political 'rationality' of the nation as a form of narrative – textual strategies, metaphoric displacements, sub-texts and figurative stratagems" [...]. Through such critiques Bhabha, Stuart Hall, Gayatri Spivak and other cultural critics work, in effect, continually to manoeuvre themselves into strategic conflicts with cultural practices in the interventionist style of one working from within an institution – as theorists and teachers in the academy – to change and transform culture. Such interventions must always be repeated in that they always succumb to the ideality of 'reading' and the monumentality of 'practice'. (p. 232)

According to this definition of Cultural Studies, a continuous questioning, or critique, of one's own reading and practice is necessary, since Cultural Studies critique is never a stable critical statement or text, but a process of discursive renegotiation of one's own critical and, by necessity, subjective position.

However, it can be argued that this self-critique collapses in the sense that it often neglects to question its own political and ideological embeddedness. There is, again, a blindness within much Cultural Studies criticism, in that its own ideological origin is implicit and hidden, rather than explicitly critiqued. What is more, the political promise of cultural change or transformation – of bringing something "new" into the analysis – as a consequence becomes somewhat ad hoc. Cultural Studies critiques of Derridean deconstruction in this way misses the mark, since the implicit ideology of Cultural Studies is exactly what a deconstructive reading would focus on. Again, as Davis and Schleifer (1992) writes:

> A deconstructive critique examines and tests the assumptions supporting intellectual insight in order to interrogate the 'self-evident' truths on which they are based. It tests the legitimacy of the contextual 'bounds' that understanding both presents and requires. Rather than seeking a way of understanding, a way of incorporating new phenomena into coherent existing or modified models, deconstructive critique seeks to uncover the examined axioms that give rise to those models and their boundaries. (p. 152)

Given this definition of what is here called deconstruction by two Cultural Studies critics, one could ask if the application of a deconstructive critique to further the ideological and political ends of Cultural Studies does not contradict the stated definition of deconstruction? Shouldn't Cultural Studies' desire for cultural transformation and change, along with its "hidden" ideological origin, be deconstructed in relation to the concepts knowledge and power that serve as the discipline's foundational theoretical instruments? One could argue that as long as the ideology and self-interest of Cultural Studies remain unanalyzed and unconscious it falls into the same objectifying positivism or ideological rigidity that it seeks to critique. Is it really sufficient to question and acknowledge one's own subjective position if the overarching ideological and political aims remain unquestioned and even unconscious?[7] One could certainly argue that it is not, and propose, instead, that it means not remaining concerned, to once again use Derrida's words. It could, however, suggest being concerned, but with a politically informed ideological concern, and not with a concern that always and already remains ethically concerned. For responsibility to be ethically relevant we must recognize the aporia at its origin, and that all acts of responsibility happen as an interruption and disruption of responsibility, an interruption and disruption which can only be translated as the political, ideological, or educational norms, rules, or laws that necessarily follow its pronunciation. The performativity of responsibility is thus the disruption of its performative act, by which a programmatic ethics is enunciated as its only possibility. In other words, as soon as I act responsibly I do so according to an ethical convention, because this act must be acknowledged as a responsible act by an other, and this other is also and always myself as other.

Levinas and Derrida: Ethics and the Other(s)

This brings me to the concept of the other as it relates to ethics and diversity. To explore how the other can be conceived of in a way that departs from the notions already addressed I will consider its development in the thinking of Emmanuel Levinas and Jacques Derrida. These philosophers can be seen to be engaged in a reciprocal critical conversation concerning the concept of the other and its relation to ethics.

Two notions of main concern in Levinas' thinking are ethics and the other. For Levinas, ethics precedes ontology, and ethics develops in my relation to the other; it is in facing the other that the ethical reveals itself. The work of philosophy, or "critique," as Levinas (2003) calls it, is a metaphysical questioning more fundamental than ontology. Hence, in *Totality and Infinity* Levinas (2003) states:

> [C]ritique does not reduce the other to the same as does ontology, but calls into question the exercise of the same. A calling into question of the same – which cannot occur within the

---

[7]As J. Hillis Miller (2005) argues in "Politicizing Art – What are Cultural Studies?": "The orientation is more toward the culture and less toward the work in itself even though the heterogeneity of each culture is in principle recognized. Rhetorical reading, or so-called deconstruction, presupposes that only an active and interventionist reading of texts and other cultural artefacts can be socially and politically effective. A merely thematic reading will remain caught in the ideology that is being contested, whatever its overt theoretical or political assertions. In the realm of words, which are the medium of cultural criticism, only an active reading wrestling with the excess of language or other signs over transparent meaning, a wrestling with what might be called the material dimension of signs, will work, that is, effect changes in the real institutional and social worlds" (p. 336). The same argument could be made, I hold, when it comes to education and its relation to literature, as well as critical pedagogy and much of Social Justice Education and the relation of these discourses to philosophy.

egoist spontaneity of the same – is brought about by the other. We name this calling into question of my spontaneity by the presence of the Other ethics. The strangeness of the Other, his irreducibility to the I, to my thoughts and my possessions, is precisely accomplished as a calling into question of my spontaneity, as ethics. Metaphysics, transcendence, the welcoming of the other by the same, of the Other by me, is concretely produced as the calling into question of the same by the other, that is, as the ethics that accomplishes the critical essence of knowledge. And as critique precedes dogmatism, metaphysics precedes ontology. (p. 43)

In other words, ethics, for Levinas, is founded on my encounter with the other, that which is not me – an ego or the "I". Thus, ethics takes place as an event in my relation to the other; when facing the other I am also, according to Levinas, faced with an ethical imperative: "You shall not commit murder". The ethical force of this expression that confronts us in the face of the other is, Levinas (2003) claims, "the infinity of his transcendence" and "the primordial expression, [...] the first word" (p. 199). In other words, the ethical is, for Levinas, the foundation or ground for being as metaphysics. It is in the relation to the other, in my conversation with the other, that the ethical originates as an originary concern, or an interest, a being between, a relation in and of difference: "But the other absolutely other – the Other – does not limit the freedom of the same; calling it to responsibility, it founds and justifies it" (p. 197).

The ethical imperative "You shall not commit murder" is, according to Levinas, an ethics of resistance: "The 'resistance' of the other does not do violence to me, does not act negatively; it has a positive structure: ethical. [...] There is here a relation not with a very great resistance, but with something absolutely other: the resistance of what has no resistance – the ethical resistance. [...] If the resistance to murder were not ethical but real we would have a perception of it. [...] We would remain within the idealism of a consciousness of struggle, and not in relationship with the Other" (p. 199). Levinas' notion of resistance, I argue, is similar to the concern that Derrida mentions. Resistance, in Levinas, is a resistance against stagnation, reductionism, and political, ideological, theoretical, or educational blindness. To put it crudely, it is a resistance against metaphysical indoctrination and repression.

How, then, does my relationship to the other figure itself? How, according to Levinas, can it be characterized? For Levinas (2003), my relationship to the other is plural, it cannot be reduced to an ego or an other as another self, which would end up as an act of self-reflection:

[T]he Other would amount to a second copy of the I – both included in the same concept. Pluralism is not a numerical multiplicity. In order that a pluralism in itself (which cannot be reflected in formal logic) be realized there must be produced in depth the movement from me to the other, an attitude of an I with regard to the Other (an attitude already specified as love or hatred, obedience or command, learning or teaching, etc....), that would not be a species of relationship in general; this means that the movement from me to the other could not present itself as a theme to an objective gaze freed from this confrontation with the other, to a reflection. Pluralism implies a radical alterity of the other, whom I do not simply conceive by relation to myself, but confront out of my egoism. The alterity of the Other is in him and is not relative to me; it reveals itself. But I have access to it proceeding from myself and not through a comparison of myself with the other. I have access to the alterity

of the Other from the society I maintain with him, and not by quitting this relation in order
to reflect on its terms. (p. 121)

In order for the concept of diversity not to stagnate, it is necessary, I suggest, to view
it through Levinas' conception of plurality. This would mean that diversity implies
an infinite conversation (to borrow a phrase from Maurice Blanchot)[8] with the other,
a conversation that would be a calling into question of its own foundation; it would,
in other words, entail remaining concerned for the other by calling the other and the
self into question. Diversity conceived like this would, I hold, be a responsible concept of diversity; it would be an ethical diversity that, in Levinas' words, in *Totality
and Infinity* (2003), "accomplishes the critical essence of knowledge" (p. 43).

Now, every cultural system follows the illogic of difference, the concept of culture itself cannot be thought without difference. Culture is always already different
from itself, it comes into being as and through difference. And if we want to assume,
as does Levinas, that my relation to the other is an ethical relationship, and that ethics founds this relationship, then I have a responsibility for the other, which means
that I am obliged to respond to the other, and this response will be framed by
Levinas's metaphysics of the good: "To be for the Other is to be Good. […] The fact
that in existing for another I exist otherwise than in existing for me is morality
itself" (2003, p. 261). The consequences of this for the concept of diversity and how
diversity is handled in higher education are, perhaps, obvious. For example, it is
only in my genuine engagement with the other that I meet the other and encounter
the alterity of the other beyond the conventional difference of me and you. I remain
concerned with and for the other; that is, I have a responsibility toward the other by
engaging in a conversation that calls into question and critiques in the interest of
the other.

This, furthermore, has implications for education and how we as teachers per-
ceive the practice of teaching and learning. But, before going deeper into those
issues, I want to continue to explore Levinas's thinking, and more specifically
Derrida's reading, or critique, of Levinas. In *The Gift of Death*, a work I quoted
from at the outset of the chapter, Derrida (1996) differentiates between Levinas' and
Sören Kierkegaard's notion of ethics, which in turn relates to how Derrida and
Levinas differ in their thinking concerning the concept of the other. In the following
I want to indicate what I see as the main point of Derrida's argument, in *The Gift of
Death*, when it comes to the difference between Kierkegaard and Levinas, and their
conception of ethics:

> Kierkegaard would have to admit, as Levinas reminds him, that ethics is also the order and
> respect for absolute singularity, and not only that of the generality or of the repetition of the
> same. He cannot therefore distinguish so conveniently between the ethical and the religious.
> But for his part, in taking into account absolute singularity, that is, the absolute alterity
> obtaining in relations between one human and another, Levinas is no longer able to distin-
> guish between the infinite alterity of God and that of every human. His ethics is already a
> religious one. In the two cases the border between the ethical and the religious becomes
> more than problematical, as do all attendant discourses. (1996, p. 84)

---

[8] See Blanchot's (1993) *The Infinite Conversation*.

According to Derrida, Kierkegaard and Levinas thus exemplify the aporia or antinomy inherent in any ethics, and consequently also in the concept of responsibility; that is, the aporia of the relation between generality and singularity in ethics. "The concept of responsibility," Derrida (1996) writes, "like that of decision, would [...] be found to lack coherence or consequence, even lacking identity with respect to itself, paralyzed by what can be called an aporia or antimony [sic]. That has never stopped it from 'functioning', as one says" (p. 84). In other words, the essence or nature of responsibility rests on its being in relation to what it is not. This contradiction, Derrida argues, is what characterizes the history of ethics and politics, as well as, one would have to add, the history of ethics and religion. Furthermore, this conception of ethics, Derrida claims, is "ethics as 'irresponsibilization', as an insoluble and paradoxical contradiction between responsibility in general and absolute responsibility" (p. 61). Derrida (1996) describes the aporia inherent in responsibility in the following way:

> Saying that a responsible decision must be taken on the basis of knowledge seems to define the condition of possibility of responsibility (one can't make a responsible decision without science or conscience, without knowing what one is doing, for what reasons, in view of what and under what conditions), at the same time as it defines the condition of impossibility of this same responsibility (if decision-making is relegated to a knowledge that it is content to follow or to develop, then it is no more a responsible decision, it is a technical deployment of a cognitive apparatus, the simple mechanistic deployment of a theorem). (p. 24)

Responsibility and the other are, in both Levinas and Derrida, closely connected, but are in Derrida's thinking also governed by an originary aporia. This is what separates Derrida and Levinas: according to Derrida, Levinas does not acknowledge the irresponsibility that provides the ground for any act or concept of responsibility.[9]

Considering what it means to be responsible entails considering what the concept of the other means. Moreover, responsibility and the concept of the other are inseparable from praxis, that is, from some sort of action. They are, in other words, performative concepts.[10] As Derrida (1996) writes:

> In order to be responsible it is necessary to respond to or answer to what being responsible means. For if it is true that the concept of responsibility has, in the most reliable continuity of its history, always implied involvement in action, doing, a praxis, a decision that exceeds simple conscience or simple theoretical understanding, it is also true that the same concept requires a decision or responsible action to answer for itself consciously, that is, with knowledge of a thematics of what is done, of what action signifies, its causes, ends, etc. (p. 25)

But, at the same time as we need to act in certain ways in order to be responsible, we must not forget and, as Derrida emphasizes, "continually remind ourselves that

---

[9] For a similar critique of Levinas, see Derrida's (1978) "Violence and Metaphysics" in *Writing and Difference*.

[10] Derrida's (1982) notion of performatives can be found, for example, in his essay "Signature Event Context."

some part of irresponsibility insinuates itself wherever one demands responsibility without sufficiently conceptualizing and thematizing what 'responsibility' means; *that is to say everywhere* [emphasis in the original]" (pp. 25–26). To put it differently, and from the perspective of the teacher, we as teachers must teach in a way that is both an act, or praxis, of responsibility, and at the same time conceptualize and thematize what "responsible teaching" means. However, and as Derrida points out, "not only is the thematization of the concept of responsibility always inadequate but that it is always so because it must be so. And what goes here for responsibility also goes, for the same reasons, for freedom and for decision" (p. 26).

This inadequacy, furthermore, installs a *sine qua non* of secrecy in the concept of responsibility. The concept is secret in so far as it is impossible to solve, or resolve, the aporia of responsibility; there is always something unknown and unknowable left even after the most meticulous analysis or thematization of it. "In fact," Derrida writes, "it comes down to linking secrecy to a responsibility that consists […] in responding, hence in answering the other, before the other and before the law, and if possible publicly, answering for itself, its intentions, its aims, and for the name of the agent deemed responsible" (pp. 26–27). This means that teaching will have to respond and answer before the other, we as teachers are answerable to the other when we respond to the other in teaching. Moreover, teaching responsibly means being aware of the inadequacy and paradoxical nature of the concept of responsibility, that is, its irresponsibility. As Derrida puts it: "The exercise of responsibility seems to leave no choice but this one, however uncomfortable it may be, of paradox […] and secrecy. More serious still, it must always run the risk of conversion and apostasy: there is no responsibility without a dissident and inventive rupture with respect to tradition, authority, orthodoxy, rule, or doctrine" (p. 27). This description of responsibility, I would like to suggest, is strikingly similar to deconstruction, in Derrida's sense of the word. Responsible teaching, in other words, is, or can be, a deconstructive event.[11]

As a deconstructive event, teaching is teaching the other, and on the most fundamental level teaching is teaching the wholly other(s). Derrida's expression for, and example of, otherness, or, diversity, which it is necessary to take into account when considering the concept of responsibility is this: "*Tout autre est tout autre*" (p. 82), that is, every other is every other, at the same time as every other is wholly other; or the wholly other is every other; or the wholly other is wholly other. But what does it mean to teach the wholly other(s) responsibly? Teaching, I suggest, can, if we want it to, adheres to the illogic of the gift, that is, a giving beyond retribution and compensation. Derrida (1996) names this illogic of the gift "the very site of the most decisive paradox, namely, the *gift that is not a present* [emphasis in the original]." And he continues to say about the gift that is not a present that it is

---

[11] Derrida describes how such an event must irrupt and interrupt any performative system if it is to take place. As soon as an event, such as, for example, responsibility, translation, teaching, happens, is given as a performative, according to a program or convention, it does not arrive or take place. Instead, it turns into "a technical deployment of a cognitive apparatus, the simple mechanistic deployment of a theorem" (p. 24), as Derrida (1996) puts it in *The Gift of Death*.

the gift of something that remains inaccessible, unpresentable, and as a consequence secret. The event of this gift would link the essence without essence of the gift to secrecy. For one might say that a gift that could be recognized as such in the day of light, a gift destined for recognition, would immediately annul itself. The gift is the secret itself, if the secret itself can be told. Secrecy is the last word of the gift which is the last word of the secret. (pp. 29–30)

In teaching, to be responsible before the wholly other(s) is to give in secret, and what we as teachers give is a putting-into-question and a "remaining concerned" as ethics; that is, "ethics as irresponsibilization," which amounts to teaching as a deconstructive event. However, this event does not ask for anything in return, it wants nothing back; it does not require compensation or retribution, for it does not come to presence as a content to be taught, but remains that silent gift, the sovereign moment, which cannot be named, determined, or included into a course of study or educational program. It does not give knowledge or constitute a body of knowledge, but is the wholly other of the will to knowledge and power.

So where does this line of thinking leave us, if our profession is teaching? What can we expect from teaching, from students, and from learning? In *Learning from the Other: Levinas, Psychoanalysis, and Ethical Possibilities in Education*, Todd (2003) draws on Levinas's notion of the radical other to argue for how taking the other as an unknowable other has tangible and practical implications for teaching and pedagogy. When it comes to Social Justice Education she writes that she wants to

> propose ways that this understanding of otherness as absolute (that is, always already a given) can help educators think about the many differences that are effected through power and social location. What I am suggesting is that social justice education might consider ways of dealing with the concept of difference outside terms of oppression in order to respond ethically to the range of lived experiences of oppression. For with this turn to alterity, there opens up two fundamental questions for social justice education: first, are we (as researchers, teachers, and readers) enacting violences upon others as we engage their stories and narratives of self-identification, despite our best intentions? That is, in seeking to learn about them, can we be negligent of learning from them? And, second, if so, how might we attend to the Other and preserve alterity as a nonviolent alternative while working toward the aim of social justice? (p. 3)

Ethics, in Todd's reading of Levinas, gives us the possibility of nonviolence. However, violence, here should not be taken solely as physical violence, but more in terms of emotional violence and discursive violence, or even, perhaps, as referring to Derrida (1978) on violence and metaphysics in Levinas, in his essay with that title, namely "Violence and Metaphysics" in his work *Writing and Difference*. I'm here pointing to Derrida's deconstruction of violence and ethics in Levinas in which "an original, transcendental violence, previous to every ethical choice, even supposed by ethical nonviolence" (1978, p. 156) has to be accounted for. What Derrida says is that even in the nonviolence of encountering the naked face, the other as wholly Other, which is the origin of ethics, there is inscribed a violence before ethics, which makes nonviolence and ethics possible in the first place. Todd relates this to education in the following way:

It is important to signal that I am employing neither a metaphorical usage of the term [vio-
lence] nor one designed to erase the differences between specific acts of violence (e.g.,
neglect, humiliation, fear, abuse, torture). Indeed, acts of violence such as these are of a
completely different order, for suffering is here inflicted through hatred, cruelty, and indif-
ference. My emphasis here is on the inevitable external force that has the power to subject,
that compels us to learn and become. In this sense, education, by its very socializing function and by its mission to change how people think and relate to the world, enacts a violence
that is necessary to the formation of the subject (this is, after all, what is meant by "formation"). Following the metaphysical formulations of Derrida and Levinas, on the one hand,
and the psychical formulations of psychoanalysis, on the other hand, violence is a necessary
condition of subjectivity. Thus the question is not so much whether education wounds or
not through its impulse to socialize, but whether it wounds excessively and how we (as
teachers) might open ourselves to nonviolent possibilities in our pedagogical encounters. (p. 20)

Thus, the encounters in which I meet the other as a potential meeting with the other
as wholly other(s) do not exclusively take place in physical meetings face to face,
but also in different types of learning situations and activities, virtual environments,
in engaging with texts of different kinds, paintings, art, poetry, and literature. It is
not what kind of diverse group I encounter that is important, but that I recognize the
ethical responsibility such a meeting demands of me. Whether we call this an ethics
of demanding approval as Simon Critchley does, or the processes of truth, as Alain
Badiou does, is perhaps of less importance. What is important, however, is that an
active and continuous ethical reflection, as an active ongoing engagement and conversation with the wholly other(s), takes place in every teaching and learning situation, and that this ethical engagement is the foundation of my relationship with
the other.

And, in our teaching, Todd suggests, instead of teaching ethics as a system of
knowledge we should engage the other to open up the relational possibilities in
which ethical and nonviolent moments of teaching and learning might present
themselves:

Teaching, then, would not be focussed on acquiring knowledge about ethics, or about the
Other, but would instead have to consider its practices themselves as relations to otherness
and thus as always already potentially ethical – that is, participating in a network of relations that lend themselves to moments of nonviolence. In this sense, the way in which we
engage the Other becomes a central question *of* ethics and *for* education. (p. 9)

Teaching is, according to Todd, to attend to the praxis of ethics and the other, or
rather the potentiality of ethics and the other. By qualifying the possibility of ethics
and the other as potentiality we are directed toward δύναμις (*dunamis*), i.e., the
movement and power of ethics and the other, each as a systematized project. It is the
violence of δύναμις as formation or education, i.e., as transformation, which is the
motivating force of teaching. And teaching, in turn, is conditioned and regulated by
phenomenality (as that which appears) and language (as meaning and λόγος).
Teaching, as the language of transformation, by which things and knowledge appear
to us as objects of learning, is only possible because of that transcendental violence
which precedes every ethical choice and every other as they are figured in the discourse of diversity and Social Justice Education. Teaching, then, is in essence

translation, as the transfer of manifest meaning, since it by an act of violence turns subject into object, without recognizing that which always remains unsaid and so untranslated. Hence, teaching translates the other into a scientific or aesthetic object to be observed, known, or sensed.

This brings about the aporetic character of translating the other, which, in this case, is translating as teaching. But, in recognizing the aporia of translation, there is no content to be taught, or body of knowledge to be learned about the wholly other, which inscribes itself as, what Derrida (1997) calls, "the violence of the arche-writing" (p. 110). Arche-writing is a writing that opens up the possibility to think the origin in the first place and so to think difference, meaning, and phenomenality. We cannot teach the wholly other as phenomenally given, as little as the teaching of death is possible. Again, we are faced with an education of death, an education that teaches nothing except in translation, and translating the wholly other amounts to a translation without origin or original. Any discourse or teaching about an other within the discourse of diversity, or Social Justice Education, is a project, work, or labor, in Bataille's sense,[12] regardless of how carefully we prepare for engaging or encountering the other. Because the wholly other does not arrive, other than as the gift of a secret, unknown and unknowable. Teaching the other, just like the teaching of death, is an enactment of aporia, it is the inevitable repetition of a decision to teach, and so to engage in the work of a project. This, in turn, brings about the designation of the other as something or someone (even if this is something *other* or someone's *otherness*) as meaning and phenomenality, such as diversity, the embodied other, or the subject of Social Justice Education. In short, our teaching inevitably succumbs to the rational division into contraries and binary opposites, and points to Aristotle's first principle of non-contradiction. And it is precisely because of this that Derrida's call for us to remain concerned, instead of disregarding aporia and the belonging together of contradictions, is indispensable. The reasons for this are, as Derrida maintains, ethical and political.

The Temptation of Ethics

In the following I would like to venture further and deeper into Derrida's thinking regarding responsibility and the wholly other in *The Gift of Death*, in order to contextualize how I have outlined the way teaching the other can figure itself in relation to different discourses of diversity.

Genesis 22 tells the story of how Abraham is tested by God; God demands of Abraham to sacrifice his only son Isaac. When Abraham goes along with God's command and is ready to sacrifice his son, God intervenes and tells Abraham to save Isaac, since Abraham as proven his fear of God. It is with the help of this biblical story, and Kierkegaard's reading of it, that Derrida, in *The Gift of Death*, develops

---

[12] See Chap. 5 of the present study.

his thinking on the wholly other, the secret, ethics and responsibility. What is, first of all, noticeable in the story of Abraham is, Derrida points out, Abrahams silence. He keeps silent about his intention to sacrifice Isaac as a burnt offering to God, and when Isaac asks his father where the lamb for the burnt offering is, Abraham replies that God will provide it. However, Abraham keeps his silence by speaking, by telling Isaac that God will provide the lamb. He accepts God's command, but does not tell his son what he is about to do, and he does this, importantly, without knowing the reason why God is asking this of him. God gives Abraham no reason for his command, but Abraham accepts it without questioning it. This is why he tells Isaac that God will provide, even though he is completely ignorant of God's motive for asking him to commit filicide. Thus he keeps it secret, that is, the secret of God's secret, which is also his own secret. By saying that God will provide, Abraham, in effect, and as Derrida notes, "responds without responding" (p. 59). "Still," Derrida continues, "Abraham doesn't just speak in order not to say anything when he replies to Isaac. He says something that is not nothing and that is not false. He says something that is not a non-truth, something moreover that, although *he doesn't know it yet*, will turn out to be true" (p. 59). It is here that the aporia of the story is forming, bringing us to consider the paradoxical nature of ethics that the story of Abraham stages. It is also, and significantly, a question of language and of translation, as Derrida makes clear:

> To the extent that, in not saying the essential thing, namely, the secret between God and him, Abraham doesn't speak, he assumes the responsibility that consists in always being alone, entrenched in one's own singularity at the moment of decision. Just as no one can die in my place, no one can make a decision [...] in my place. But as soon as one speaks, as soon as one enters the medium of language, one loses that very singularity. One therefore loses the possibility of deciding or the right to decide. Thus every decision would, fundamentally, remain at the same time solitary, secret, and silent. Speaking relieves us, Kierkegaard notes, for it 'translates' into the general" (pp. 59–60).

Abraham, then, is torn between saying nothing, or divulging his intention, and accounting for what he is about to do. Thus, if he does not say anything and stays silent about killing Isaac, he fails to act on his responsibility toward his son, his family, and society, that is, what Derrida, with Kierkegaard, calls general (or universal) ethics. However, if he admits to what he is going to do and exposes the secret between him and God, he breaks with absolute responsibility, namely the responsibility he has toward God, and so, by entering into language, he loses his singularity and unique responsibility which can only be retained by remaining silent and keeping the secret. In Derrida's words:

> He keeps quiet in order to avoid the moral temptation which, under the pretext of calling him to responsibility, to self-justification, would make him lose his ultimate responsibility along with his singularity, make him lose his unjustifiable, secret, and absolute responsibility before God. This is ethics as 'irresponsibility', as an insoluble and paradoxical contradiction between responsibility *in general* and *absolute* responsibility. (p. 61)

Kierkegaard calls this an ethical temptation, which Abraham must resist, and in doing so keeping his secret responsibility toward God. There is, in consequence, an unavoidable contradiction between general and absolute responsibility, our responsibility toward God, or the absolute other, and our responsibility toward one's family and society, in other words, the responsibility one must show toward the law of the home; in Greek, the two words οἶκος (*oikos*) meaning home, and νόμος (*nomos*) meaning law give us the word economy. This contradiction must be endured, Derrida says, since it is inevitable:

> In both general and abstract terms, the absoluteness of duty, of responsibility, and of obligation certainly demands that one transgress ethical duty, although in betraying it one belongs to it and at the same time recognizes it. The contradiction and the paradox must be endured *in the instant itself*. The two duties must contradict one another, one must subordinate (incorporate, repress) the other. Abraham must assume absolute responsibility for sacrificing his son by sacrificing ethics, but in order for there to be a sacrifice, the ethical must retain all its value; the love for his son must remain intact, and the order of human duty must continue to insist on its rights. (p. 66)

Thus, Abraham will always be a murderer, there is no doubt and no way of denying it. What Abraham does is an atrocious act. But, it is here that Derrida's argument diverges from that of both Kierkegaard's and Levinas's ethics, and where he introduces the formula "*tout autre est tout autre*." With this ambiguous and untranslatable sentence Derrida want to point to the secular implications of thinking the absolute other. Since, as Derrida insists, the duty to speak and account for one's actions is not only an ethics that relates to religion and family or society. It is a duty deeply entrenched in the practice of philosophy and science, and builds on the principle of rationality and knowledge as the public expression of and accountability for what is to be known. It is in this sense that Abraham breaks with ethics, he does not assume responsibility for what he is doing by making it public, he does not present his case. At the same time, he obeys the command of the absolute other, which can only be done by keeping silent. As Derrida puts it:

> Abraham's decision is absolutely responsible because it answers for itself before the absolute other. Paradoxically, it is also irresponsible because it is guided neither by reason nor by an ethics justifiable before men or before the law of some universal tribunal. Everything points to the fact that one is unable to be responsible at the same time before the other and before others, before the others of the other. If God is completely other, the figure or name of the wholly other, then every other (one) is every (bit) other. *Tout autre est tout autre*. (pp. 77–78)

This is so, since the decision to take responsibility for the wholly other puts me in the position of being, at the same time, irresponsible toward the other others. Every one of those others being altogether other in their absolute singularity. In terms of translation, Derrida's formula "*tout autre est tout autre*" is a case in point. What we translate is the absolute other, an absolute and unique singularity, and as such it breaks with the responsibility we have toward that which is translated. At the same time, we are also obliged to translate in order to make ourselves and what is translated understood, we have a responsibility toward the others to make what cannot be translated readable. We have a responsibility to relate and render that which is translated as truthfully as possible, and in a way which conveys what we understand to be the meaning of what is translated. But in doing so we betray the translated, we do not stay true to its singularity, but instead transform it into what it is not. This kind of translation, or rather transgression, occurs each time we translate, and also when we attempt to use an absolute other as an example, model, or illustration. In that moment the absolute other loses its unique otherness by being organized into a matter for rational knowledge, understanding, analysis, and explication. The aporia of translation enacts the irresponsible resignation of that which cannot be said in any other language, the aporia here being the silence of language that the act of translation breaches. If the untranslated keeps its silence and its secret, that which is unknown, it cannot be accounted for in a language that presents it as what it is assumed to be, but nevertheless eludes. There is, in other words, always something left that cannot be determined and accounted for, controlled and systematized, taught and learned.

Transgressions: Translating the Other

What happens, then, when we want to apply and put to practice the consequences of this aporia of ethics and responsibility? What practical consequences does it have for how we can relate to the other, the marginal, or subaltern? What are the consequences for how we understand the other and ethics within, for example, Social Justice Education? To address these questions further, I would like to attend to Sara Ahmed's (2004) study *Differences that Matter: Feminist Theory and Postmodernism* and Gayatri Spivak's preface to Mahasweta Devi's (1995) *Imaginary Maps*, to which Ahmed is also referring. First, however, let me once again invoke Derrida, in order to situate the aporia of responsibility in terms of theory and practice. To repeat, in *The Gift of Death*, Derrida (1996) formulates the aporia which suspends the theory and practice of responsibility in the following way:

> Saying that a responsible decision must be taken on the basis of knowledge seems to define the condition of possibility of responsibility (one can't make a responsible decision without science or conscience, without knowing what one is doing, for what reasons, in view of what and under what conditions), at the same time as it defines the condition of impossibility of this same responsibility (if decision-making is relegated to knowledge that it is content to follow or to develop, then it is no more a responsible decision, it is the technical deployment of a cognitive apparatus, the simple deployment of a theorem)" (p. 24).

This formulation of the aporia of responsibility leads up to Derrida's reflections on the story of Abraham, and the ethical decision that leaves us torn between our responsibility toward the absolute other and all other others.

Now, in *Differences that Matter*, Sara Ahmed addresses the other and ethics by critiquing Derrida's reading of Levinas and the feminine. She argues that Derrida reduces sexual difference to difference as such. Ahmed (2004) writes:

> Derrida, in making sexual difference "the difference" that challenges Levinas, repeats this prioritising of sexual difference over and above other kinds of difference that may "derive" from ethics (a process which enables him to assume the figure of "the woman reader"). I would argue that a feminist reading of this dialogue must not repeat the very same gesture – to recognise the violence when sexual difference comes to stand for difference *per se*: a

process that makes other differences themselves derivative (other differences matter). The importance of such a refusal to repeat the gesture through which philosophy comes to mourn the (dead) body of the woman, is to begin with the possibility that differences themselves already mark the other to whom I am endlessly obligated (rather than seeing the other as a mark of a difference – including sexual difference – which obligates me). (pp. 62–63)

Ahmed is referring to Derrida's reading of Levinas in his essay "At This Very Moment In This Work Here I Am"; however, I would like to confront Ahmed's reading on the grounds of what Derrida says about ethics, responsibility, and the other in *The Gift of Death*. In fact, in *The Gift of Death*, Derrida is claiming the exact opposite of what Ahmed holds Derrida accountable for, that is, what Derrida is saying in *The Gift of Death* is that there is no absolute difference, not even sexual difference, since "difference" becomes an issue only after a decision, ethical or otherwise, has been made. Hence, all difference is "derived" because difference is manifested as such or *per se* in a specific context, which in this case is Derrida's reading of Levinas. This does not mean that all other differences do not matter, but that a decision is necessary, since as Derrida states *"tout autre est tout autre,"* which implies that we must make a decision about the other whenever we encounter the other, we cannot avoid it. This means that Derrida's reading of Levinas is responding to Levinas in a singular and unique way, which by necessity will sacrifice all other others, including the feminine others or subaltern others, including the other possible sexual differences. Thus, in deciding to respond responsibly to Levinas, Derrida, at the same time, ends up being irresponsible toward all other others, whoever they might be, for example Ahmed, since Derrida did not decide on Ahmed's reading of difference and sexual difference.

But, what, then, is the (more ethical or responsible) alternative, according to Ahmed? Ahmed invokes Spivak for a feminist ethical response to an ethics of the other. She writes:

How might a feminist ethics of otherness proceed differently? To begin with, a feminist approach may address the particularity of an-Other by assuming that *a* philosophy of otherness is impossible as such. Such a particularity may not simply be figured. This is particularly clear in Spivak's reflection on her translation of Mahasweta Devi in *Imaginary Maps*. Here, Spivak formulates a model of ethical singularity, not of the other *per se*, but of the subaltern woman, who remains other to the various privileged categories of otherness (migrant/exile/diasporic/postcolonial) within Western knowledges. Such a singularity takes the form of a mutual engagement and hence involves both accountability and responsibility. (p. 63)

First of all, a possible ethics is already presupposed, that is, Ahmed suggests a possible praxis or program for a feminist ethics. This ethics, she writes, "may address the particularity of an-Other by assuming that *a* philosophy of otherness is impossible as such," which is precisely what Derrida states in *The Gift of Death*, and which he decided to do in his reading of Levinas in "At This Very Moment In This Work Here I Am." However, Derrida emphasizes that the "particularity" or singularity, the uniqueness, of being responsible for the absolute and wholly other is governed by aporia. Accountability only becomes a possibility if we break with the responsibility we give toward the wholly other, since to be accountable implies an ethical order before which we can be judged. As Derrida (1996) says of Abraham: "Abraham's decision is absolutely responsible because it answers for itself before the absolute other. Paradoxically, it is also irresponsible because it is guided neither by reason nor by an ethics justifiable before men or before the law of some universal tribunal" (p. 77). Thus, Ahmed wants to replace Derrida's reading of Levinas, or rather avoid repeating what she holds is reductive in Derrida's reading of feminism, with a feminist ethics which would focus on ethical singularity, drawing on Spivak's notion of ethics. Ahmed seems, in consequence, to disregard Derrida's singular encounter with the absolute other and demand accountability, which as we have seen entails precisely an entering into language. Ahmed proposes a theoretical model for an ethical feminist program, which she claims would avoid repeating Derrida's reductionism, but, at the same time, she overlooks the very singularity she proposes being the foundation of her ethics, in addition to not engaging in a singular reading/translation as a unique encounter with the absolute other. She seems, then, to profess a universal ethics of singularity, while disregarding the aporetic double bind of generality and singularity of any responsible and ethical decision.

Since Ahmed is basing her ethics on Spivak, I would like to turn directly to the text by Spivak which Ahmed invokes to develop her feminist ethics. We find Spivak's text in Mahasweta Devi's (1995) *Imaginary Maps*, written as a "Translator's Preface," where Spivak develops her thoughts on ethics, reading, and translation. It should be noted that we find in Spivak's (1995) preface the notion of aporia mentioned, and she defines it quite succinctly in an endnote, in which she differentiates it from a dilemma. An aporia, she writes, is "insoluble – each choice cancels the other – and yet it is solved by an unavoidable decision that can never be pure. Dilemma is a logical, aporia a practical item" (note 15, p. 210). It is this aporia that lies at the heart of Spivak's subaltern gendered ethics. It is an ethics highly influenced by Derrida's thinking, without which it would, arguably, not be possible. Derrida's influence on Spivak's, at times, elliptical writing, however, is often implied and the reader is often left without much help when it comes to sorting out when Spivak is, *de facto*, invoking Derrida. Be that as it may, Spivak's engagement with Devi's three stories is acknowledging the singularity of a responsible engagement with the other, and it highlights the necessary generality of the way in which we must act, that is, make decisions, in order to accomplish ethical change. Spivak's ethics is an ethics that takes its point of departure in the singular responsibility we have toward the absolute other, a responsibility which is the foundation on which general and public change can build. For example, what Spivak says we should learn from Devi's stories is precisely how a singular ethics makes possible a general ethics of transformation: "I have no doubt that we must *learn* to learn from the original practical ecological philosophers of the world, through the slow, attentive, mind-changing (on both sides), ethical singularity that deserves the name 'love' – to supplement necessary collective efforts to change laws, modes of production, systems of education and health care" (pp. 200–201). What Spivak is proposing, in other words, is close to what, for example, Todd suggests when it comes to Social Justice Education and, indeed, to Ahmed's feminist ethics. In short, it is a question of achieving social change. In Spivak's thinking ethical singularity is necessarily

connected to societal, including juridical, change, that is, singular absolute responsibility is the *sine qua non* of any general ethics, so that any substantial, sustainable,
and positive social transformation must begin in singular ethics. As Spivak
maintains:

> Ethical transcoding of strategy is not impossible in our part of the world. Otherwise we
> remain caught in a collective disavowal that paradoxically strengthen the long-term possi-
> bility of the very thing we seek to avoid: the virulent misogyny of the right. [...] Without
> this acknowledgement and the responsible and caring process of the establishment of ethi-
> cal singularity (which can only exist between equals) that is its practical consequence, no
> collective action on the basis of legal calculation, itself absolutely necessary, will last. (note
> 18, pp. 210–211)

Here it is clear that Spivak's aim is to prescribe a general ethics based on ethical
singularity; in order for there to be accountability there has to be ethical singularity,
on which societal transformation forms. Injustice, or irresponsibility, is thus uncovered and revealed by an engagement with the absolute other, even though this
engagement cannot be revealed as such, it remains secret. However, it is precisely in
such engagement, in its external manifestation, while keeping its intimate secret
with the other internalized, that injustice is exposed. In this way, injustice in the
form of, for example, racism or misogyny, can be made legally and ethically
accountable.

How, then, does Spivak's ethical singularity differ from the absolute singular
responsibility toward the wholly other that Derrida proposes? Spivak defines ethical
singularity in the following way:

> "Ethical singularity" is neither "mass contact" nor engagement with "the common sense of
> the people." We all know that when we engage profoundly with one person, the responses
> come from both sides: this is responsibility and accountability. We also know that in such
> engagements we want to reveal and reveal, conceal nothing. Yet on both sides there is
> always a sense that something has not got across. This we call the "secret," not something
> that one wants to conceal, but something that one wants to reveal. In this sense the effort of
> "ethical singularity" may be called a "secret encounter." [...] In this secret singularity, the
> object of ethical action is not an object of benevolence, for here responses flow from both
> sides. [...] This encounter can only happen when respondents inhabit something like nor-
> mality. Most political movements fail in the long run because of the absence of this engage-
> ment. In fact, it is impossible for all leaders (subaltern or otherwise) to engage every
> subaltern in this way, especially across the gender divide. This is why ethics is the experi-
> ence of the impossible. Please not that I am not saying that ethics are impossible, but rather
> that ethics is the experience of the impossible. This understanding only sharpens the sense
> of the crucial and continuing need for collective political struggle. For a collective struggle
> *supplemented* by the impossibility of full ethical engagement – not in the rational sense of
> "doing the right thing," but in this more familiar sense of the impossibility of "love" in the
> one-on-one way for each human being – the future is always around the corner, there is no
> victory, but only victories that are also warnings. (p. xxv)

As is evident for what Spivak says, it is the political struggle that is of main priority,
since it is supplemented by ethical singularity, that is, the impossibility of full disclosure between subjects. There are a few crucial identifiable differences between
Derrida's and Spivak's thoughts on ethics. Let me touch on three of them. First of
all, Spivak emphasizes the activism or "collective struggle," that is, ethics as a

theorem giving rise to a program or procedure "supplemented" by ethical singularity. As we have seen, Derrida's contention is that all others are absolute others and that my responsibility toward the absolute singular other excludes making it public, since once I enter into language and so make my response to the other open to scrutiny I also breach my responsibility to the absolute other. That is, every responsibility carries with it its own irresponsibility. Second, ethical singularity can, as Spivak writes, "only exist between equals" (note 18, p. 211). As is clear from Derrida's reading of the story of Abraham, ethical singularity does not presuppose equality. One can hardly argue that God and Abraham are equals, yet the story portrays an instance of a responsible engagement with the absolute and wholly other. Third, the secret in Spivak's case is concerned with that which necessarily eludes transfer in the communication between two subjects, while the secret, in Derrida's case, is that which remains secret even for the one taking responsibility. One cannot know a secret, since to know it means that it is no longer secret, which turns my responsibility toward the absolute other into irresponsibility. There can be no accountability of the secret, hence Spivak's claim that ethical singularity involves both responsibility and accountability does not adhere to Derrida's version of what it means to be responsible toward the absolute other. As Derrida (1996) puts it: "If I obey in my duty towards God (which is my absolute duty) *only in terms of duty*, I am not fulfilling my relation to God. In order to fulfill my duty towards God, I must not act *out of duty*, by means of that form of generality that can always be mediated and communicated and that is called a duty" (p. 63). Thus, responsibility becomes duty if I know and am able to mediate and expose my responsibility so that I can be held accountable for it; in other words, my responsibility toward the absolute other is and must always remain secret. This, precisely, is the responsibility that Derrida is invoking when in his reading of Levinas he claims to betray Levinas, that is, Derrida is not reading Levinas out of duty, but is responding to him as absolute other, which means responding in secret, as a singular encounter which can only be approached by engaging with Derrida's reading as absolute other. However, as a text of philosophy it inscribes itself into that generality of scholarship that demands accountability, which is why, in the end, Derrida can be said to betray Levinas.

The listed differences between Derrida's and Spivak's notions of ethics, responsibility, and the secret also point to how Ahmed's feminist ethics differs from Derrida's. It is not, perhaps, as Ahmed holds, a question of reducing the other to an idea of difference as such, but rather of being attentive to the singularity which governs my responsibility toward the absolutely other, as well as the aporia which, inevitably, always puts me in a position where I betray the other by entering into the medium of language and so declaring myself accountable. Now, the feminist ethics of Ahmed and the ethical singularity of Spivak, as well as the kind of Social Justice Education that Todd suggests, all end up, I argue, exposing what is secret to profess a certain ethical stance which leads to an implicit or explicit ethical program or convention to follow. When these three philosophers translate the impossibility of ethics and the aporia of responsibility into praxis and engagement for a certain cause or idea, they at the same time transgress Derrida's reading of ethics and responsibility. The social and political practice of ethics to achieve, for example, emancipation cannot avoid the irresponsibility of this transgression, since as Derrida emphasizes: "We must continually remind ourselves that some part of irresponsibility insinuates itself wherever one demands responsibility without sufficiently conceptualizing and thematizing what 'responsibility' means; *that is to say everywhere*" (pp. 25–26). In other words, responsibility eludes being exhaustively conceptualized and thematized, but demands that we remain concerned, precisely, every time we attempt to explain it or put it into practice, even for the best of reasons. And it mandates, furthermore, that we endure the aporia that it confronts us with, since the aporia and its translation open up for the vigilance that reading, translating, teaching, and learning demand. "The exercise of responsibility," says Derrida, "seems to leave no choice but this one, however uncomfortable it might be, of paradox, heresy, and secrecy. More serious still, it must always run the risk of conversion and apostasy: there is no responsibility without a dissent and an inventive rupture with respect to tradition, authority, orthodoxy, rule, or doctrine" (p. 27). Nevertheless, whatever their (inevitable) transgressions (transgression taken in the sense of a passage through, form ethical singularity to ethical generality, from thematization to praxis) when it comes to ethics and responsibility toward absolute other, Todd, Ahmed, and Spivak provide us with exemplary illustrations of how to translate the absolutely other.

Conclusion: The Aporia of Teaching

In conclusion, I would like to return to Todd's discussion of ethics and the other, and specifically her reflections on institutional rules and regulations, responsibility, and our response to the other within contexts of teaching and learning. What Todd describes as an aporia, and she indeed uses the word aporia, is the double responsibility that teachers have, on the one hand, toward institutional rules and regulations and the attendant institutional violence that accompany them, and on the other hand, their responsibility toward the other, meaning each of their students. What Todd suggests, as we struggle to come to terms with this aporia, is an ethical practice that in terms of our teaching practice urges us to attend to the other as someone who is in essence unknowable, and it is my responsibility as a teacher to attend to the other as unknowable, or as Todd puts it, this is "an ethical attentiveness to the Other that comes prior to understanding" (p. 145). This means that we should not simply rehearse ready made responses and thought through answers to provide the other with, but instead be open and actively listening to the unpredictability of the other. As Todd writes: "What I have to be mindful of is the way in which my affect affects my capacity for response, affects my capacity to be confronted with the challenges to become altered in my encounter with the Other" (p. 145). This openness and willingness to redefine and reevaluate myself as a teacher is a form of responsibility toward the other, in that I do not impose a way of being on the other, but rather engage with the other in a manner in which learning and transformation becomes the gift of the unexpected. Todd states:

What is at stake here is the development of a capacity for the continual renewal of the self in relation to another who signifies. The emphasis becomes not on embodying predefined images of what responsibility should look like, as though it were merely a performance of a code, but on the alertness and vigilance we bring to our own responses in the context of listening. Thus it is not so much that consciousness has no role to play in being vigilant, but that responsibility itself does not emerge from conscious intent.

We as teachers should, in other words, engage ourselves in a process of learning and "renewal" based on a vigilance toward not only the other as each of our students, but also toward texts, films, online content, games, etc. What Todd describes, in short, is a form of responsible, concerned, close reading. Todd's version, or perhaps vision, of Social Justice Education is in itself a responsible approach to developing an ethical teaching practice. But, as she admits, her suggested ethical practice is not an easy one to achieve, but certainly worth striving toward, so that it becomes an ethical response to the other in order to develop, as she puts it, "a capacity for the continual renewal of the self in relation to another who signifies" (p. 146).

However, just as Ahmed's as well as Spivak's ethics, Todd's proposed ethical practice is precisely that, a practice which translates the aporia of singularity and generality into a program of action in which the secret and unknowable other, as absolute singularity, is sacrificed, precisely, by entering the world of signification. This, since an ethics put into practice is by necessity accountable also before the other others and not only for the absolute wholly other that this ethical practice nevertheless wants to be responsible for. But, as Derrida insists, being responsible for the absolute other is at the same time being irresponsible for all the other others, while an ethics governed by rules is responsible before the other others, it is irresponsible before the absolute other. Such is the inevitable aporia of responsibility, an aporia which we cannot escape, an aporia that nevertheless ought to concern us, and as Todd suggests, keep us alert and vigilant, in teaching as well as learning.

References

Ahmed, S. (2004). *Differences that matter: Feminist theory and postmodernism*. Cambridge University Press.

Badiou, A. (2002). *Ethics: An essay on the understanding of evil* (P. Hallward, Trans.). Verso.

Baez, B. (2004). The study of diversity: The 'knowledge of difference' and the limits of science. *Journal of Higher Education, 75*(3), 285–307.

Blanchot, M. (1993). *The infinite conversation* (S. Hanson, Trans.). University of Minnesota Press.

Critchley, S. (2007). *Infinitely demanding: Ethics of commitment, politics of resistance*. Verso.

Davis, R. C., & Schleifer, R. (1992). *Criticism and culture: The role of critique in modern literary theory*. Longman.

Derrida, J. (1978). Violence and metaphysics. *Writing and difference*. (A. Bass, Trans.). University of Chicago Press.

Derrida, J. (1982). Signature event context. In J. Derrida (Ed.), *Margins of philosophy* (A. Bass, Trans.) (pp. 307–330). Harvester Press.

Derrida, J. (1996). *The gift of death* (D. Wills, Trans.). University of Chicago Press.

Derrida, J. (1997). *Of grammatology* (G. C. Spivak, Trans.). The John Hopkins University Press.

Derrida, J. (2005). Violence and metaphysics: An essay on the thought of Emmanuel Levinas. In J. Derrida (Ed.), *Writing and difference* (A. Bass, Trans.) (pp. 97–192). e-Library: Taylor and Francis.

Freire, P. (1996). *Pedagogy of the oppressed* (M. Bergman Ramos, Trans.). Penguin.

Levinas, E. (2003). *Totality and infinity: An essay on exteriority* (A. Lingis, Trans.). Duquesne University Press.

Lewis, T. E. (2012). *The aesthetics of education: Theatre, curiosity, and politics in the work of Jacques Rancière and Paulo Freire.* Continuum.

Miller, J. H. (2005). Politicizing art – What are cultural studies? In J. Wolfreys (Ed.), *The J. Hillis Miller reader* (pp. 330–338). Stanford University Press.

Spivak, G. C. (1995). Translator's preface. In M. Devi (Ed.), *Imaginary maps* (G. C. Spivak, Trans.) (pp. xxiii–xxiv). Routledge.

Todd, S. (2003). *Learning from the other: Levinas, psychoanalysis, and ethical possibilities in education.* State University of New York Press.

Chapter 8
Coda: Aporia and the Excess of Translation and Education

In the preceding chapters, I have attempted to develop the notion of, what I call, the aporia of translation. I have done so by exploring how such aporias of translation figure themselves in texts and contexts where literature, philosophy, and education intersect. Chapter 1 of the book introduced the main themes of the study, which provide a "roadmap" for the reader, together with chapter summaries. In Chap. 2, I addressed the education of death as it figures in Thomas Bernhard's novel *Gargoyles*; in Chap. 3, I explored the notions of censorship in literature, philosophy, and education, and its relation to aproias of translation; in Chap. 4, I analyzed cultural translation, critical thinking, and discourses of rationality and logic, from the perspective of aporia; in Chap. 5, I proposed a reading of Heidegger's notion of learning in his analysis of Stefan George's poem "Words"; in Chap. 6, I addressed John Ashbery's poetry and aesthetic education; and in Chap. 7, my focus was on the notion of the other, diversity, social justice education, and aporias of responsibility.

Every translation, it might be argued, is an excess of language, and every process of education is in excess of itself, to the extent that both of these movements surpass their respective conceptual determination. There are a number of conceptions and translations of excess; for example, excess as *Überschuß* (Husserl), *Übermaß*, *Überfluss* (Heidegger), the exorbitant (*l'exorbitant*) (Derrida), *sûrcroit* (Marion), and expenditure (*dépense*), excess (*excédant, excès, surabondance*) (Bataille). Of these conceptualizations of excess, I would like to focus on Heidegger's thinking concerning excess as *Übermaß* and *Überfluss*, which on the one hand signals a change in or development of his philosophy, and on the other hand provides me with a language to address excess in and of translation and education. In addition, Heidegger points to how a simultaneous poverty in inherent in the notion of excess, which I would like to explore in relation to translation and education.

I begin by noting that in Chap. 1 I referred to a short essay written by Heidegger in 1945, in which Heidegger talks about poverty (*Armut*), which is also the title of

© Springer Nature Switzerland AG 2022

E. Schwieler, *Aporias of Translation*, Contemporary Philosophies and Theories in Education 18, https://doi.org/10.1007/978-3-030-97895-2_8

the essay. In the *Gesamtausgabe* (73.1),[1] the essay is preceded by Heidegger's notes on the subject, found under the heading "Armut." Now, in these notes there are two sentences that I want to pay particular attention, namely: "*Das Reichtum ist das Überfluß des Seyns (des Da-seyns) über alles 'Haben' aus der Unerschöpflichkeit der Armut im Eigentum.* [...] *Die Armut is die Überfuß (das Überfließen-lassen) des Unnötigen*" (p. 711). To attempt a preliminary translation of these two sentences, we could say that "Wealth is the excess [literally an overflowing] of the Being of beings (or rather the Being of Dasein), beyond all kinds of 'having', which belongs to the inexhaustibility of the poverty of possessions, ownership or property. [...] Poverty is the excess or overflow (the letting-it-overflow) of the needless or unnecessary." It is necessary here to point, first of all, to the ambiguity of the word *Überfuss*, which can mean abundance, excess, luxury, but as *Überfussig* also redundant, superfluous, unnecessary, waste, that which is not needed. This ambiguity affects how we read the second sentence in that *Unnötigen* is that without need, which means that poverty is both a state of need and an overflow or excess of what is needless. Heidegger thus says that poverty is not the opposite of wealth or abundance, but that wealth is the essence of poverty, while povery is the essence of wealth. The contradictory nature of Heidegger's thinking concerning poverty and wealth is clearly expressed in the sentence: "*Indem wir arm werden, werden wir reich*" (p. 710), which can be translated as "When we become poor, we become rich." Heidegger points out that poor and rich are commonly considered opposites, so that being rich and poor at the same time would be a contradiction, according to Aristotle's first principle of non-contradiction. But, Heidegger says, if we look closer at these words and their meanings we find that they are, in fact, not opposites. How we understand these words hinges on the word "Haben," to have. What does it mean to have something? As, for example, in having knowledge or having an understanding of something. To have something, in this context, says Heidegger, does not mean to possess it as a possession that I own and that thus belongs to me. Instead, Heidegger states that "*Armer werden heißt jedoch nicht, Besitz verlieren und in die Entbehrung greaten, sondern Armwerden ist das Wesen der Armut lernen*," that is, "Being poor does not, however, mean to lose possessions or belongings; rather, being poor is to learn the nature or essence of poverty" (p. 710), and when it comes to wealth, he states "*Reichwerden heißt nicht, an Besitz gewinnen, sondern: das Wesen des Reichtum lernen*," meaning "Being rich does not mean to gain, win or acquire possessions or belongings, but to learn the nature or essence of wealth or abundance" (p. 711). Thus, Heidegger relates being poor and rich to learning, and not to "*Haben,*" as in having or being in possession of something. As he says, "*Arm als Seyn ist ein 'Haben', das alles hat, weil es nichts Entbehrt – es sey den das Unnötige –, welches Nicht-Entbehren das Seyn der Inständigkeit ist*," that is, "Poor as Being is a 'having' that has everything, since it does not lack anything – it is thus

---

[1] This volume of the *Gesamtausgabe* has not been translated in its entirety. However, a translation of the short essay "*Armut*" can be found in Schalow (2011) under the title "Poverty." In consequence, I rely on my own translations of the passages in Heidegger's text that I refer to.

the needless, the superfluous – according to which insistence[2] is the Not-Lacking of
Being" (p. 711). Being, as Heidegger describes it here, is both poor and rich since it
lacks nothing in an overflowing abundance of what is not needed, that is, wealth as
having possession of belongings or poor in the sense of lacking belongings. This is
what Heidegger expresses in the first two sentences I quoted. To repeat: "*Das
Reichtum ist das Überfluß des Seyns (des Da-seyns) über alles 'Haben' aus der
Unerschöpflichkeit der Armut im Eigentum.* [...] *Die Armut is die Überfuß (das
Überfließen-lassen) des Unnötigen*," which in my translation becomes "Wealth is
the excess [literally an overflowing] of the Being of beings (or rather the Being of
Dasein), beyond all kinds of 'having', which belongs to the inexhaustibility of the
poverty of possessions, ownership or property. [...] Poverty is the excess or over-
flow (the letting-it-overflow) of the needless or unnecessary" (p. 711).

Now, this oscillating movement of poverty and wealth, each providing the contradictory and paradoxical, or rather aporetic, translation of the other, stages what is
at stake in the act of translation. A translation and its original are not opposites but
must be seen, precisely, as Heidegger's thinks of poverty and wealth. The poverty of
a translation is also its richness because it is, in a sense, superfluous in that it cannot
claim to possess the original as its own, it is not its *Eignetum*, to use Heidegger's
German. This in turn levels the hierarchy between translated and translation, so that
there is no original in the strict sense of this term. They rather work as the wealth of
the other, as well as the poverty of the other – wealth since it extends the other's
meaning, and poverty in that the meaning is also restricted by its otherness. This
brings to them both a simultaneous balance and imbalance, which is equal in its
inequality. One could, perhaps, say that they emancipate one another. They are, in
short, in excess of each other. In my translation of the two sentences I began by
translating, these sentences perform precisely that which they describe, namely the
overflowing excess of wealth and poverty of meaning, dependent on the seeming
opposition between the terms as well as how they can only be understood by not
considering them as contradictory. Hence, wealth and poverty does not rely on contradiction or opposition as the foundation of understanding, as the play between
signifier and signified, as it is said that we understand something to be what it is by
knowing what it is not. A translation becomes its own by being other form itself as
well as different in itself, not as the opposite or contradiction of something else.
Translation is deprived of the proper, a translation is thus the altogether other, without home or dwelling constituted by the force of an aporia which forces a choice. A

---

[2] Richard Polt (2006), in his *The Emergency of Being: On Heidegger's* Contributions to Philosophy,
unpacks Heidgger's notion of *Inständigkeit* in the following way: "Insistence in the *Contributions*
resembles authenticity in *Being and Time*: it is a stance that enables proper ownness. Genuine self-
hood – belonging to one's self – requires belonging to being. Heidegger calls this stance a paradoxical 'out-standing insistence' (*ausstehende Inständigkeit*). We understand being only by
with-standing its abandonment and standing ready for its call (64). This means dwelling in the
place and time where appropriation may happen. This 'masterful knowing' (44, 62, 64, 281–82) is
both the 'innermost' (64) and the 'outermost' happening (57); it gathers us into intimate belonging
to our particular moment and site, yet it also takes us to the strangest limits of our ability to
embrace what is and what is not" (p. 127). Polt's page references are to Heidegger (1999).

translation is absolutely free in its poverty. As with my translated sentences, where almost every word is in need of translation even in the original language (because the contradiction and ambiguity within one specific word and between words and sentences resist to be determined), it is then we are faced with the excess of aporia, the impasse, the unpassable, where there is no way out, no method to help us determine a course of action. As Heidegger points out, this entails that we do not possess these concepts as objects of knowledge and understanding, but that we are continuously only beginning to *learn* what they are in their essence. For Heidegger, this means that we must begin to ponder the question of how to think what the matter (*Sache*) for thinking consists in. We have to prepare a way for learning, which we can only do if we begin to learn what the matter for learning and thinking is.

If this presents a way to read translation from the perspective of the aporia and excess, then what about education? Is there are way to read education in terms of wealth and poverty, in the manner of Heidegger's thinking regarding these notions? To address these questions, I would like to refer to another text by Heidegger, in which he mentions excess explicitly, namely the lectures collected under the title *Four Seminars*. The title refers to seminars given in Le Thor in 1966, 1968, and 1969, and in Zähringen in 1973, and the collected volume consists of seminar protocols taken down in French and then translated into German. The German translation was supervised by Heidegger and eventually included in the *Gesamtausgabe* as volume 15. The English translation, by Andrew Mitchell and François Raffoul, is based on the GA translation, "always with an eye to whatever light the French 'original'" provided (Heidegger, 2012, p. viii). The process of translation of *Four Seminars* is, needless to say, interesting, considering the themes of the present study. However, *Four Seminars* is interesting also from another perspective, namely that it constitutes what could be called a summing up, or even the consummation, of Heidegger's thinking. In short, the seminars deal with the themes running through Heidegger's work from *Being and Time* to his later work which emphasizes the importance of poetry and *Dichtung* to his thinking. As Mitchell and Raffoul notes, the seminars present "Heidegger's own ruminations upon his path of thought, from the early focus upon the 'meaning of being' all the way to his late conception of a 'topology of being'" (p. xvi).

How, then, does Heidegger conceive of excess in *Four Seminars*? First of all, Heidegger in these seminars speaks of excess as *Übermaß* rather than *Überfluss*. *Übermaß* signaling, with the word *Maß*, a measure, extent, amount, so that it is a question of an exceeding measure or amount, more than an overflowing as in *Überfluss*. What specifically is emphasized by using *Maß* instead of *Fluss*? What is it that exceeds its measure, according to Heidegger? His answer is similar to his thinking concerning poverty and wealth, namely that excess belongs together with withdrawal, so that the excess of Being and the withdrawal of Being describe the same situation. Just as with poverty and wealth, excess and withdrawal are not placed in a contradictory relationship, but translate one another: Excess is withdrawal and withdrawal is excess. For there to be excess there has to be a withdrawal, and for a withdrawal to occur there must be an excess. Heidegger talks about such excess-withdrawal when it comes to technology, and also when it comes to philosophy as such. Technology, on Heidegger's view, is excessive in that it causes a self-withdrawal of Being, so that technology is foregrounded by its coming to presence, and so takes over Dasein's way of being. At the 1969 Le Thor seminar, Heidegger suggests that what characterizes humanity (at the time of the seminar) is that it is disposable and in consequence replaceable. Heidegger gives the examples of fashion and news; fashion, which is no longer synonymous with adornment and embellishment, but with the replacement of fashion lines from 1 year to the next; and news, or as he says, "current affairs," which are constantly updated and become obsolete as soon as they are communicated. Humanity's relation to Being is consequently forgotten; Being withdraws and the excessive presence of technology takes its place. Heidegger states that "modern man finds himself henceforth in a fundamentally new relation to being – AND THAT HE KNOWS NOTHING OF IT" (p. 62). This, moreover, constitutes what Heidegger calls positionality (*Gestell*), of which Heidegger says:

> In positionality, the human is challenged forth to comport himself in correspondence with exploitation and consumption; the relation to exploitation and consumption requires the human to be in this relationship. Man does not hold technology in his hand. He is its plaything. In this situation, there reigns a complete forgetfulness of being, a complete concealment of being. Cybernetics becomes a replacement for philosophy and poetry. Political science, sociology, and psychology become prioritized, disciplines which no longer bear the slightest relation to their own foundation. In this regard, modern man is a slave to the forgetfulness of being. (p. 63)

Hence, Being is covered over by technology's excessive measure; at the same time, however, technology also means the possibility to uncover or reveal Being in Being's excessive measure, since this excess goes beyond the calculating algorithms of technology to leave a trace or hint of Being as such. Thus, technology is both the danger and possibility for human Dasein.[3] In a similar manner, philosophy itself is excessive in its reply to the fleetingness of technological being. To experience Being uncovered is what Heidegger names ἀλήθεια, and in discussing how it is possible for Dasein to uncover Being, Heidegger asks "what occurs in the fact of arising-into ἀλήθεια? What is at once co-named in the word φύειν [*phuein*: grow, produce; hence, appear]?" (p. 38). Heidegger's answer is excess: "It is the *overabundance*, the *excess* of what presences" (p. 38), which in the German translation of GA 15 reads: "*Das ist die* Überfülle, *das* Übermaß *des Anwesenden*" (p. 331). Now, this abundance and excess of what presences, the φύειν of ἀλήθεια, is at the same time, Heidegger maintains, a privation, which does not mean it is a negation, but precisely that it co-exists with the term it marks as a privation. This is how Heidegger explains the ἀ of ἀλήθεια, that is, the ἀ is both a mark of privation and excess: "Clearly, what is decisive in all this is that the privation, the ἀ of ἀλήθεια, corresponds to this excess. Privation is not negation. The more strongly it becomes what the word φύειν indicates, the more powerful is the source from which it springs, the concealment in unconcealment" (p. 38). Heidegger talks of such co-existence of contradictory

---

[3] For a developed discussion of technology and education as it relates to Heidegger's later thinking, see, e.g., Magrini and Schwieler (2018), and Ekberg and Schwieler (2020).

terms by using a word from Heraclitus, namely ξυνόν (*ksynón*) which Heidegger translates as belonging together, sharing. Thus, the concealment in unconcealment, the ά of άλήθεια, becomes stronger the more it is revealed or unconvered. It is in this way that philosophy is excessive and at the same time privative: "Consequently, it must always be emphasized that the dimension of the entirely excessive is that in which philosophy arises. Philosophy is indeed the answer of a humanity that has been struck by the excess of presence [*übermaß der Anwesenheit*]" (p. 38). This presence beyond measure is in consequence at the same time a withdrawal of Being, so that what philosophy in essence is concerned with is not Being as such, but with the meaning of the beings of Being.

It is in this way, too, that education, as I noted at the outset, surpasses its determination. As I have tried to show in the preceding chapters, by focusing on education as a transformative process in which learning, knowledge and understanding presuppose certain meanings, or traditional or canonical readings of texts in literature and philosophy. The pedagogical moment or situation thus takes precedence over the text, which is used as a static object, a commodity or product, to be learned from in a preconceived way. As such, the text used for educational purposes loses its otherness, it is censored, and so reduced to a replaceable object and only functions as an example or illustration of something other than itself. This situation, I argue, is yet another example of the consequences of positionality or enframing, that is, what Heidegger calls *Gestell*, resulting from the influence of technology on our way of being. This would, furthermore, mean that education as a discipline can be added to the list of disciplines Heidegger mentions (political science, sociology and psychology) that have lost their relation to their foundation. To relate back to the foundation of a discipline we must learn its essential way of being. And to think essentially, according to Heidegger, is a thinking in which Being as such is revealed, that is, it is an opening up toward άλήθεια. The excess of education as positioning is in this way at the same time the withdrawal of its foundation, so that learning becomes a "having," which means to acquire knowledge as a possession that can be calculated, assessed, and accounted for. To learn essentially would mean first of all to prepare to learn what is to be learned in its essence, which would mean letting that which has withdrawn appear. And it appears in the contradictory state of aporia, as that which does not let itself be named, but nevertheless calls for us to translate it.

Does the excess of education and translation, and of tracing these notions back to their aporetic foundation, remove them from considerations of ethics, justice, emancipation, and politics? I suggest it does not. What it does is to reframe these concepts and expose some of the preconceptions that have structured how we think and conceive of them. It suggests an alternative way of approaching the question of what they can be. Moreover, my approach does not deny meaning or signification as impossible, which would, of course, be sophistry. However, my approach points to the aporetic nature of determining meaning. That certain things mean this or that in our everyday lives is something indisputable, so too is the verity of scientific facts. In other words, I do not argue for any kind of relativism; my aim has rather been to explore texts and situations in which education, philosophy, and literature seem to expose moments of aporia, where translation, even seen as hermeneutic interpretation, is disrupted, and we are forced to reconsider established determined, or canonical readings of these texts and situations. This approach goes against such rationalism as, for example, the referred to reading of the first sentence in Camus's *The Stranger* that claims to be able to assign a determinate meaning to its protagonist and the novel a whole, an understanding of the novel that is then taught and assessed as objectively ascertained. Or in education, the application of a canonical reading of a literary or philosophical text in order to generate educational and/or political change or transformation, without considering the uniqueness and specificity of the text in question. This is, for example, my aim with considering Bernhard's novel *Gargoyles* with its questioning, if not denouncing, of formal education and its ability to teach human experience in an essential way. The death of education is precisely this questioning of formal education and a staging of what an aporetic translation of education, such as Bernhard's novel, might bring to light.

In sum, the excess of translation and education is an excess inherent in aporia, that is, the insoluble character of aporia gives rise to an excess that cannot be contained in a single concept, theory, method, or discourse. Each system or discipline, then, such as a philosophical system, a system of ethics, a theory of education, or the academic discipline of education itself, by defining and determining itself, opens up unto aporia, which means the system, theory, or discipline is always and already in excess of itself. This impasse is the supplement of origin, it is the call which J. Hillis Miller speaks of as the imperative to teach.

References

Ekberg, N., & Schwieler, E. (2020). Evolving *Bildung*: Streaming media, art, and technology. *Popular Communication*. https://doi.org/10.1080/15405702.2020.174460

Heidegger, M. (1999). *Contributions to philosophy (from enowning)* (P. Emad & K. Maly, Trans.). Indiana University Press.

Heidegger, M. (2012). *Four seminars: Le Thor 1966, 1968, 1969, Zähringen 1973* (A. Mitchell & F. Raffoul). Indiana University Press.

Magrini, J. M., & Schwieler, E. (2018). *Heidegger on literature, poetry, and education after the "turn": At the limits of metaphysics*. Routledge.

Polt, R. (2006). *The emergency of being: On Heidegger's contributions to philosophy*. Cornell University Press.

Schalow, F. (Ed.). (2011). *Heidegger, translation, and the task of thinking: Essays in honor of Parvis Emad*. Springer.

Printed by Printforce, United Kingdom